Winning Squash Racquets

Winning Squash Racquets

Jack Barnaby

Allyn and Bacon, Inc.
Boston   London   Sydney

Library of Congress Cataloging in Publication Data

Barnaby, John M
    Winning squash racquets.

    Includes index.
        1. Squash rackets (Game)   I. Title.
GV1004.B32   769.34'3   78-25730
ISBN 0-205-06175-3

Production Editor: *Joanne Dauksewicz*
Designer: *Paula Carroll*
Manufacturing Buyer: *Linda Card*

Printed in the United States of America.

Dedication

This book, which is a sort of summation of my professional knowledge of squash racquets, could have been dedicated to many individuals and groups. There are my fellow coaches who made winning difficult, exciting, a real challenge. There are the Harvard men who furnished a ceaseless stream of talent, enthusiasm, idealism, and unexcelled sportsmanship. There is Corey Wynn, who contributed so much that he became known as "Harvard's secret weapon." There is Harry Cowles, who taught me so much that retaining half of it enabled me to have a successful career. There are the Friends of Harvard Squash and Tennis, many of whom did not play for me but have given loyal support for years. There are the administrators, both at Harvard and throughout the country where the game is played, without whose understanding and support achievement would have been sorely limited.

Yet there is another—a person who has contributed his services for many years. I refer to Everett Poeckert, operator of The Tennis & Squash Shop, whose work in caring for the needs of our players was tops in quality. Although he was a member of the Harvard gang for about forty years, this fact has never been publicly recognized. His work has won him everyone's admiration and respect, and his personality has won him our affection and esteem. Now retired to Cape Cod for a well-earned rest, it is hoped that this dedication will bring him not only my best wishes, but those of some forty generations of "Harvard hackers," as well as some happy memories.

Jack Barnaby
Center Harbor, N.H.

Contents

*Constructive Practice - Get the Concept Right First -
Rationalization - Mind over Muscle - Racquet Skill Is the Key -
Learn to Handle the Racquet - Summary*

Preface

For years the success of the Harvard team and individual Harvard players has led to demands for an explanation. What methods develop players faster and carry them farther? How could one college dominate a sport without recruiting, without any relaxation in notoriously tough requirements for admission, without any "athletic scholarships?"

There has also been a need for an historical treatment of the subject. Having watched many of the top players over a period of almost half a century, some written tribute to their extraordinary excellence seemed to be in order. The magic of many of the former greats, from Palmer Dixon to Hashim Khan, is, it is hoped, at least partially revealed in the section on great players. This is perhaps timely because of the advent of the swarm of fine players that now dominate the enlarged game and tend to make one think the past was nothing compared to the present. In numbers this is true; in quality the past is unexcelled.

A third need has been for a textbook that, like a cookbook, gives the definition and recipe for each shot in the game, and the basic techniques that underlie all shots. Slicing, the fact that the racquet and weight move in different directions, the full use of spin in finesse shots, and a thorough refutation of the 'flat' theory (which has limited the development of scores of talented players)—these subjects, of rock-bottom importance to excellence in the game, have never been carefully explored and laid before interested readers. It is hoped a good start has been made in this volume.

Finally, the book is a frank summation of the knowledge gained over a teaching and coaching career of forty-four years, and it is hoped this might be of interest and use to others.

Some may find the book a bit too personal and a bit too much laden with Harvard experiences. Since all the author's experience was at Harvard (1932–1976) this was quite unavoidable. I am well aware that great players were developed elsewhere—particularly in Philadelphia—but I am also aware that a writer should confine himself to what he knows well. Hopefully someone else, with far more intimate knowledge, will write the Philadelphia story and do justice to "Whitey," Hunter Lott, and all the others. No one would greet such an effort more warmly than the writer of this book which is, in an historical sense, unashamedly limited.

Acknowledgments

I wish to thank Victor Niederhoffer for his contribution of the chapter on squash doubles. There being no doubles courts at Harvard, my experience was limited to playing about once a year at some other location in a casual way. Yet doubles is a great game and I did not wish to omit the subject.

Doing work of this sort takes time, thought, and a lot of fussing about organization, illustrations, etc. No one is busier than Vic Niederhoffer. No one could have begged off with more incontrovertible excuses involving other pressures. But Vic didn't beg off. He did it, and did it well, and I know many will join me in my sincere gratitude for his effort in filling this huge gap in my knowledge. The champ has met another challenge with success.

Winning Squash Racquets

Introduction

According to one story, squash racquets started in the corner of an English prison building. When a kindhearted person passed on some used racquets and balls from a different game to the bored inmates, they proceeded to improvise a court and a game. Be that as it may, squash racquets is now a very popular wall game and its popularity continues to grow with increasing speed.

Why has squash racquets persevered, grown, survived depressions, and the invention of other games to emerge now as a leader in its field? Court tennis, called the "Game of Kings" and long recognized as the "aristocrat" of all wall games, began to die when the income tax was born. A court costs hundreds of thousands of dollars. Rackets, squash tennis, fives—all these have dwindled sadly as squash racquets has grown with slow but stubborn momentum. Recently this growth has undergone a marked acceleration. There is no question that squash is now an important sport—the only question is how big it will get.

There are many reasons for squash racquets' great success. First of all, squash has decisive economic appeal. Courts are expensive but durable, and after the initial cost, expenses are comparatively low. Secondly, squash fits neatly into a busy existence. A half hour to an hour gives good exercise—a nice work out. You don't need a weekend to play, as you do for golf or skiing. If the club or the Y is handy, you can go from work to squash to supper—and almost be on time at home. This practical appeal, besides the fact that squash can be played by the old as well as the young, means that squash can, and often does, become a long-lasting source of pleasure and exercise in the lives of many people.

But the real secret is the game itself. It is so adaptable almost anyone can play it. Read chapter 19 on "The Game's Great Players" and you will find that squash is for all types: sluggers, scramblers, touch artists, the patient or impatient, the aggressive, dogged, sly, or smoothly cool. Whatever type you are, squash can be played that way—it's the game for you. Size doesn't matter at all. Champions range from five feet five to six feet five. Excellence depends on mobility, skill, and thought. Whatever your natural bent, you can be that kind of a player and rise to the limits of your intrinsic athletic potential.

Some players use squash racquets as an outlet. After being polite all day to frequently irritating people, a person can get in there and beat hell out of the ball. Some players get hooked by the technical difficulties. The game is not easy and, as in golf and tennis, the challenge involved in acquiring real skill can be intriguing. "I *will* get to make that cussed drop shot that's so hard to execute well!" Then there are those who like to run. These people often play badly but delight in scrambling madly for the placements that are made off their mediocre shots, defiantly getting the ball back until their opponent errs. They don't seem to be irked at all by their own ineptness—they find joy and satisfaction in defying you to beat them. They take all the dirt you can feed them, and swallow it with amazing satisfaction. They even go home quite satisfied saying, "I showed him!"

There's the touch artist—the man who dreamt of being Toscanini and never quite made it. He wields his "baton" with infinite delicacy, plays with (hopefully) supreme precision, agonizes over his errors when he attempts the impossible—but then soon tries it again. He always makes some of the plays he planned and the errors are quickly forgotten—he made *beautiful* shots. The artist in him is uplifted, win or lose. But we mustn't leave out the strong man—the man who *crushes* his hapless victim with might and main, blasting the ball with all he's got on every shot, ignoring opportunities for finesse shots and glorying in his power. The brute loves squash. There is such satisfaction in hearing the ball go *smack* against the wall every time he lays into it. It's bone crushing—what could be more fun?

Then, too, there is Mephistopheles, the sly baffler. He continually thinks and thinks, and connives, playing high long balls that are harmless but hard to kill, gradually lulling his opponent into a sense of false security until the time comes for that little surprising short shot that *catches* him. He is not a Bobby Fisher, but he thinks he is: "I outsmarted him. I brainwashed him. I set him up and dispatched him with my slim rapier thrust. And he still doesn't know how it all happened. Ha!"

There's the gamesman, too. The fellow who wrote the book on how to win without actually cheating missed his greatest gold mine when he left out squash, a game that offers more shadowy, borderline areas of behavior than any other. This subject is in itself too large to be capsuled here, and will be treated in the chapter on "Sportsmanship." At any rate, the principle of gamesmanship has been and is often carried to heroic heights at all levels of play, from class D to championship play.

Are there other types? Doubtless, there are many. Yet squash is for them, too, because the game can be played in so many different ways. This infinite variety, while not quite as sexy as Cleopatra, nonetheless offers an endless subject for conversation. Many players derive a considerable part of pleasure from analyzing, dissecting, and extolling or downgrading the efforts of others, spending far more time carrying others to inexorable verbal victory or defeat than they ever spend in the court. After all, there is no limit to the excellence of one's talking game. No shots are missed, fatigue is unknown (tongues have incredible endurance), strategy is farsighted and tactical implementation knows no bounds. Which one of us has ever failed to win a title over a beer? The Monday morning quarterbacks in squash are not outranked by those of any other sport. After being whipped by a mediocre rival, an hour of squash talk can be an unsurpassed restorative for the damaged ego.

If squash is such a wonderful game to play, to watch, and to hash over, then why has it been a comparatively obscure sport with only a small following? Courts are costly, so rapid expansion is precluded by that first big financial hurdle. The nature of the court makes it impossible to seat more than two hundred people so they can view a match. How can a sport go "big time" when only a handful can watch? Finally, because the ball is small and moves so fast, it is not easily picked up by TV, so to date the game's marvelous spectator appeal cannot be exploited. Thus, squash is for players and not for viewers in great numbers. It is primarily a participant sport, not a spectator sport—and the spectators are what count in big-time tennis, football, basketball, baseball, and hockey. There is no big money in small numbers. Perhaps these difficulties may be overcome in the future. If so, squash might well balloon like the current tennis explosion. At present, people think about it and talk about it, but no one actually seems able to do it. A technical breakthrough in television might suddenly change the situation. It's impossible to know. But without a doubt, squash is as absorbing a sport for spectators as any that exist. The potential is there, in spades.

Objectives

It is helpful to set idealistic goals and move as far towards them as possible, therefore the objectives in this book are quite ambitious. The plan is to set forth the basic nature of the game, the techniques needed to execute the necessary shots, and from there to move on to the subtleties of advanced tactics and match play. Additionally, reasonable attention is given peripheral considerations such as the difference between men's and women's tactics, some suggestions on spectating, sportsmanship, the styles of past great players, and that fascinating but much overrated factor in match play—psychology. Above all an attempt is made to treat these matters more systematically and logically than has been done in the past. How? By relating tactics to areas of the court, by relating technique to tactics and percentages, and by sharply distinguishing between core knowledge (governed by the laws of physics) and athleticism (subject to personal mannerisms and therefore infinitely variable). The aim is to establish and lay bare what is true and inescapably necessary for everyone, whatever his style. It's important that teachers and students alike get a grasp of the game without becoming confused by attempting to imitate champions whose talents and idiosyncrasies may be irrelevant to the students' abilities. Teaching, skill tests, suggested questions for possible written tests in physical education courses—all these are included to facilitate use of the book. The foregoing is quite a list. But, as has been said, squash racquets is quite a game, and to do justice to this marvelous sport is really the ultimate objective.

The Basic Game

Squash is a game of position. The successful player always holds the center, thereby being the shortest distance from all possible shots. The fight for the center can be termed the *rally*. Neither player expects his shots to be winners; rather, each hopes to drive his opponent out of the center and take that position himself. Each player tries to keep his opponent behind him by intercepting the other's shots by use of the volley. The rally terminates when one player makes an error or, more commonly, a poor shot that comes out into the center. Such a shot is usually referred to as a *setup*.

Note: the very common impression people have that the ball should always be played as low as possible is false. From the back of the court the ball should seldom be played low, because depth is needed to force the other player back into the corner. A low ball will not go deep. Therefore, play high enough to get depth (one to three feet above the tin) when behind an opponent. Play lower only when out in front. This is basic percentage play, and it is not only safer (less risk of tins), but more aggressive, too, because of the depth. It also inhibits your opponent—no short balls.

At the end of the rally one player usually has an open ball, an opportunity to place the ball quite far from his opponent, to run him around and eventually win or punish him severely. The ball is out in the center, and his opponent must therefore be off to one side or the other. How does the striker take advantage of this situation? The simple answer would seem to be to place the ball to the open side.

This answer is the most sound for those just learning the game. But a squash court is rather narrow, and a player always stands as near the middle of the width as he can, thus cutting the width in half to begin with. The only long dimension is the diagonal: from deep left to short right, or deep right to short left. When the striker has a setup, the opponent has usually just dug the ball out of a back corner, so he is not only off to one side but is also behind the striker. Thus the best shot is frequently short to the open side, not long. This brings the finesse shots into play: drop shots, corner shots, and attempts at nicks up front. If the striker makes a short shot and his opponent retrieves it, the striker immediately plays long, again running his man the greatest distance permitted by the dimensions of the court. This combination—short followed by long—is known as the *up-and-back-play,* and it is basic to good tactics beyond the intermediate stage. Why not just play every other ball long and short, thus running an opponent mercilessly from start to finish? Because a short shot, if badly executed, has a backfire effect. It gives an opponent a chance to do to you what you had planned to do to him. The risk inherent in the short ball—letting him out in front of you—is against the percentages, unless it is very well done so that he has trouble reaching the ball and cannot do much with it. Therefore, the more conservative rally is a necessary prelude to any decision to precipitate a crisis by playing short. The good player wants to "mix them up" but is hesitant to do so until the advantage of a setup gives greater assurance of the necessary perfection in executing the finesse shot.

The rally brings to the fore another basic shot: the *lob*. Frequently during a rally an opponent's shot will be very forcing. You do not have time to set up the feet and weight well enough to make an equally forceful return. But the ball must be kept deep to avoid giving an opponent that short ball we call a setup. The only way to get depth without power is to play high, i.e., a lob. While a lob can and should be intercepted by the volley, the lob cannot be "killed." It's too high in the air. Striking down close to the telltale on such a volley is definitely nonpercentage, resulting in more errors than winners. Thus, while not aggressive, the lob is a great point saver and a much underrated part of basic technique.

It may be argued that the lob is too negative. It merely postpones defeat, and players should be more constructive and positive. This is a good point, and it would be difficult to refute this contention if the game always permitted a choice. But when two players are evenly matched, it is reasonable to assume that each player will find himself in serious trouble at some point during half the points played. All he can do is get it back, digging it out of the corner or barely getting under it just before it takes that fatal second bounce. In all such situations the ability to toss up a lob that creeps along the wall is essential to avoid certain defeat on subsequent shots. A player with a good lob is frequently down but never out. He "hangs in there" and frustrates his opponent's efforts to finish him off. He is adept at "pulling the point out." It is much easier to finish off a player who lacks the ability to lob when in trouble. The lob is the backbone of defensive play, and as such must be included in any catalogue of basic shots.

Two other skills are basically necessary: service and return of service. Since one of those two shots is a player's first shot on every point, the importance of these two skills is so obvious it needs no stress. The function of the service is hopefully to gain an initial advantage. The return of service strives to frustrate and cancel out this play, hopefully establishing parity in the subsequent exchange.

The rally and the intermittent crisis situations involve a lot of mobility, turning, twisting, and balance. The heart of the physical skills needed is the ability to make a fast start. The ball is quite dead. When played low it takes two bounces rather quickly, in sharp contrast to the comparatively long floating bounce of a tennis ball. Most shots are only a step or two away, but you have very little time to take those steps. Therefore very simple and minimal moves of both the feet and racquet are essential to success at any level beyond that of the rank beginner. There is no time for anything complicated or elaborate, however persuasive such procedures might appear in print. The most compelling element in the game is tempo. The more advanced the play, the higher the tempo, and the greater the necessity for absolute simplicity. A discussion of how a player should handle himself (as contrasted with how to use the racquet) will be found in chapter 8 on "Footwork and Balance."

Thus squash racquets demands a varied yet disciplined technique. You must have an effective service and return of service, accurate deep drives, a good volley, a controlled lob, and at least some skill in executing finesse shots in order fully to exploit opportunities. You must also be able to move quickly and execute all these (except service) so simply that very little time is needed, since an opponent worth his salt won't give you much time.

To acquire all of this is quite an assignment, and this is merely the basic game. Nothing has yet been said about advanced tactics: deception, surprise, contrasting shots, cross-ups, counterattack, the shot-off-the-shot, match strategy, and the psychological aspects of match play. These will be explored later in the chapter entitled "Advanced Tactics and Match Play." The tactics are academic until one has acquired the techniques necessary to execute the thoughts. But the fun involved is well worth the effort needed to acquire the skills, and the process of acquiring them can in itself be a considerable pleasure, not a chore (see the chapter on "Teaching and Learning"). So to those who might be frightened into faintheartedness by the apparent magnitude of the task of learning one might say that though really good things don't come cheaply, in this case the price itself is a reward, and not a cost.

Summary

1. The server tries to establish an initial advantage.

2. The receiver tries to return high and deep to cancel this advantage.

3. The rally is a battle for the center in which the ball is played well above the telltale without thought of outright winners, in the hope of forcing a setup.

4. The setup brings about a crisis: one player now plays quite low for a placement, the other tries desperately to retrieve this ball in such a way as to reestablish parity. If he does, the rally resumes. If not, the point is over.

PART I

Technique

1

Grips

Technique is the servant of tactics. Whatever a player does he should do in a way that best serves the tactical objective. Therefore, the discussion of each aspect of technique will be related to the most common tactical purpose for which the stroke or shot is used. Basic tactics have already been discussed (see the section on "The Basic Game"). This chapter will be helpful if what is advised seems questionable from a tactical point of view. For a more lengthy exposition of the subtleties of match play refer to the chapters on "Advanced Tactics" and "Tactics and Match Play."

Grips

There is eternal argument about grips. I have no illusion that I am about to utter the last word on an apparently inexhaustible subject, but I do have an objective. The discussion about grips has been and is too frequently based on the examples of successful players rather than on logic. A really good athlete, who is also a good competitor, will be successful even with poor grips; but he will seldom be a champion. He will do well *in spite* of his grips, not because of them. Unfortunately people learning the game tend to imitate without discrimination. They believe that whatever a winner does must be good. What follows will hopefully eliminate this misconception and will be based on two factors alone: the biomechanics of the hand and its logical application to the demands of the game (i.e., what

11

you wish to do to the ball). I hope to be able to establish facts that are basically true for every player whatever his talent.

Forehand Grips. There are three basic forehand grips: eastern, western, and continental. When the palm of the hand and the face of the racquet are in the same plane this is called an *eastern grip* (Fig. 1.1). When the face of the racquet is turned down (closed) compared with the palm, this is a *western grip* (Fig. 1.2). When the face of the racquet is turned up (opened) compared with the palm, this is a *continental grip* (Fig. 1.3).

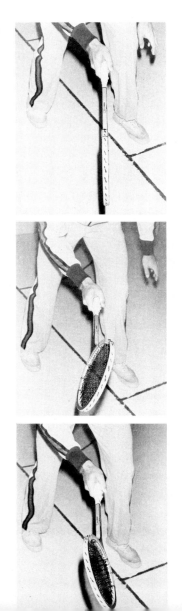

Figure 1.1 *Eastern Forehand Grip.* The palm of the hand and face of the racquet are in the same plane.

Figure 1.2 *Western Forehand Grip.* The face of the racquet is closed (turned down) compared with the palm.

Figure 1.3 *Continental Forehand Grip.* The face of the racquet is open (turned up) compared with the palm.

Note that in all three illustrations the hand does not change, it is the racquet that is different.

Backhand Grips. As with forehand grips, backhand grips are also termed as eastern, western, or continental grips. When the hand is held in its natural karate hitting position and the face of the racquet is almost perpendicular to the floor, this is an *eastern grip* (Fig. 1.4). When the face is more nearly closed, this is a *western grip* (Fig. 1.5). When the face is definitely open, this is a *continental grip* (Fig. 1.6).

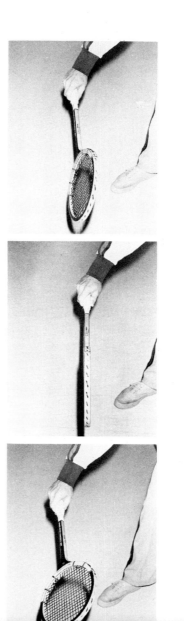

Figure 1.4 *Eastern Backhand Grip.* The hand is in its most natural position. The racquet is very slightly open so that the ball will clear the telltale but will still be low.

Figure 1.5 *Western Backhand Grip.* The ball of the thumb is flat behind the handle. The racquet face is more closed than in Figure 1.4 so a low ball may be put into the tin.

Figure 1.6 *Continental Backhand Grip.* The face of the racquet is decisively open. Using this grip, you will seldom play too low, but it is often less aggressively flat than an eastern. This grip is excellent for slicing.

The Forehand

If you deal a flat blow with the fore or front of your hand—i.e., the palm—you will swing your arm with the palm of the hand perpendicular to the floor. Try it any other way—with the palm faceup or facedown—and it tends to become awkward to whatever extent you deviate from this "natural" swing. Therefore you should swing this way (Fig. 1.7a).

Now put the racquet in the hand, so that the face is very slightly open or tipped back (Fig. 1.7b). Why? Most shots in squash must be played up a little to avoid the telltale and to give a little backspin to bring them down after they strike the front wall. The resultant grip will be almost an eastern grip but not quite: it will be very slightly continental. This has long been recognized as the basic grip for the forehand. The forehand *can* be played with other grips, but an extreme continental will open the face too much—the ball will go too high. A western will close the face too much, resulting in errors in the tin—the ball will go too low. With the proper grip you get the desired effect without departing from the most natural swing.

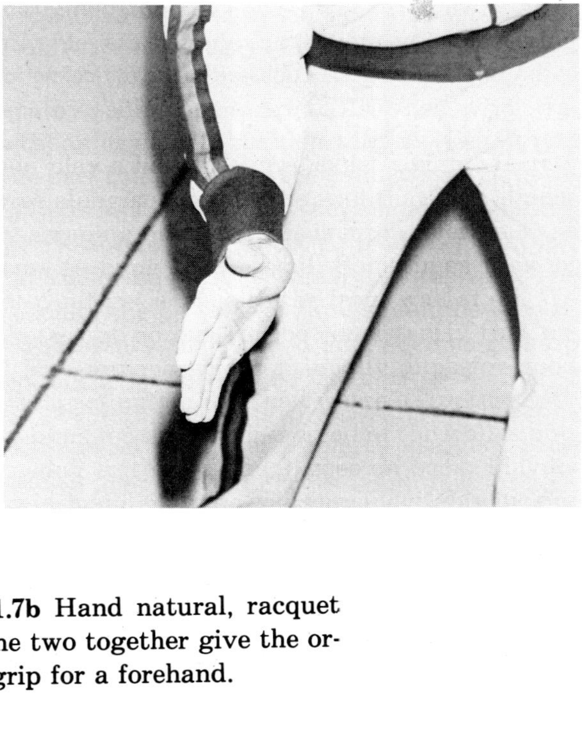

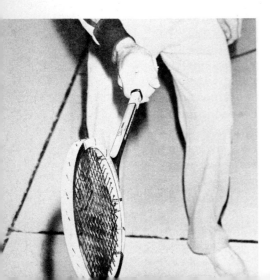

Figure 1.7a The most natural way to deal a forehand blow is with the palm roughly perpendicular.

Figure 1.7b Hand natural, racquet right—the two together give the orthodox grip for a forehand.

The Backhand

Unlike the forehand, which is played with the fore or front of the hand, a backhand is *not* played with the back of the hand. It is played with the edge of the hand, as in karate. Realizing this—it is astonishing how many people don't—is fundamental to understanding a backhand grip. The natural way to deal a backhanded blow is with the edge or heel of the hand (Fig. 1.8a). If, as with the forehand, you now place the racquet in the hand with a slightly opened face, you will have almost, but not quite, an eastern grip. It will be a very slight continental (Fig. 1.8b). Again, to vary from this by using a western or an extreme continental will tend to make the ball go too low or too high if you use your natural swing. The arm does tend to swing naturally: that's the way it is built to operate and it naturally seeks this groove. To make any other grip do the same job requires a distortion of nature and, while it can be done, it increases the difficulty of achieving consistently good execution. Therefore even though it can be done, and is done, it is considered wrong.

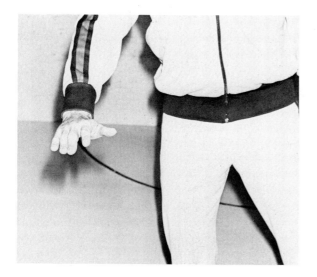

Figure 1.8a The "karate" position is the most natural way to deal a strong backhand blow.

Figure 1.8b Hand natural, racquet right—the two together give the most effective backhand grip.

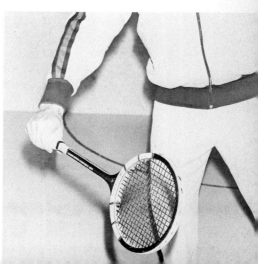

Variations

The basic grips are recommended for all beginners and intermediates. As soon as this stage is reached, all players should learn to use eastern grips for volleying high balls. Why? You now wish to play the ball down, not up, and a more closed racquet face is desirable. This is equally true for both forehand and backhand. The first thing to learn is to play the ball up to avoid errors and to handle the majority of shots, which tend to be reasonably low. Besides this, however, you should have the ability to cover the ball and play it down when occasion demands. This cannot—repeat *cannot*—be done merely by changing the aspect of the hand without changing the grip. Try it. It is next to impossible to take a volley well in front of you with a continental grip (forehand or backhand), and play it low along the wall (a very effective play). The ball keeps going higher than is desirable, because again the hand and arm seek their natural groove. You have to change the racquet's position because it is a biomechanical necessity (Figs. 1.9a, b).

Note that these grips are not *the same as those shown in Figures 1.7 and 1.8.*

Figure 1.9a The forehand volley with an eastern grip closes the racquet face and makes it easy to play down on a high ball.

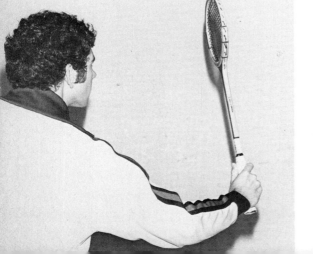

Figure 1.9b The backhand volley with an eastern-to-western grip closes the racquet face and enables the volleyer to play down with aggressive flatness.

Retrieving Grips

Whenever a player is passed and is reaching far behind himself to retrieve the ball, drastic grip changes are unavoidable. The only way to get the ball to the front wall is to dig flat underneath it. This is impossible (note that word—impossible) unless, on the forehand, the player uses such an extreme continental that it is the equivalent of an eastern backhand grip (Fig. 1.10a), and, for the backhand, a slightly western forehand grip (Fig. 1.10b).

Every advanced player does this frequently in a tough match. He instinctively changes the racquet to get the extremely open face required to make the only sensible shot (a lob). When the ball is in front of or even with a player such changes are not necessary, but when the ball is well behind him it is physically impossible to avoid them. Players and teachers should recognize this, and learn it and teach it, because effective retrieving is not possible without it.

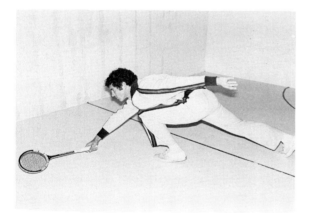

These pictures do not exaggerate what advanced players constantly do when in trouble.

Figure 1.10a Retrieving with a forehand. Note the drastic grip change to get completely under the ball.

Figure 1.10b Retrieving with a backhand. Note the drastic change (to an eastern forehand) to get under the ball.

Shortening the Grip

In playing a ball that barely comes off the back wall, such as a good lob service that was not volleyed (as it should be), some players will move their hand literally halfway up the handle to reduce leverage, put the racquet head behind the ball, and flick a lob down the wall. This can be effective in avoiding the less desirable play of sending the ball into the sidewall on its way to the front wall. (This makes it come out into the center—a poor play.)

Logic

Many players are quite adamant in asserting that they use one grip and never change it. This is seldom if ever true; and if it is true it is a weakness, not a strength. A racquet held in such a way that it will produce a fine backhand with a completely natural swing will *not* produce a fine forehand with a completely natural swing. A small change in the position of the butt under the palm is necessary. The amount of change needed is markedly increased when the player changes from playing a high backhand volley to a high forehand volley. The greatest change is necessary when the player goes from forehand retrieving to backhand retrieving.

The logic behind this is simple. The aspect of the hand cannot be changed very much without drastically weakening the strength of the natural swing. Therefore, in order to get different effects, such as playing sharply up or down, you must change the racquet. Put another way, you cannot tamper much with the natural functioning of the hand and arm without encountering real trouble. It is "against nature." The basic grips are fine for beginners and lower intermediates, but they are not the last word or suitable for all plays.

Does this all seem too complicated? It is actually quite simple. Use your physique the way it is built to be used most efficiently. Learn to adapt the racquet to your physique to play moderately up (basic), moderately down (good volleying), and extremely up (retrieving). Conversely, do not try to make your hand, wrist, and arm act unnaturally in order to change the aspect of the face of the racquet (open or closed). The hand has its limitations. The racquet must absorb the rest of any change needed in playing the ball to the best advantage.

Importance of Grips

This cannot be overemphasized. A poor grip on either side immediately limits a player's possible improvement. Many very talented people fail to realize more than half their potential excellence just because they have "funny strokes"—and a funny stroke, nine times out of ten, is the result of holding the racquet in a "funny" way. What does "funny" mean? It means holding the racquet in a manner that requires distortion of the natural swing in order to get a good result in the action of the ball. The best example, and a very common fault, is the tendency of many beginners to use an eastern forehand grip in playing a backhand (Fig. 1.11). This particular example makes very obvious the unnatural and weak actions forced on a player by a poor grip. Other departures from the natural are less glaringly obvious and are often harder to spot—but the principle holds throughout the entire gamut of technique.

Figure 1.11 The worst backhand grip. In order to meet the ball squarely, the player must hit in the weakest possible manner. Many players have been doomed to permanent mediocrity, in both tennis and squash, because they adopted this backhand grip. It is a common fault, and quite fatal.

Resistance to Change

We are all creatures of habit and resist change. If you have "funny" strokes you are urged to read the chapter on "Teaching and Learning." Many people try a new approach and at once feel they can't do it that way and give up, thereby preventing the realization of their own potential for improvement. It is hoped they will gain new understanding and the courage to try again from reading this exploration of learning problems common to everyone. The tendency is for the individual to leap to the conclusion that he's different, that he just can't do it. This is not true. We are all the same, we all resist change, we all say at first, "I can't do it that way." Yet this should be no cause for discouragement. Instead, it should arouse your determination, because the job *can* be done, by you as well as by anyone else.

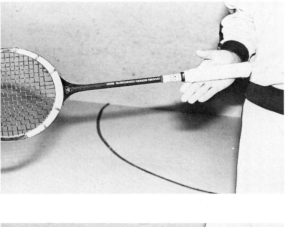

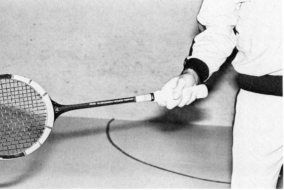

Figure 1.12a Note the diagonal position of the racquet in the hand. This results in "feel" and "touch" because the fingers come into play.

Feeling the Grip

All grips should be somewhat diagonal in the hand, so that the butt is firmly against the upper palm but that part of the grip nearer the head of the racquet is somewhat in the fingers, particularly the forefinger and thumb (see Fig. 1.12a). A racquet held at a right angle to the palm, so all the grip is in the palm, seldom gives a good "feel." The grip is comparatively clumsy and unskillful, and is often referred to as "clubbing the racquet" (Fig. 1.12b).

Figure 1.12b The racquet is held at a right angle so it is totally in the palm, rather than partially in the fingers, as shown in Figure 12a. This "clubby" way of gripping is not recommended.

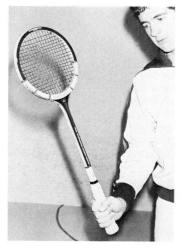

What does "feel" mean? It means that there is rapport between the player and the face of the racquet when he is not looking at it (he is watching the ball). On a forehand, this comes from "feeling" the back of the handle, i.e., the flatness which is in the same plane as the face of the racquet. If a player feels this, he knows, without looking, exactly how the face of the racquet is slanted and therefore whether the ball will be struck so as to go up, down, or level. On the backhand, the side of the first joint of the thumb and the side of the second section of the forefinger correlate with the front and back flatnesses of the handle, which again are in the same plane as the face of the racquet (Fig. 1.13).

Without this "feel" the ball flies all over the place, goes too high or too low, and the player doesn't know what will happen next. That is why beginners often make many ludicrous shots even though they are intelligent people. There is no connection, or "feel", between their minds and how the face of the racquet is coming to the ball. Without this communication anything can happen, and often does. Therefore, it is crucially important to spend a good deal of time on getting grips that have some "feel," or practice time will be substantially wasted.

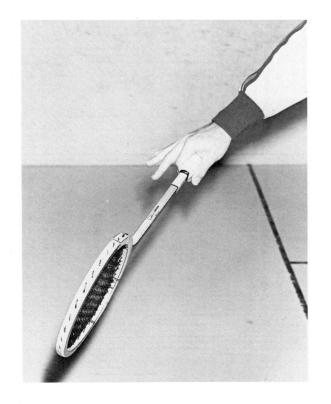

Figure 1.13 To get "feel" with a backhand grip, hold the racquet with two fingers only and do not look at it. See if you can tell how it is slanted by the feel of surfaces held by your thumb and forefinger. Note carefully that the side of the thumb, more than the ball, is used.

Changing Grips

The essential change between a basic forehand and a basic backhand grip is not visible since it's under the hand. The butt of the racquet is somewhat in the crotch of the palm for a forehand, and more towards the little finger for a backhand. That is, the butt moves a little more under the hand for a backhand. There is little change in the position of the thumb and forefinger. Cocking the racquet back for a backhand will effect this change automatically if you loosen the grip of the third, fourth, and fifth fingers to *let* it happen. You can't *make* it happen: you must allow it to happen. Similarly, if you have just played a backhand and the ball returns quickly to your forehand, cock the racquet and *let* the change occur. A little fiddling with the racquet will give you the feel of making this change as an automatic part of preparing to play the ball. With a little experience it becomes an instantaneous twitch.

Summary

1. Technique is the servant of tactics. Therefore, the two should constantly be related.
2. Grips should relate logically to physique and tactics.
3. Eastern grips are flat. Western grips close the face. Continental grips open the face.
4. Forehands are played with the palm of the hand.
5. Backhands are played with the edge of the hand.
6. Basic grips are slightly continental. Volley grips are more eastern. Retrieving grips are extremely open. All should be learned.
7. Getting "feel" is indispensable to good aim.
8. Everyone resists change. This doesn't mean they can't change.
9. Changing grips is easily learned.

2

Spin

Spin is almost as important to technique in squash racquets as it is in billiards, a game in which it is often referred to as "putting English on the ball." As in billiards, the angle of the bounce off the wall can be decisively influenced by spin. Spin can be used to augment the effectiveness of many shots. It can also be used to reduce the chances of error by allowing the player to play a safe distance above the telltale and still get the same result that can only be obtained by playing very low with a "flat" stroke—i.e., one without any appreciable spin. Thus spin is one of the great components of "percentage play."

Percentage Play

Squash racquets is above all a percentage game. Unlike football, where one brilliant play can redeem all in a twinkling, the reward for the most difficult and incredible shot is still only one point. And every failure costs a point. There is an inexorable quality about squash. You may make six perfect shots and I three, and you make four errors and I none—you have outplayed me in terms of super shot making two to one, but the score is seven to six and I am ahead. Therefore every play, every shot, every plan must be judged on a basis of percentages. If you perform this play one hundred times, how many times will you come out ahead? If the result is negative that shot in that context should be discarded, no matter how tempting the possibility of success on individual points may be. The objective is not to win any one point but to win more points than your opponent over an extended period, namely a match. Therefore the concept of percentage must govern your entire attitude, not only regarding tactics but also technique.

Backcourt Spin

In playing from the back of the court you must play quite hard. If the ball goes slowly, an alert opponent will intercept it, and you will seldom get in front of him in that dominant position from which attempted winners are possible without undue risk. At the same time you do not want your ball to rebound off the back wall since this gives your opponent plenty of time to set up and make a fine return. If you play well above the tin and hit quite hard without spin the ball will frequently come off the back wall, so your forcing shot doesn't force him very much. If you play quite low you will continually risk error in the tin, and will inevitably miss a few too many in the course of the match. If, by contrast, you put some backspin on the ball by crossing it a little from the outside in, the ball will be pulled down a little from the front wall. You can play a little higher, never make an error, and still play as aggressively as possible. Doing this is what is known as "slicing the ball." It is not by accident that it is a characteristic of the strokes of almost every champion. They achieve the objective of making near zero errors by playing far enough above the telltale so that even if they miss their aim (in height), the ball will still be fair. They achieve the objective of making the ball go dead by using spin.

Forecourt Spin

When out front with a setup a player may wish to make the ball take two bounces as far forward as possible. A player with flat strokes can achieve this only by aiming extremely low and, on a drop shot, by playing extremely gently. Again, the use of heavy spin will give not only equal, but actually better, results even if aimed a few inches higher. Sharp backspin will pull a drop shot down decisively so it takes its first bounce nearer the front wall. Sharp side spin will throw a ball around the corner from wall to wall faster than a flat ball, and will make it deader too—i.e., less likely to reach the third wall. On a three wall nick, sidespin can be used to throw the ball sideways when it reaches the front wall so that a higher percentage of successful nicks inevitably follows. Sidespin can be used in lob serving from the backhand side to the forehand. This allows the player to play the front wall nearer the sidewall and still have the ball rebound straight so it nearly clings to the wall and is very difficult to volley.

Topspin

Even topspin has its use on rare occasions. Some like to use it on a lob service, particularly in a high ceilinged court, to make the rebound go higher and therefore drop more vertically into the receiver's corner. Again, sometimes on a desperate move up front when a player does *not* want the ball to go short but cannot hit hard due to reaching, some topspin applied with a quick wrist flick will give a higher and therefore deeper rebound off the front wall. That extra depth can save the point or win it outright.

Nicks

A standard play in advanced squash is to try for a nick off a setup. A true nick, in which the ball actually hits the wall and the floor simultaneously and literally doesn't bounce at all, is very rare. The word *nick* means that the ball strikes the sidewall very near the floor so that it instantly bounces once and takes a quick little hop to its second bounce, and only the fastest moving player can get to it before it is "down." A ball that is hit without spin will rebound much more horizontally than a ball with heavy backspin. Therefore the "flat" ball will more often strike the sidewall high enough so it takes quite a while to take two bounces, and with enough scrambling, anyone can reach it. Moreover, even if it does nick it will necessarily nick at a point well back from the front wall, therefore making it easier to reach. A ball with heavy backspin tends to go down from the front wall. Therefore it will nick more often—that is, strike the sidewall low. Equally importantly, it will strike the sidewall nearer the front wall, so the retriever has farther to go (see Fig. 2.1).

More about Percentages

These distinctions are often a matter of inches rather than feet. However, squash is a fast game and the court is small. A few inches is usually the difference between an ace and a ball that comes back to frustrate the attacker and drive him into aiming too low for an error. The masters of spin are most often those who develop an effective offense without cancelling out half of it or more with their errors. Flat strokes and shots will often be brilliant and gain individual points, but they do not pay off over a five game match when opposed by spin strokes. They are nonpercentage.

The following discussion will deal with individual strokes and shots, and in each case will emphasize the spin that makes a certain shot most effective without the undue risk that leads to errors. The whole technical approach in this book is based on aiming *away from* the tin. If you aim at it you'll hit it, and you'll lose. Spin makes percentage play possible.

The Nature of Spin

This seems quite simple, yet it is frequently misunderstood thereby causing much frustration. *Topspin* does not mean to hit the top of the ball. It means that the top of the ball is turning forward as the ball travels through the air. You should think of it as a "forward spin" and forget the "top" part. It is quite easy to play below the middle of the back of the ball,

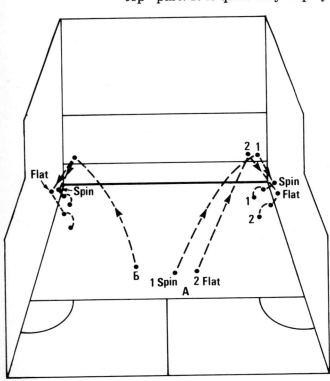

Figure 2.1 Flat and Spin Drop Shots Contrasted. The spin drop shot will drop more sharply down and can therefore be aimed closer to the wall for a semi-nick farther forward (A). The more horizontal rebound of the flat shot is illustrated (B). If a short nick is aimed for, the ball will strike the sidewall higher and come out, causing a setup. It's a matter of inches—but inches make the difference in class A squash.

almost on the bottom of the ball, and still spin it forward—and many players actually do this with a topspin lob service.

Likewise, *backspin* does not mean to cut under the ball. It means that the top of the ball is turning backwards as the ball travels. It is easy to cut down on the top of the back of the ball from above, with a chopping stroke, and play it right into the floor and still have a lot of backspin. Yet whenever someone suggests "cutting the ball," players cut the bottom off it and send it almost into the ceiling. You should always play the *back* of the ball: the center of the back to aim straight, a little toward the top of the back to play down (many volleys), and more toward the bottom of the back for basic drives. Only on a high lob do you play the very bottom of the ball—i.e., when you wish the ball to go sharply up.

Much of the prevalent misunderstanding is due to the interaction of the racquet and ball. When a player cuts the ball it rolls up his racquet and goes higher than his swing. When he spins the ball forward it rolls down his racquet and goes lower than his swing. Not realizing this and not allowing for it causes many players to hit much too high when they first attempt to slice the ball (and too low when they first attempt to use topspin in tennis). A little experience and practice teaches a player to "hold down" his sliced shots (and "lift up" his topspin tennis shots). In sum, they have to get used to it so the allowance becomes automatic. Only playing the ball a lot gives

Figure 2.2 Spins. Note that weight always goes "through the ball"; i.e., in the same direction. Only on the flat hit (A) does the racquet go through the ball. On all strokes, the direction of the racquet takes it off the ball, not through it, and spin increases as the divergence increases. Strokes C and D are the same, except that C cuts from high to low and D cuts from side to side (from outside in—in this case, a forehand slice—right to left).

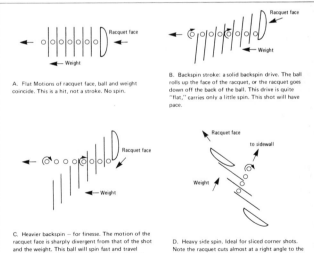

A. Flat Motions of racquet face, ball and weight coincide. This is a hit, not a stroke. No spin.

B. Backspin stroke: a solid backspin drive. The ball rolls up the face of the racquet, or the racquet goes down off the back of the ball. This drive is quite "flat," carries only a little spin. This shot will have pace.

C. Heavier backspin — for finesse. The motion of the racquet face is sharply divergent from that of the shot and the weight. This ball will spin fast and travel slower—desirable for finesse. This is a chop (high to low).

D. Heavy side spin. Ideal for sliced corner shots. Note the racquet cuts almost at a right angle to the direction of the shot and the weight.

E. Topspin. The ball rolls down the racquet, or the racquet goes up the back of the ball. Used extensively in tennis, rarely in squash.

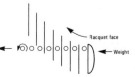

this "feel" for adjusting to the effects of spin on the height of the flight of the ball as it leaves the racquet. However, understanding what is occurring speeds the learning process (see Fig. 2.2).

Summary

1. Spin is vastly important in squash technique. It is an important ingredient in percentage play. In the back court spin aids in making a hard hit ball go dead. Up front it makes short shots shorter. Playing the ball flat is nonpercentage.

3

Technical Generalizations

There are many aspects of technique that apply to recurring playing situations. Each is also a tactical situation, usually calling for the same answer. While there are exceptions, anyone learning the game should first acquire habits that will serve well in the majority of circumstances. Only after a player has such a solid grounding should he think about brilliant surprises and exceptional plays. An exploration of these rules of technique and their relationships to tactics and general play is in order.

Play Up

The tactical objective of most drives is to force an opponent back into a corner. Therefore the ball must go deep. It must therefore strike the front wall well above the tin (one to three feet) or it won't carry that far. Since most balls are rather low when you play them, a slightly open-faced racquet is needed on contact so that the ball will rise on its way to the front wall. A second objective that every player should keep in mind is to aim away from the tin. Cultivating this habit breeds steadiness and will cause opponents to refer to you as being "tough." That is, you may not achieve a raft of winners, but you won't give points away.

Let the Ball Get Low

If a player wishes to play up away from the tin, as contrasted with playing down towards it, it follows that he should allow the ball to drop low before playing it. By doing this, he can aim up and still not play so high that he is ineffective and unaggressive. Also, by allowing the ball to drop low he gives himself more time to set up properly—i.e., to prepare the racquet, arrange his feet and balance, aim, and think. The first thing a beginner should learn is to take as much time as the ball permits. To say it another way, he should try to stroke the ball better, not sooner. If a player could wait five minutes and then make a fine shot, his opponent would be in trouble. It is the excellence of his drive that bothers the other fellow, not the fact that he hits it a half second earlier. Playing the ball as quickly as possible usually rushes the striker into sloppy execution instead of hurrying the opponent.

Crouch

To play a drive in this manner requires that both the striker and his racquet must be low. He should crouch decisively, so that his knees are bent and his back is bent sharply at the waist. This is usually described as "getting down to the ball." It is a most important habit to form early in the game, for almost all shots.

Use a Small Swing

Beginners and anyone trying to mend a faulty stroke should use a *very* small swing. The elbow should be kept low and should never kick out backwards on the forehand since this closes the face of the racquet and causes the striker to tend to play down instead of up. There is actually no backswing at all: the racquet is cocked with the wrist and taken back by the turn of the shoulders, not by a swing. The racquet is kept quite close to the proposed point of contact so the stroke is a snap of the wrist with only a little arm motion, as contrasted with a full swing. The follow-through should be low and the face of the racquet should be kept a little open all the way to the finish. This assures the player that the ball will go up and will have a little backspin, so it will rebound downwards from the front wall.

Many readers will be quick to point out that this swing, as described, is *not* what many top players use. This is true. Most leading players use a fuller swing to get more power and take their racquets rather high in preparing the stroke. Then they play the ball by scooping it up with a bolo-like swing that drops down behind and below the ball before contact. But it will be noted that with these advanced players the racquet still comes to the ball from below, slices it a little for control, and follows through quite low. These are the core characteristics of a good stroke. The more advanced, fuller swing simply takes the racquet farther away to get a better start for more power. This can be added easily later on, *after* the core of knowledge has been mastered. A beginner or someone in trouble should concentrate on the guts of the problem, get it right, and ignore power until the objective is achieved.

Wild Beginners

There are other cogent reasons why this "no swing" stroke should be the basis on which a player builds. The worst thing about beginners is that they tend to flail around with full arm swings that literally make them a bodily threat to their opponents on nearly every shot. Squash is played by two people who occupy the same space. The opponent is not far away across the net, as he is in tennis. He is by necessity quite close to the striker. The first thing a beginner should learn is a low, very restricted backswing and a low restricted follow-through. There should be no thought wasted on maximum power. The beginner must learn *at once* to be an acceptable companion in the court, or, even with all the goodwill in the world, he will injure someone and get a bad reputation. "Joe is a great guy—but don't get in a squash court with him. He's murder!" This is problem number one and must take precedence over all other considerations. The restricted swing does this at once.

The Double Threat

The second reason for a restricted swing is important to all advanced players including champions. If the racquet is taken far away from the ball, so it has a rather large approach to the ball, it is next to impossible to make anything except a large shot. By contrast, if the racquet is cocked rather close to the ball, any shot can be made, from a little drop shot or snippy corner shot to a hard snap that gives full depth. Surprise and deception, the "double threat" that characterizes top play is based on having a restricted swing. It is quite noticeable that the many-times champion, Vic Niederhoffer, takes less backswing than most of his opponents. It is also noticeable that he is probably the most deceptive player in the game today. Each shot is played after a preparation that allows for and therefore threatens every shot, short and long. Each is made with a last minute snap that is almost impossible to "read," i.e., anticipate. His technique is well worthy of everyone's close attention.

Neatness

A third reason for a small swing is neatness. Most players' shots are sadly inexact. A restricted swing and good footwork permit a degree of accuracy far higher than that given by a large swing. A slugger with a big swing makes a huge amount of noise in the court but is comparatively ineffective, "full of sound and fury, signifying nothing." A neat player, who can hit sharply (as contrasted with powerfully) and can put the ball more exactly where he wishes, is almost always superior in skill as well as being more agreeable to play with. He plays you, he doesn't intimidate you.

Skill in the Corners

A fourth reason favoring a restricted swing is the cramping effect of the walls. In tennis there is nothing but air all around you. In squash many balls are near the back wall. There is no room for a large backswing, the only way to handle such a ball is with a wristy swing with severely limited arm motion. Beginners clatter around the walls and are helpless as they try to use their tennis swing in a back corner. It won't fit, and they at once ask, "How do you get those shots? I can't play them." The small swing is the answer, and if they use it all the time, even when there is more room, they will learn the indispensible trick of handling balls near the back wall far more quickly. The small swing works everywhere in the court. The large swing works only in the open away from the back wall.

Therefore safety, sportsmanship, neatness, skill in the corners, accuracy, and deception all require that players should first learn a sternly disciplined small swing that is fundamentally sound and dependable.

What if a player decides he wants to be more of a hitter? All he needs to do is prepare the same way, then take the racquet farther away from the ball. When he does this the arm and the racquet will necessarily rise since it is swinging in an arch hinged at the shoulder. This expansion of the small disciplined swing is easy to add. It is much more difficult to cut down and reduce a habitually big swing. The best way to acquire any style is to start with a neat small stroke, then enlarge it as much as may suit one's purpose.

Hand Skills

A further argument favoring the restricted swing follows from an understanding of what a player is learning to do. The skills involved in all the shots are primarily skills of the hand and wrist. Anyone can swing his arm around. The secret of excellence is the skillful handling of the racquet. Think of that word *handling*. It means to use with the hand—not with the arm or body. Once a player has the hand skill it is comparatively easy to add more arm, more weight, more power. Since the hand skill is the core of the problem it is advisable to stress it from the start, for everything else is peripheral rather than central.

Preparation

The manner in which a player prepares his racquet determines what he can and cannot do. This is a most important fact although it is not appreciated by many players and even some teachers. If a player prepares his racquet badly he has two choices: (1) play the ball badly, or (2) don't play it at all. Since no one will accept the second choice, what it means is that to prepare incorrectly guarantees a poor shot (on a percentage basis), no matter how hard the player tries, how much he concentrates, or how much he practices. That is why there are so many inconsistent players, i.e., those with a good stroke on one side but a poor stroke on the other side. They may play for a decade—and still the weak side is weak. This is always due to faulty preparation.

It follows then that you should stop putting all your concentration on how you play the ball, and instead focus on how you get ready to play the ball. You must first make it *possible* to play the ball well. This is a new concept to many people. It is actually one of the keys to successful learning and teaching.

Early Preparation

Preparing the racquet instantly—as early as is humanly possible—is of great importance. Why? The reason is somewhat subtle but nonetheless true. Once the ball is near the contact point you must concentrate on timing—on choosing when you will "pull the trigger" or strike. This timing requires all your attention. The mind will not focus on more than one thing at a time. You cannot simultaneously think about preparing the racquet and timing the ball. It is one or the other, and since the timing is absolutely essential (after all, you don't want to whiff the ball), you must focus your attention only on the timing once the ball nears the planned point of contact. It follows that you must prepare the racquet as long as possible before the ball gets close, or, in spite of any good intentions you may have, you won't think about it at all. In that case, it will do anything rather than what you had planned or intended it to do. If the instant you identify a ball as coming to the forehand or backhand you also prepare the racquet, you can think about it and control it before the timing problem takes over. The whole secret of learning a new technique or correcting an old one is quick preparation. Only early preparation can be thoughtful as contrasted with instinctive or habitual.

Aiming

Aiming takes time. We have all read stories about firing instantly from the hip with deadly and infallible accuracy. The fact is that outside of pulp magazines no one can, on a percentage basis, hit the side of a barn without taking some time to aim. Squash is a fast game, so how do you find the time to aim? You can make the time by very quick preparation, so the racquet is ahead of the ball, lined up before the ball arrives. This way, final adjustments can be made to achieve as exact an aim as possible.

The Three Aims

There are three aims in squash racquets: the ball must go in the proper direction, not to the left or right; it must go the desired height, not above or below; and it must go the correct distance, not too short or too long. The third aim—for length—is much neglected by many players. Their ball may go accurately down the wall, but go too far and come off the back wall, thus robbing it of much of its effectiveness. Or it will go short and fail to carry an opponent back into the corner. The opponent steps sideways, plays, and steps back: the drive did not get him out of the center even though it was crisp and had good direction. The best players have good length as well as direction. The ball goes way back and usually does not come back out. It dies in the corner. It is important to realize that this third aim is essential for true excellence.

Footwork and Balance

In most shots length is controlled by weight. A deep drive must be pressed hard enough into the front wall so it will carry almost to the service line before taking its first bounce. This feeling of pressing while one plays the ball comes from shoving with the legs. It is just as essential on a drop shot as on a drive. A good drop shot is "feathered" with the racquet to give it backspin so it will go down as soon as it touches the front wall. It is simultaneously pushed with the legs just hard enough—but no harder—to reach the front wall. It can be compared to shooting a basket in basketball: the player must aim straight, must aim up so the ball will drop down into the basket, and it must be pushed just far enough so it drops in—not short or long. The push comes from the legs on all except the fanciest shots.

Balance and Touch

If this is true, setting up the feet and balance ready to shove is essential to good "touch." It is quite surprising how nearly impossible it is to make a good drop shot when off balance. The ball goes too hard and rebounds as a setup, or drops short in the tin. Therefore preparing the feet, as well as the racquet, and maintaining good balance are as important as having a good eye. What is generally not appreciated is that these factors become *more* important as the finesse of the shot increases. You can be on one leg and leaning away and make a pretty fair drive with your arm and wrist. You cannot make good drops, corners and nicks this way. This seems illogical because so little actual force is used on finesse shots. But the factor of length—very exact length—depends on the legs and balance, and this is the key to achieving successful offensive plays instead of mistakes that backfire. If you want to be known as a "touch" player, learn to set up your feet for balance so that you can perfectly control the weight shift that gives good length.

The Open Follow-Through

The importance of the follow-through is based for the most part on one fact: what the head of the racquet does at the end of the swing almost always begins while it is playing the ball. It is almost impossible to roll over the follow-through (close the face of the racquet) and slice the ball. It is also almost impossible to follow through with an open face without slicing the ball. Since you want to slice the ball a little and the follow-through largely controls this spin factor, you should develop an open follow-through.

The Follow-Through Makes the Spin

Many players do not understand that the spin is controlled by the follow-through. It becomes more clear if one realizes that spin is created by *leaving* the ball, not by coming to it. If the follow-through is rolled over, the top edge of the racquet leaves the ball first, the ball tends to roll down the racquet, and forward spin (topspin) is created. If the follow-through is kept a little open, the bottom edge of the racquet leads off the ball, the ball rolls up the racquet, and slice (backspin) is created. Sidespin is created by leading off the ball, from the outside in, with the bottom edge of the racquet (from right to left for the forehand, from left to right for the backhand). But the point being made here is that the *last* part of the swing—the follow-through—is what controls all this, and therein lies its fundamental importance.

Balance Again

Of course you must handle yourself (as distinct from the racquet) properly also. If your weight shifts backwards, a high follow-through will result with any stroke. If you "pull up," your follow-through can be high with any stroke. Thus, good balance in addressing the ball and "keeping your head down" (as in golf) are important.

Racquet Work Is the Key

However, too frequently a high follow-through is blamed on bad balance or pulling up when in actuality it is because of bad racquet work. If a player rolls over his follow-through, the ball tends to go down. He must follow through high to clear the telltale. After all, he doesn't want to hit the ball into the floor just to keep his head down and have nice balance. So he does follow through high, which tends to take his head and weight high instead of keeping them low. By contrast, if a player slices the ball he must follow through low and keep his head down or the ball will go much too high and be a bad shot. Thus good racquet work—a proper follow-through—tends to force good balance and a low racquet on a player, while bad racquet work tends to make a dangerous, high follow-through inevitable.

This is not a case of the hen and the egg. The follow-through is definitely the cause and the good or bad performance the result, not vice versa. This should be stressed by all teachers because it determines to a large extent whether a player will be fun to play against or a menace to be shunned. Far more injuries to the face occur when players roll their strokes. I have played for forty-seven years, was taught by a fine coach to follow through open, and have never once struck anyone higher than the elbow. It is not because I'm such a nice guy. Many times when taking the ball off the back wall, and an opponent's whereabouts must be assumed rather than perceived (because you are looking back at the ball), I have hit an opponent unintentionally with my follow-through—but never high. The nature of the open follow-through stroke just about precludes the possibility. I was merely lucky enough to be well taught when I first took up the game. The more of such early schooling the better.

Stroke—Don't Hit

The word *stroke* contrasts sharply with the word *hit*. Stroke means to wipe or pass across something, as when we caress a cat. Hit means to go straight through something, as when a boxer delivers a punch. He tries to enter at the jaw and go right through the back of his opponent's head, accelerating all the way. (Boxing is indeed a cruel sport!) Likewise, a baseball player hits the ball. He goes right through it, hoping to knock it a mile. A squash or tennis player does not hit *through the ball* in spite of the generally accepted cliché: "Always hit through the ball." The racquet goes off the ball with a wiping effect. If it doesn't, then there is no spin, and the player does not have a stroke, he has a hit. That is why baseball players are referred to as good hitters, while someone who is good at racquet games is said to have "good strokes." Why is the idea of hitting through the ball so totally accepted? Because there is some truth in it: the weight should always go through the ball. The trouble with the cliché is that people learning the game invariably think it means the racquet should go through the ball—and this is not so unless everything that has been said about spin is wrong. A hit gives no spin.

Think of stroking a dog's fur. The hand goes sideways along the dog's back, while the weight of the hand presses down or "through" the dog. A hit tends to be instantaneous and only touches one spot on the dog. A stroke has much more duration and is a combination of wiping and pressing. These two processes are very different. That's why there are two different words to express them.

In squash, with few exceptions, a slice stroke is used. The racquet cuts across the ball from the outside in, or, on a high shot, from above downwards. This gives a dragging or drawing effect so that the ball rolls along the strings and is spinning as it leaves the racquet. The spin is what enables a player to control the subsequent action of the ball. With heavy spin and limited pressure (weight) he can make it go down from the front wall and take two bounces far up front (finesse shots). With a lot of pressure and less spin he can make it bounce first at the service line and then very near the back wall (a deep drive). On a shoulder high volley he can press the ball out towards the front wall, and pull down to get backspin so the ball will "lay down" after it hits the front wall. The length of every shot is best controlled by the use of varying amounts of spin, and spin is created by going "off" the ball, not by going "through the ball."

Therefore, the cliché, to be properly understood, should be amended to read: "Play through the ball with the weight, play off the ball with the racquet."

It is true that squash can be played by merely hitting the ball. The length can be controlled quite a bit by sheer "touch"—play higher or lower to get more or less length, play harder or softer to get more or less length. But the substantial additional control given by stroking (i.e., using spin) has always resulted in superior results for those who use it. Champions use spin, and anyone else is better for it at his own level of athletic ability.

In tennis the value of stroking is very obvious. If the ball is not stroked, and is hit hard, it sails over the baseline and is out. A tennis player is really poor if he doesn't learn to wipe or stroke the ball. In squash it is less obvious. The ball will be a fair ball (i.e., not an error) but it will tend to fly around too high and constantly come off the back wall. Also, a hitter's finesse shots will lack finesse; they will not die as quickly or as far up front. They will therefore be ineffective by comparison. People who hit "flat"—with no spin—will frequently be heard to say, "I can run and keep the ball going but I don't have any shots." This is another way of saying, "I am a pretty good athlete and can fight hard, but I cannot make the ball take two bounces within a given area." Such players can, and sometimes do, make a remarkable improvement by learning to stroke the ball. Others resign themselves to thinking that they "just don't have as much natural 'touch' as those fine players." This is usually not true. They merely are uneducated in the most basic skill in the technique of the game, which is to stroke rather than hit.

Summary

1. Percentage play is playing up—away from the tin.
2. Let the ball get low.
3. Control, deception, neatness, hand skill, and sportsmanship all favor a small swing with a low racquet from start to finish.
4. A player's preparation determines what he can do.
5. Early preparation makes possible more thought, better aim, and faster learning.
6. The follow-through controls the spin. The open follow-through gives slice, which is what we want, and also gives better balance and keeps the racquet low.
7. Stroke the ball, don't hit it.

4

Basic Drives

For the most part, basic drives are made from the back of the court. A player should aim well above the tin for several reasons, and the first is to give a margin for error. In the course of a match one must play the ball hundreds of times from the backcourt, but few of these shots are attempts at winners. They are position shots, and a good player should be very steady and make literally no errors at all in this sparring contest. A reasonable allowance over the tin is essential—about a foot for a hard drive, higher for drives with less pace.

Depth

A good drive takes its first bounce at or just before the service line. In fact, a drive will bounce just about the length of the service court. Therefore if the first bounce is just in front of the service line, the second bounce will be very deep but the ball will not come off the back wall.

Force and Inhibit Your Opponent

This depth serves two purposes. It continually forces your opponent to back up into the corner, thereby getting him behind you and sometimes forcing him to hit the sidewall with his return. This will give you a setup out in the open. Such forcing play is obviously desirable. The second objective is more subtle but equally important—it plays the ball *through* an opponent as contrasted with playing it to him. A ball that lacks depth will take its first bounce well in front of your opponent, and will bounce *to* him. He can do anything with such a ball as he moves sideways to intercept it. He can make short or long shots, even if it is a hard hit ball with considerable pace. However, if the ball takes its first bounce near the service line, it will bounce past him, or through him. Yes, he can get this ball and play it, but he is moving back and cannot set up to make finesse shots nearly as well as he can on the shorter ball. The depth inhibits him, reduces his options to merely keeping the ball in play, prevents him from using his pet weapons out front.

This double effect of good depth is very much appreciated by fine players but is much neglected by average players. They merely play the ball crosscourt or down the line, thinking only of direction. They give no thought to how *far* it goes down the wall and have no concept of making the first bounce at a certain depth. They wonder why, although they are very fiery, they cannot make headway against a top player. Poor depth is often the answer.

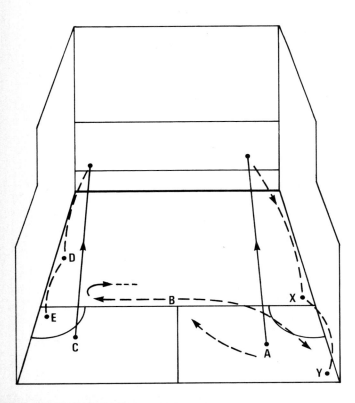

Figure 4.1 The Basic Straight Drive (A). Note the height on the front wall to get a deep first bounce at service line X, and total depth on the second bounce (Y). Player B is forced back, Player A gets in front. A poor basic drive is illustrated (C). Note the risky lowness on the front wall, the early first bounce that slows the ball and allows Player B to play it without being carried back. He holds the desirable forward position and may even make a placement off this ball. Good depth is safer *and* more agressive.

Hitting too short has been stressed here because the other fault—playing too long so the ball continually rebounds—is very obvious to one and all (Fig. 4.1).

Width

Squash players tend to think in terms of the court. This leads them to believe that a fine crosscourt or straight shot goes directly to the deep corner where the sidewall meets the backwall. You should not think this way. Squash players do not play the court, as a golfer plays the course. You play an opponent. Your shot should relate to him, and be as far from him as possible. He is usually in the center (on the T, where the two service lines meet). The farthest distance from him is the sidewall to his left or right. All drives should be aimed to touch the sidewall between the straight and curved service lines. A ball aimed for the actual corner will be easily intercepted. It goes too close to the center on its way back. A ball that doglegs around an opponent cannot be intercepted, forces him back, and wins the center position (Fig. 4.2). On a crosscourt, your concept of width

Figure 4.2 The Basic Crosscourt Drive. Note the shot dog-legs around the opponent P, so he cannot intercept it but is carried back to the corner near D. Note that the ball is played to the right of the center of the front wall (X) to get this width, and high enough to get a deep first bounce (B). Note that the striker pivots, twisting on his right foot, stepping over (from 1 to 2) with his left foot *after* striking the ball. This helps turn the ball to the right, so no special wrist action is required to play crosscourt as contrasted with a straight drive.

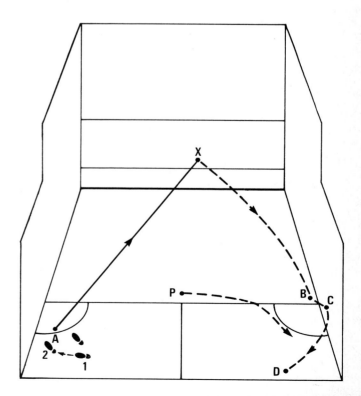

should be to play around your opponent; and you should relate to him this way, rather than relate to the symmetry of the court.

Even a straight drive should be aimed to graze the sidewall starting just behind the service line. If a ball is played this wide and has reasonable pace it cannot be intercepted before it bounces; and just after it bounces it's on the wall and cannot be played then either. Therefore, the ball *must* be played from the back corner so that your opponent will be taken out of the center and forced far back. Then, you will have gained the center and obliged your opponent to go back behind you.

Use the Walls

This concept of playing to the wall opposite your opponent is basic to good tactical thinking. You can't beat the telltale, so stay away from it. You can't put the ball away when playing from behind your opponent, so don't try. What you can do is keep the ball going so it's as near that sidewall as possible every time it gets back to the red line. Thinking in this way is quite different from thinking "aim for the back corners," a thought that relates to the court, not the man.

Luck

Every now and again you play a ball that goes exactly right. It gets back to the red line then grazes along so close to the wall that it is almost unplayable except in a sloppy scraping manner. This is often referred to as a "glue ball" because it seems to cling to the wall. Sometimes it is an outright winner—an opponent can't get it back to the front wall at all. We all yearn for these perfect shots, but no one can be consistently that accurate in such a fast game. *But,* anyone who continually aims for good width on his straight shots is at least putting the ball where it *can* turn into a lucky glue ball, while he who aims for the corner instead of the wall is putting the ball where it cannot cling to the wall as it goes on back. Players who continually try for good width and play the walls are inevitably luckier than those who play the court, i.e., the corners.

Similarly a crosscourt shot will often nick with the sidewall *if* it is aimed very wide. It will never nick if it is aimed for the corner. It is nowhere near the sidewall when it bounces, so how can it nick?

Don't complain about your luck or lack of it. If you play well you will be lucky. If you play badly the absence of luck is not due to Dame Fortune but to your own poor play. If you play the ball to where the luck is located you'll get your share. If you don't, you'll soon become convinced everyone else is luckier than you. And you'll be right!

The Forehand Drive

Use a very slightly continental grip, almost an eastern grip. Cock the wrist as much as is comfortable. Keep the elbow low and somewhat forward. Crouch, bending the knees, and keep the racquet low, making sure the face of the racquet is slightly open. Point the left toe somewhat forward, and brace the right foot to shove forward. Study these details by referring to Fig. 4.3. They are more easily understood through a photograph than through a text.

Figure 4.3 The Basic Forehand. Note the crouch, balance, open racquet face, the minimal backswing with the arm, and the fully laid back wrist. Note that the face of the racquet does not roll over or under throughout the stroke—it stays the same. Note the pointed front foot, facilitating weight transfer and shoulder turns. Many fine players add flourishes. The pictures purposely omit all individualism.

The stroke begins by a slight forward push of the butt of the racquet. Then the wrist snaps the racquet around. Here is where most mistakes are made: players tend to roll the wrist. It is important that the face of the racquet remain open throughout the stroke. This means the ball will roll diagonally up the racquet—it will be sliced. The shoulders will naturally turn into the ball as the arm goes forward and the wrist snaps. The racquet will naturally follow through to the left, adding to the slicing effect by drawing off the ball. The ball will go upwards a bit as it goes to the front wall but will be pulled down by the spin so it will tend to "lay down" rather than rebound high.

The Backhand Drive

Use a slightly continental grip so the face of the racquet is just a bit open. You should be crouched with your right foot advanced, somewhat pointed forward. There is little need to restrict the swing on the backhand. If the arm is taken back across the body so the elbow is at the stomach and close to the body, no further swing can be taken except by turning away. The presence of the body prevents it. By contrast, there is nothing to prevent a forehand from being a haymaker, because the body does not get in the way as it does when the backhand is used.

Again, the stroke should begin with the butt of the racquet moving forward to overcome inertia. The wrist comes into play a little later. There is less wrist in a backhand than in a forehand. It more nearly resembles a karate swing with the edge of the hand.

Backhand Wrist Motion

The use of the wrist in the backhand is often misunderstood. The wrist will flop up and down, causing the hand to slap. This motion is used (horizontally) for the forehand but not for the backhand. The wrist will also twist back and forth, without uncocking itself as it does for the forehand. This second wrist motion is correct for the backhand, and the "reversed" forehand motion is possibly the worst way to play a backhand. Study the sequential figures illustrating the two strokes and this difference will become clear (Figs. 4.4a, b).

Figure 4.4 The Basic Backhand. Note that everything is the same as it is for a forehand: the low racquet, open face, crouch, and pointed front foot. Note the one big difference—the contact point is about the width of the shoulders farther forward, because the hitting arm is now the front arm instead of the rear arm. The follow-through is again low and open.

Pivot for Crosscourts

The crosscourt drive is executed in the same manner as the straight drive with two exceptions. The ball is taken a little farther forward (sooner), allowing the racquet to get around the outside of the ball so as to make it go across, as well as up and down, the court. It addition, it is a great help to pivot a bit as the shot is played in order to turn it to the left with a forehand and to the right on a backhand.

This can be accurately compared to a third baseman who fields a grounder to his right, near the bag. He fields it and throws. If he throws to home plate, he just throws. If he throws to first he pivots as he throws to turn the throw to the left. If he throws to second, he pivots more decisively to throw even more to the left. The pivot is accomplished by rotating on the ball of the left foot and turning the shoulders.

Playing in this manner can be quite deceptive, since the preparation is identical and there is no clue as to which of several shots is planned. From the same position you can play a straight drive, a crosscourt drive, a reverse corner, or a crosscourt drop; thus you are threatening to put the ball into any one of all four corners of the court. (You could also play a three wall nick, a boast, a sidewall drop shot, or a lob, but these are merely different ways of putting the ball into the various corners; and such great variety adds nothing to the basic threat.) More will be said about this in the chapter on "Advanced Tactics." The point here is to urge you to make your basic technique such that it can develop later into a subtly deceptive method.

Off the Back Wall

Sometimes the ball doesn't come out enough to be playable. Sometimes it takes surprisingly queer bounces around the corner. Sometimes it will rebound glued to the sidewall. Also, every time you let the ball go to the back wall you're letting your opponent get in front of you—a loss of the more advantageous position. So a good tactical precept is "don't let the ball go to the back wall."

Yet a lot of balls get by all of us, so knowing how to handle them is a basic necessity. Here is where mastery of the simple small swing and the pivot become extremely important. Out in the open, far from the back wall, a player can use any old swing, large or small, and do pretty well even if not really well. But many balls get by everybody and *must* be taken off the back wall. Here a big backswing encounters an immovable obstacle and gets a player into great difficulty. The small restricted swing can play any ball that rebounds a foot and a half or more.

Take the Ball Low

The proximity of the back wall is what makes this shot difficult—you lack sufficient room to swing. So the first thing to learn is "always let the ball drop low before playing it." This means wait as long as possible so you will get as much space as the rebound permits. You should wait until your racquet will almost—but not quite—strike the floor when you play the ball.

Crouch

Since you are planning to take the ball very low you should prepare as low as possible. You should turn partly toward the back wall, crouching down so that the back knee is nearly on the floor. The racquet hand should be nearly on the floor and the face of the racquet should be open. Study the illustration and note these details: the back foot dropped back, the restricted swing, the low open racquet, and the deep crouch (Fig. 4.5).

Always Play Up

Any ball that is allowed to drop well below the level of the tin must be played up to be a fair ball. All the previous instructions—the low open racquet, etc.—are clearly preparations to aim up. And that is exactly what you must do, not most of the time, but every time with no exceptions.

Use the Pivot

The illustration (Fig. 4.5) shows that you turn somewhat beyond a sideways position so you are diagonally facing the back wall. This enables you to take the racquet back along the back wall to be out of the way of the ball as it goes to the wall and rebounds. This, however, is not a strong position from which to play. The normal position is stronger. So, as the ball rebounds you should follow it with a slow pivot and actually play the ball from the normal position as shown in the figure. If a crosscourt shot is

Figure 4.5 A Backhand Crosscourt off the Back Wall. The position of the feet (almost facing the back wall) permits an unimpeded backswing. The racquet moves parallel to the back wall, so it never bumps into it. The low crouch helps keep the open racquet very low, practically scraping the floor. The second picture is important—the racquet is rotating towards the ball and the shoulders have begun to turn, but the feet are still the same. The movement of the feet (quite drastic in the last two pictures) *follows* the movement of the racquet and shoulders. In the third picture the rotation has begun to take the left foot around with it. The right foot is rotating too, twisting on the ball of the foot. The last picture shows the rotation completed. The left foot has "walked around the ball" and is now to the left of the contact point. Observe that the actual backhand stroke is unchanged. It is the same stroke as that shown in Figure 4.4, but with a drastic pivoting motion added. This pivot can be carried even further, so the player aims at the right sidewall and executes a reverse corner. Note the low, open follow-through. In actual play, the follow-through would *appear* to be higher because of the instant recovery of position.

desired, you keep on pivoting so you face the front wall at the conclusion of the swing.

Tough Ones

Sometimes a ball rebounds so little that it is impossible to get in behind it and follow it even with a very neat restricted swing. First of all, you shouldn't have let the ball go to the back wall to begin with and you are now in deep trouble. However, the ball *can* be retrieved by snapping under it with the wrist and aiming as high and as far forward on the sidewall as possible. This will be a poor shot that comes out and sets up—but it is better than nothing. If the ball doesn't come out even enough to permit this, it is unplayable and therefore a winner.

Into the Back Wall

Playing the ball into the back wall always results in a feeble setup for your opponent. It should never be done except when nothing else is possible. In such cases, the thing to remember is to aim sharply up so that the rebound off the back wall will carry all the way to the front wall. Here is one case where slice defeats the objective. Topspin helps give you the long flight you want, so you should use it on this rare shot.

Off the Sidewall

A ball coming off the sidewall can be played at any time. However, it is always wiser to let it come as far out as possible. Treating it like an off-the-back wall shot, by waiting as long as reasonably practical, brings several advantages. The farther out it comes, the nearer the center it gets, and this is advantageous since more shots are possible. Your position is the best possible, and your opponent's position is the worst possible; he is "boxed out" to whatever extent the ball comes out. Another gain is time. You have an opportunity to prepare with perfect footwork, balance, and racquet work. Many balls that come off the sidewall are setups. You should never hurry a setup, because to hurry it impairs the accuracy necessary to taking full advantage of it.

Another advantage in playing sidewall balls in this manner is that it avoids the problem of different techniques. You play all balls off all walls the same way. The exception to this rule applies to balls directly off the front wall which are intercepted in order to hold the forward position.

Off the Wall on the Fly

Balls that strike the back wall on the fly, without first having bounced, and balls that do the same off the sidewall will go down quickly to the floor and tend to race out into the court, contrasting sharply with the floating flight of a ball that has bounced before reaching the wall. You have less time on such shots, but the technique remains unchanged. Take as much time as the ball gives you, and let it come well out. A good rule is, insofar as possible, do not go to the wall to play a ball—let it come out to you. This yields better position, increased opportunities, and increased accuracy in execution.

Around the Corner

Many balls strike the sidewall, then the floor, then come off the back wall. There is no basic change in technique with one exception. The ball rolls off the sidewall and in so doing acquires considerable side spin. It therefore tends to jump towards you as it comes off the back wall. To allow for this, you must back up and get much farther away from the ball than you would expect. If you don't do this, the ball will get much too close and your stroke will be very cramped.

If the ball strikes the sidewall, then the back wall before striking the floor, it will race out much straighter, so you must get much closer to it. The difference in the two rebounds is so great that sometimes even an experienced player will fail to return the ball at all if he anticipated the "wrong" rebound. All beginners and intermediates should drill to learn how the two rebounds act.

Summary

1. Basic drives should be aimed well above the telltale for safety from error and for good depth. A first bounce at the service line achieves this by playing through an opponent, not to him.
2. Playing too short is as bad as playing too long.

3. Playing for the walls at the service line brings luck.

4. Slightly continental grips and a low, small, open-faced swing are desirable on drives.

5. The wrist twists on a backhand—it doesn't flop.

6. Pivoting helps crosscourts and deception.

7. When playing off the walls, crouch, take the ball low, keep the racquet low, play up, pivot for strength and direction. Avoid playing into the back wall. Drilling is desirable.

5

Serve and Return

These two shots, the serve and return, begin every point. They frequently set the tone and determine the winner even though the point may involve several exchanges before it is terminated. What could be more important? Many players think of the service as merely a means of putting the ball in play. This is a very limited concept that does little justice either to the opportunities or the dangers involved in this initial exchange. The service and the return are always important and in many matches they can be, and have been, determining factors. It is not a matter of outright winners but of gaining an initial advantage (or disadvantage), which on a percentage basis inevitably leads to winning or losing a majority of points over an extended period.

Six Serves

The following describes six different services and the most advisable answer to each. In general, the server has a plot—he intends either to tie the receiver up in a back corner or rush him into a hasty and therefore sloppy return. The receiver's task is to foil the server's scheme. In almost every case this means to volley the ball, thereby nipping the plot in the bud by not letting the ball go where the server intended it to go. The server's plan is offensive; he hopes to establish an advantage. The receiver's plan is defensive; he hopes to establish parity so as to have an even chance in the subsequent exchange.

Of course there are exceptions to these generalizations. Sometimes a service can be a winner if accurate and not taken on the fly by the receiver. Likewise, a badly executed service can offer an opportunity for a very offensive return. Basically, though, the server has the initiative, he calls the play, and the receiver must adapt to and defend against the server's choice.

Varying the Serve

Even by ranking players the service is frequently not exploited to any great degree. Players seem often to be personal about it. They will say, "I prefer the lob (or some other) serve." This is not really the point. If one service can be found that will decisively bother a given opponent, it is extremely important to discover it. Perhaps the threat of variety is more important; it keeps the receiver on edge, unsure of what will come next.

If a receiver can be reasonably sure as to what to expect, his problem is half solved to begin with. He can position himself to receive this particular service without worrying about others. For example, if a player lob serves every time, the receiver can move well into the service court and be in good position to volley every time. By contrast, if the server varies with a crisscross serve, the receiver, if he is in towards the wall to volley a lob serve, suddenly finds the ball coming at him off the wall, very fast and at an angle hard to judge. He is likely to miss or make a sloppy return. If he stands back by the center line, a serve to the corner may get in there before he can move in to intercept it. It gets into the corner, he has to dig it out, and the server has a marked advantage.

There are many combinations of contrasting serves. These will be more fully explored in the chapter on "Advanced Tactics." The point being made here is that every player should, as he progresses, acquire a variety of serves that will make it possible for him to use the service as a formidable weapon in his offensive play. He can use the serve to press weakness, to take the other fellow by surprise, and to keep him in a state of uncertainty that is a psychological advantage throughout the play.

Receiving Service: Position

If the server has all these options what chance is there for the poor receiver? What can he do about it, beyond hoping that his opponent is unable to execute them well? There is one answer: stand on the center service line, about two-fifths of the distance from the back wall to the forward service line, holding the racquet up head high ready to volley. (Fig. 5.1) This exact position is the *only* position from which every service can be handled effectively. The receiver must crouch and point his feet toward the sidewall, ready to move in, stay where he is, or back up a little. From this position he can move in quickly to volley any service to the corner (lob, chip, straight hard). He can take one hop back to handle a down-the-middle hard serve or a crisscross serve, so the ball never comes suddenly to the "wrong side" for which he is not prepared. He can advance diagonally and attack (with the volley) any service that is in the open due to bad aim by the server. There is no easy way for the server to confound him.

Bad Receiving

By contrast, there are some very common errors in receiving, all of which should be avoided (see Fig. 5.2). If a receiver stands well into the service court a crisscross serve will suddenly come to the wrong side and will frequently force a poor return. If he stands too far forward, it is possible to get a lob or chip serve in behind him so all he can do is retrieve it rather

Figure 5.1 Receiving Service. Besides the player's position, other details should be observed: the slight crouch, elevated racquet, the watchfulness (eyes on the server) so any sudden change will not catch him napping. Also note the server—he looks as though he plans a chip, but he could easily and quickly drop his racquet and serve a lob, or raise his racquet and serve very hard. He is watchful too, ready to take advantage of any weakness he may perceive in the receiver's position, attitude, or apparent anticipation.

Figure 5.2 Receiving Service. Here the player is doing everything wrong: he is standing straight, on his heels, his racquet is low (not ready to play), his eyes are on the front wall (unaware that his opponent is preparing to slam). He is also positioned in the middle of the court, thus letting the server have the options of serving to his right, left, or at him. Few players get everything wrong, as in this photo, but many players commit some of these errors. Each, by itself, is a serious mistake that may cost points.

than make an acceptable return with good depth. If he faces the front wall he will, because of the position of his feet, have difficulty in getting his return along the wall. He will tend to play crosscourt back to his opponent. If he holds his racquet low, and a hard service is aimed at him or into the corner, he will not have time to lift it to volley. The ball will go to the back wall, perhaps nick, or run out close to the wall or far out if aimed high, so he has to chase it and is out of position and off balance.

Study the illustrations carefully. The only position that fails to open up inviting options to an astute server is the one shown in Fig 5.1, since it prevents "wrong side" serves and makes it possible to volley or half volley every known delivery. There are other possible receiver positions and there are other ways of reacting to the server's choices, but from any other position the necessary reactions are more difficult and therefore inevitably produce a higher percentage of ineffective returns.

The Receiver's Objective

The return of any decent service should *always* be aimed high and deep along the wall. Note the emphasis on the word always, which means with no exceptions whatever. The receiver should have no grand delusions about how he hopes to put it away or make a low forcing shot. The most common error in tactics is the continual attempt to do more than is possible with a good service on a percentage basis. Note that this applies only to a good service. (One can and should do all kinds of things to a poor service.) A well-played service always prevents an early "out front" volley. Therefore the server is in front, and the receiver's objective should be limited to getting the ball back *deep* along the wall, with the double purpose of forcing the server back and avoiding the mistake of giving him a ball out front since that can be fatal. The receiver should confine his thinking to avoiding error, playing for parity in position, and avoiding offering the server a chance to make a winner.

This is defensive thinking. People tend to prefer to think offensively. "The best defense is a good offense" is a popular cliche. But in this situation it is wishful thinking and does not square with the facts. The facts are that the server has the initiative and the advantage in position, while the receiver is in a defensive position and is not sure what is coming. Whether a player prefers to think offensively is beside the point. The point is that, prefer it or not, he is on the defensive and should therefore think in those terms. He should forget about winning points with his return. Rather, he should stop losing them by playing low, which gives his opponent a short ball and a good chance to win them. The ball should be played high enough on the front wall so that the first bounce will be at or behind the service line. A return that comes off the back wall is to be preferred to a short ball that can often be placed for a winner. Therefore it is better to play too high than too low. This is one of the many situations in which it is more effective to play high than to play low.

Tricky Returns

Many players are fond of attempting tricky returns off their opponent's serve, such as a volley reverse-corner shot, or a three-wall nick, or a crosscourt drop shot. When an advanced player plays a less experienced player, these tricks are frequently successful and appear to be very subtle examples of advanced tactics. In fact they can be summmed up as "junk." They are nonpercentage and almost always fail against a worthy, alert server who is an equally advanced player. They are futile attempts at finding an easy way to win, and against good competition there isn't any easy way. A player who gets in the habit of doing this sort of thing will continue to do it when there is real pressure in a tough match. It is therefore a bad habit to form and should be shunned even against poor opponents who don't know the answers.

Aim Straight

A crosscourt return is usually not advisable unless an opponent is much weaker in his play from one side as contrasted with the other. Since the receiver is playing defensively, a crosscourt will seldom carry enough pace to prevent its interception by an aggressive volley. Thus we return to the first lesson: always aim high and deep along the wall.

Exceptions

Once a player is competent and has acquired good tactical and technical habits, there are many variations the receiver may use in his attempt to wrest the initiative and the forward position from his opponent. They involve calculated risk, deception, and sudden moves, which will be dealt with in the chapter on "Advanced Tactics." These variations are omitted here because this discussion is about basics, and the first thing to acquire is a clear understanding of the basic situation and the proper reaction to it. As one great teacher remarked, "Rules are made to be broken, *after* you know them." The tendency of most players who are learning is to strive constantly for the exceptional and brilliant rule-breaking play, and the result is that because it is attempted so frequently, it ceases to be exceptional and becomes an unsound policy. Brilliance does not by itself make percentage play. It must be sustained by a sound foundation, and it is the foundation that should be cultivated first and foremost.

The Lob Serve

This should be executed by holding the racquet head extremely open faced near the floor and lifting the ball smoothly up through the ball. It should not be flippy or wristy. It should be smooth. Many players like to put a little topspin on the ball serving from the right, to make the rebound higher and more floaty to an opponent's backhand; and they use a little side slice when serving from the left. This "side" enables one to aim closer to the sidewall and still not have the ball come out. The sidespin tends to make it come back straight and cling to the wall, increasing the difficulty of the receiver's volley (Fig. 5.3). The ball should be aimed as high on the front wall as possible without serving a fault into the ceiling or lighting fixtures. The ball should float back to a point on the sidewall a little behind the service line, so high on the sidewall that it is impossible for the receiver to volley it before it reaches the sidewall. The receiver is then obliged to back up and take it after it has come off the sidewall, which means he is back in the corner and at a disadvantage.

Perfect depth is of great importance. A good lob service is nearly unplayable if allowed to drop to the floor. It lands very near the back wall and rebounds so little that it is a winner or near winner that forces the receiver to flip it up weakly into the sidewall on its way to the front wall. When it comes out it is usually a perfect setup.

The control of the depth is achieved through smooth execution, in which the arm, body, and legs all lift the ball into the front wall just hard enough so the ball will almost, but not quite (by a few inches), reach the back wall before it strikes the floor.

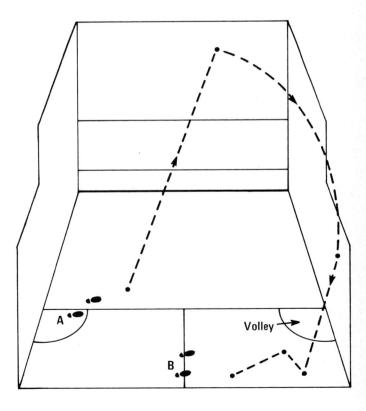

Figure 5.3 The Lob Serve. This should be as high as the ceiling and fixtures permit. The ball should touch the sidewall just behind the service line at a point high enough to prevent any volley before it hits the wall. The ball should then die along the back wall. The proper return would be a volley between the sidewall and floor.

Receiving the Lob

The only acceptable answer is the volley. If the ball can be played well before it reaches the sidewall this should always be done. The receiver can then get in front of his opponent. A good lob serve will not permit this since the ball is on the wall by the time it comes within reach. Therefore, the receiver should move into the service court along the back wall, lower his racquet, take the ball after it is well off the sidewall, and volley it *up* to a point somewhat above the service line on the front wall. This way, it returns fairly high along the sidewall and presents the server with the same problem—a high volley or a ball deep in the corner if he does not volley.

Common Errors

Most players, in learning, tend to move diagonally forward to volley. This is fine if the lob serve is a poor one that can be taken before it reaches the wall. It can be fatal against a good one. The ball is on the wall where it is physically impossible to play it. It then drops down *behind* the receiver and his best chance is a desperate "get." The first move of the receiver should be straight into the corner along the back wall, so he gets between the back wall and the ball and has the ball in front of him at all times. The receiver can then see the ball coming and can easily make the judgment on whether to move forward and take it early, or if he can't take it early, to let it come off the wall and then volley it. His first move should be very quick. He should make it as soon as he is sure that a lob serve (and not a sudden switch to something else) is what is coming. He is in the corner by the time the ball reaches the front wall and can instantly perceive that the ball can or cannot be taken early. If it can, his second move is to sidle quickly forward, keeping his feet in the backhand position and his racquet high for the volley.

Another common error is to move in and attempt to volley the ball while it is on the sidewall or very close to it. Since the ball is on the wall and cannot be hit, an outright error results almost every time. It seems a stupid thing to do, but if a player moves in diagonally he often has no other choice—so he does it. Or, he may decide to volley it early but be too slow about it. Thus, by the time he is volleying, the ball is near the wall.

This brings up a very important rule for the receiver. He must either be quick and volley the ball well before it gets to the wall, or he must wait until it is well out from the wall where he has room for his racquet. The receiver must be decisive in his choice. Anything in between is fatal since he is playing the ball when it literally cannot be played. His attitude must be expectant, he must choose between two sharply contrasting actions: get to that ball and play it as far before the wall as possible, or wait, let it come well out, and volley it back up high. The failure to do one or the other decisively is usually the root of the trouble many players have in getting a lob serve into play in a decent fashion. The first move must be along the back wall—so that he has a choice. The second move must be definitely one or the other.

The Slice Service (Chip)

This is often referred to as a "chip" service. It is best played from the left side because sidespin enables the server to bring it back straighter along the wall. It should strike the front wall just above the service line and land just within the service line very close to the wall. If allowed to bounce, it will cling to the wall and go dead at the backwall (Fig. 5.4).

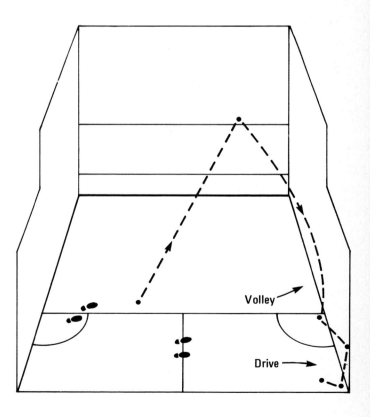

Figure 5.4 The Slice Serve. Try to hit the ball exactly as shown—near the line on the front wall and barely in the court near the wall in the service court. An inaccurate slice serve is a very poor shot. The proper returns are (1) to move fast and volley, or (2) to drive after the bounce.

Volley

Drive

The best answer is the volley. Once it gets creeping along the wall the receiver can be in real trouble. The receiver must move forward very quickly to volley it before it gets in there.

This service brings about a battle of wits between the two players. If the receiver shows signs that he plans to rush in to volley, the server can "play the wall," i.e., aim the ball so it strikes the wall at or before the service line just when the receiver plans to volley. If the receiver has committed himself to a diagonal rush to cut the ball off, he is often forced to swing at it anyway, trying to scrape it off the wall, usually with very bad results. But the receiver can counter by pretending to be very eager, causing the server to play the wall. The ball then comes out and the receiver has a chance to make a good solid forehand drive.

This service is very effective against all who are not prone to volley. It can be used from the right side also but will not cling to the wall quite as well unless one cuts around it (i.e., carves the ball). Even then the angle is less effective because one is serving from near the wall (the racquet hand) instead of more from the center. The flight of the ball is more into the wall and out rather than along the wall.

The Hard Services

All hard services should be executed in the same manner. This not only simplifies technique but enhances deception, since when the server raises his racquet above his head to pound the ball the receiver knows a hard ball is coming, but he doesn't know which one. Good hard serves are very accurate shots. They do not merely go fast, though speed is necessary to rush the receiver. They also go to specific spots requiring good control on the part of the server. A tennis swing should not be used. In other words, don't haul off with the down-up-and-cock technique common to serving in tennis. Instead, hold the racquet high, slightly in front, just as one would to swat a fly high on a wall (Fig. 5.5). The racquet should be taken straight back and cocked from this position. The ball should be tossed in line with the racquet and the target—that spot on the front wall which will give the perfect rebound. The ball should be played flat but with a slight wiping effect down the back of the ball. The wrist action (there should be a lot of it to get a "crack") should be slightly delayed so the ball runs up the racquet a bit. This is important, since it lets the ball go higher and reach the back wall on the fly. Too early wrist action results in continually hitting the floor on first bounce because the wrist brings the ball down. All straight hard

Figure 5.5 To prepare for serving hard, use the racquet like a flyswatter. Take the racquet straight back and forth (for greater directional accuracy.) There is no down-up-and-scratch-the-back tennis service swing.

serves should strike the back wall on the fly so they race out. The ball should be aimed high enough so it will always "reach" (Figs. 5.6, 5.7).

For a crisscross serve the ball should be aimed as near as possible to the service line on the front wall, and the wrist action should be purposely early. You now want the ball to strike the front wall, the sidewall, then come *down* into the court (Fig. 5.8). Many players continually miss the court with their crisscross service because they play it as a straight service. It goes right across the court they aimed at and lands in the other one—merely a noisy fault.

For the rarely used around-the-corner service, you must swing around the ball from right to left with a more horizontal motion. The ball should be tossed lower and as far out to the center as you can reach, to improve the angle (Fig. 5.9). The follow-through on all hard serves should be to the left side.

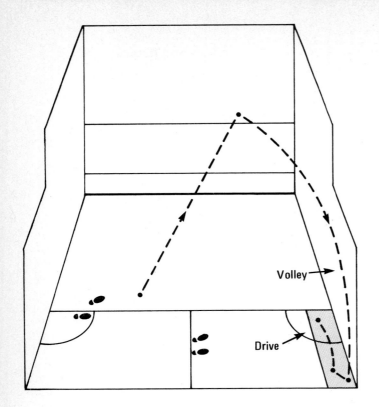

Figure 5.6 The Hard Serve to the Corner. Hit the back wall first, so the ball will run out along the sidewall. The best return is the volley. (The target area is shaded.)

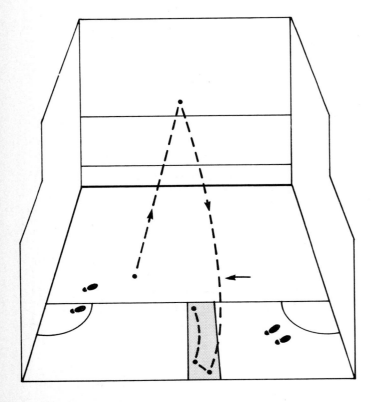

Figure 5.7 The Hard Serve to the Center. Get the ball near the center line as shown. (The target area is shaded.) The best return is a volley.

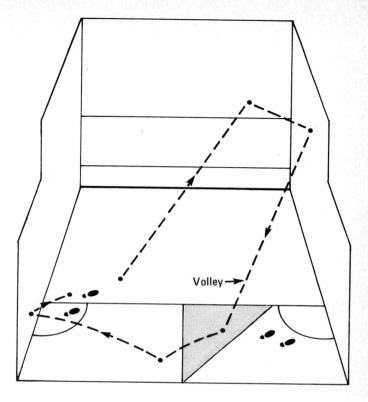

Figure 5.8 The Hard Serve, Criss-Cross. Aim lower to hit the floor first. Practice your angle until you consistently hit the shaded area. The best return is the volley. If the receiver lets it go around, jump to the center to get out of the way.

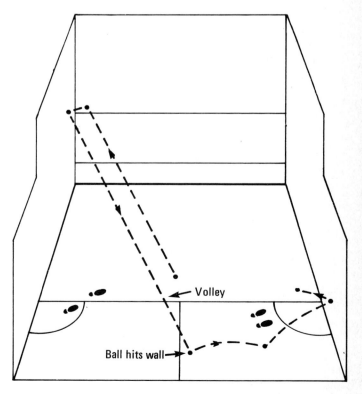

Figure 5.9 The Hard Serve around the Corner. Reach out as far as possible (without foot faulting) to get the angle. Aim high, close to the sidewall. The best return is the volley.

Because you are pounding the ball and following through low, the ball tends to go somewhat lower than your aim. It is advisable not to aim very low on the back wall, but to aim a foot or two above the floor. Many of these will tend to go lower and be very fine low, rebound, or nick serves. If you aim very low, a large percentage of your shots will strike the floor first and float up so the receiver has plenty of time to play the ball well. A little higher on the back wall is still an effective service that hurries an opponent. A ball that strikes the floor first is a poor service just about every time unless it is a lucky glue ball as it comes out.

Serving with the Backhand

Serving with the backhand is generally inadvisable because the receiver is forewarned that a soft service is coming. Yet some players like to do this to get a better angle off the front wall. Serving from the right court with the backhand means that the serving hand, and therefore the racquet, is near the center. The forehand service puts the racquet nearer to the wall. Therefore, with the backhand, a sliced lob service can be brought back from the front wall closer to the sidewall due to this improvement in angle.

Straight to Corner

The standard hard service goes straight to the corner, strikes the back wall first (not the floor or the sidewall) and runs out low, close to the sidewall. Many players become experts at placing it very close to the sidewall and close to the floor on the back wall, so at times it will nick and at other times glue to the wall. In any case it runs out fast and hurries the receiver hopefully into sloppy play. One important variation is to aim high on the back wall, making it run far out, so the receiver must chase it towards the front wall and is open to being passed on the other side on the second shot.

The answer, as always, is the volley. If the server is good, and the receiver lets him place the ball where he wishes, the server will place it in a very inconvenient spot for the receiver. The volley prevents this and puts the ball in play in a respectable manner. The volley should be aimed for depth, that is, quite high on the front wall. Many players try for a low aggressive shot. However, they usually fail in their aim and merely make a sloppy setup. The action is so fast they do not have time to aim with the exactness needed for such an ambitious return.

Straight to Center

This ball is played exactly like a straight to corner service, but is aimed within a foot of the center service line. It is a surprise serve, calculated to "get the jump" by aiming straight at the receiver when he is worried about other options the server has been using, particularly the straight-to-the-corner service. If he is moving in to volley a straight-to-corner service he may well be caught with the ball suddenly on the wrong side and must twist quickly to adjust. Sometimes a player is even hit by this ball for an outright winner. The volley is the best return.

The Crisscross

This brings the ball into the center, hopefully unexpectedly, and, by using the sidewall, brings it there via a dogleg route that can be a disconcerting surprise. It is extremely effective against players who position themselves well inside the service court to cut off serves to the corner. The ball gets to them so soon after it strikes the sidewall that they don't have enough time to judge it and line it up. Sloppy play and errors result. If they do not volley it or half-volley it, and let it go, it acquires a lot of spin from glancing off the walls and the receiver has a tough time chasing it around the other corner. His chances of a good return are poor.

Most players who take up squash have played tennis. They have experience in volleying a ball that comes straight back off the front wall. They are often baffled by a ball that doglegs at them off a wall, changing its direction sharply on the way. It is quite surprising how badly many otherwise competent players will react to this service.

The answer is again the volley or half volley, which should as usual be aimed high enough to get good depth. But the crucial problem is to have the *time* to judge the ball so as to volley decently. Here the position of the receiver is of extreme importance. If he is on the center line he will have plenty of time to judge the ball. If he is well into the service court he will not. The ball will be "on him" too quickly as it comes off the sidewall. Therefore, even if a server is using a lot of straight serves, the receiver should still take up the proper position on the center line, so he is ready for anything, not just corner serves. An astute server will be quick to observe when the receiver is set up for a surprise service to the center.

Round the Corner

This is another way to bring the ball into the court from an unexpected direction. Again, the answer is the deep volley.

Beginner Serving and Returning

A beginner has so much to learn that it is advisable to teach him just the lob serve at first. After he is a bit used to the walls, can play forehand and backhand drives, can volley some, and has some concept of position, receiving, and how to play a point, then it is time to start teaching him to acquire other serves and make his service a more varied weapon.

Receiving should immediately be given considerable attention since many other players will blast hard serves at an inexperienced player. He *must* learn to block-volley the hard serve so as to get it back and not just miss it. This knack of the block volley, a no-backswing little poke, is one of the first things all beginners should learn. The player literally puts his racquet *to* the ball (as contrasted with drawing it back) and pokes the ball back high down the wall. Volleying the lob serve again requires training. Beginners always swing at it, instead of putting their racquet on it and pressing it with the weight. This will be more fully covered in the section on the volley. It is basic to developing any kind of a controlled return.

Summary

1. Serving and receiving plays begin every point, well or badly. They are therefore of supreme importance.

2. There are six serves that can be used either to tie an opponent up with the walls in the corner (the lob and chip), or rush him into sloppy play (the hard serves). If varied judiciously they can make the service a great asset in a player's offense.

3. The receiver should foil the server's plan by intercepting whenever possible with a volley.

4. The receiver should play for depth, therefore should never play low on the front wall.

5. A most important aspect of receiving is proper position. Without this the receiver is vulnerable to clever variation.

6. Bad position is the most common fault in receiving; failure to volley is another; aiming low is a third; and attempting tricky low placements is a fourth.

7. Exception should not be taken to the "play for depth" rule until a player has mastered this basic tactic.

8. The six services are the lob, chip, hard straight to corner, hard straight to center, crisscross, and around the corner.

9. The lob and chip serves require smooth touch and great accuracy in width and depth.

10. The hard serves are effective partly because of speed, but are three times as effective if they are also very accurate.

11. Hard serves should be made without a tennis backswing.

12. The straight serves should be aimed higher than the crisscross.

13. Beginners should be taught the lob serve and should be given more instruction on volleying all serves so they can get the ball in play when receiving it.

14. Knowing volleying technique is an immediate basic need while knowing a great variety of serves is not.

6

The Volley

The use of the volley is on many occasions optional. On many other occasions it is an absolute necessity. Many serves and other shots will go dead and be unplayable if allowed to bounce. They are shots that are either volleyed or not played at all. This is particularly true of lob serves which are used by everybody. Therefore a beginner should learn to take the ball on the fly almost as soon as he gets in the court. The intermediate player is well advised to volley almost whenever he can, since by so doing he stays in front of his opponent and that's an advantage. The advanced player uses the volley as an important offensive weapon. His opponent digs the ball up and he immediately whacks it to the other side, running and rushing his opponent about the court with continuous pressure. Some of the greatest players have based their game substantially on a policy of continuous volleying, thereby setting up such a tempo that an opponent seems never to be able to get set and make a good shot. Thus, the ability to volley is a necessity for beginners and champions.

Negative Techniques

To explain the technique of volleying it is necessary first to consider some negative techniques, because almost without exception, inexperienced players have definite ideas as to what is involved, and these concepts are for the most part the exact opposite of good technique. You do not swing at the ball. If you do, you whiff and hit wood shots. You do not have a backswing. If you do, you have to swing to get the racquet onto the ball, with bad results as described above. You do not use much wrist. If you do, you get a flappy shot that will often have speed but will seldom have accuracy. The wrist should be used freely only on a desperate, reaching, off-balance volley that does not permit proper positioning, good balance, and use of weight. The average inexperienced player thinks he should draw back, swing at the ball, and use a lot of wrist. He therefore commits all the sins enumerated in this paragraph and wonders why he is a poor and ineffective volleyer.

Positive Techniques

The racquet should be lifted forward *to* the ball (the opposite of a backswing). It can almost be said that the swing starts as the racquet meets the ball. While this is an exageration it has much truth in it. The racquet is put forward, towards the ball, and when the racquet and ball meet, the ball is pressed to the front wall with a comparatively stiff-wristed jab of weight (legs) and arm. The racquet should be prepared a little above the ball (except on low volleys, but most volleys are taken high), and the face of the racquet should be slightly closed. The follow-through, which is almost the entire shot, should be diagonally down and across the striker, to the left for a forehand, to the right for a backhand. This gives a dragging or drawing effect on the ball, which gives it a little backspin and helps it to lay down and not fly about, because it pulls the ball down from the front wall (Fig. 6.1a).

Contrast

The technique just described is in sharp contrast with the technique advocated for basic drives. On most volleys the ball is to be played somewhat down; therefore the racquet head should be close-faced and slightly above the ball. The action is very fast, so instead of taking the racquet back away from the ball, you push the racquet towards the ball in the preparation. Instead of waiting for the ball to get fairly low, you intercept it, stepping forward to it diagonally whenever possible, and play it while it is high (Fig. 6.1b).

Figure 6.1a Preparing for a Forehand Volley. Contrast this picture with Figure 4.3. Note the many opposites. Here the racquet is high, closed, and in front towards the ball. For the drive the racquet is low, open, and laid back away from the ball.

Figure 6.1b The Follow-Through on the Forehand Volley. Observe how little wrist has been used—a little but nothing like a full snap. The racquet has gone down the back of the ball and a bit across to the left at the finish. The racquet face stays closed all the way. The shot is a very simple, rather stiff jab, quite similar to a tennis volley, and *not* a great deal more wristy, as everyone continually says about squash.

This contrast is extremely important in achieving technical excellence. Most aspiring players spend almost all their time learning to play the ball up, i.e., developing good basic drives. They form good muscle habits for this purpose, then use them on the volley. But then their volley goes too high and is ineffective. They begin to dislike volleying, because they feel they are not good at it. This all follows from a failure to realize that to be well-rounded a player must learn to lift the racquet, close the face, and play *down*, as well as learn to keep the racquet low, open, and play *up*. There is no one way to do both well. The section on drills contains specific instructions on how to get this switch incorporated into your playing habits. Drilling the volley is strongly recommended as a substitute for some of the endless work players put into their ground strokes, particularly if you are someone whose basic strokes are superior to your volley.

Stroking the Volley

The volley is definitely a stroke, not a hit. The ball should be pressed sharply to the front wall and as this is done the racquet should pull down the back of the ball, so there is backspin and the ball will "lay down" after it strikes the front wall. Many players have great difficulty in mastering this concept. They snap their wrist through instead. It does little good to deal with a negative technique by telling them not to use their wrist. Instead, if they have a positive thought, namely to push with the weight and pull the butt of the racquet (the part that is held in the hand) through (down and across), then they have a definite idea of what they should do—and a substitute for the wrist action. Note that in Figure 6.1, in the last picture, the butt has gone through and taken the racquet with it, but the wrist has *not* snapped around. This is usually the best volley, and should be learned first. If a snap of the wrist is necessary to get good aim, such as a sharp crosscourt angle, then indeed the wrist should be used. However, most volleys are best placed along the wall, and a stiff-wristed crosscourt is possible by taking the ball earlier. So the general rule to use very little wrist is subject to few exceptions.

Stiffness

I have placed considerable emphasis on the necessity of wrist stiffness for a good volley because many players think of squash as a "wristy" game. Compared to tennis this is true, but compared to badminton, squash requires far less use of the wrist. The concept that all one's shots in squash should involve snapping the wrist is a gross exaggeration. The volley is one of many squash shots that are less wristy than popular belief would have you assume.

A stiff volley can be placed with almost pin-point accuracy. The face of the racquet is put on the ball and presses the ball to exactly that spot on the front wall which will give the best possible rebound direction. A wristy volley means the head of the racquet is coming around as the ball is played. This constantly changes the direction of the shot. While it *can* be done, it is extremely difficult to time this swing so that it will meet the ball at the one instant that will give perfect aim. Some players with unusual gifts in timing and touch can achieve far better percentage results than this passage would lead you to believe, but they are few in number. The vast majority of players are quite inaccurate with a loose volley and only occasionally get a good one that goes exactly where they had hoped. In sum, volleying with the wrist is sloppy, stiff volleying gives accuracy.

Volley Grips

It has been emphasized that the volley usually involves taking the ball higher and playing it down to avoid making a high shot that lacks severity and often comes off the back wall. It is quite difficult to lift the racquet, put it forward above the ball, and close the face if one uses a slightly continental grip as recommended for basic drives. The hand tends to remain in its natural position, which means the face of the racquet does not close but remains open. Playing the ball down is much easier if a player shifts his grip slightly so that he has an eastern grip. Many good players say (and believe) that they don't change their grips, but they actually do more or less instinctively so that the ball will go down, not up. The change is quite slight but makes all the difference in keeping the shot low, because the change closes the face of the racquet. Note the grips as shown in Figures 6.1 and 6.2. They are straight easterns, not slight continentals, for both forehand and backhand.

Whenever a player is unable to keep his volley down, learning this slight shift will effect a seemingly miraculous cure. Suddenly he can "bury" the ball along the wall on shots that he could never before deal with in a forceful manner. His offense picks up markedly and his confidence soars. He can really punish his opponent when he gets him down, because he has freed himself from the rigid and limited concept of having only one grip for all shots. If you wish to test this out, refer to the section on drills which

Figure 6.2a Preparing for a Medium-High Backhand Volley. Note the ball of the thumb behind the handle, thus closing the face of the racquet to get more on top of the ball. Observe the abbreviated backswing.

gives specific instructions on how to go about acquiring the skill. After a short period of getting used to it (the ball often goes too low at first and hits the tin) your volley will become much more lethal.

The High Backhand Volley

This is often considered the toughest shot in the game. The reason is that if it is not done properly it is a weak shot. On the forehand a player has his natural throwing motion to give strength; so even if he is badly positioned and off balance, he can still swat the ball and give it a good whack even if it is inaccurate. Not so on the backhand. His natural throwing motion is weak, and he feels rather helpless. To get strength he *must* position

Figure 6.2b The Finish on a Backhand Volley. As in the forehand, note the absence of the wrist, the presence of the forearm jab and body weight. Also observe the increased bend at the waist. The extreme simplicity makes consistency easy, yet there is that little subtlety—a slightly altered grip. This is what gives that aggressive feeling of "burying the ball" along the wall.

himself behind the ball, take the ball in front of him, and press it with his weight while his racquet pulls down from high left to low right. Note that in Figure 6.3 very little wrist is used. The ball is pressed forward by the use of the legs and a bending forward of the body. Considerable "drag" is put on the ball by the down pull of the arm, and this down pull also aids in bringing weight forward into the shot. A backhand volley played in this way can be a solid forcing shot, with much more pace and accuracy than is possible with any flick of the wrist. It is a combination of push (with the weight) and pull (with the arm and racquet) so the butt (not the head) of the racquet leads through low to the right side. On a lower backhand volley the arm and racquet pull sideways from left to right and the weight presses forward (as when volleying a lob service that has come off the sidewall). If you find this concept hard to understand, the discussion of slicing at the beginning of the next chapter should be helpful.

Figure 6.3 The High Backhand Volley. Use two hands to prepare the racquet. Use an eastern grip. Get behind the ball, not to the side of it. *Do not* snap the wrist at the ball. Push the butt of the racquet towards the ball (see the first and second pictures) by leaning with the weight, swinging the upper arm some, and straightening the forearm. The right arm then pulls down to the right side. This puts "drag"(slice) on the ball and the bending puts more weight into the shot. Note that the weight has gone so completely forward over the right foot that the left foot has left the floor and started a step as the stroke finishes. It is important to note that this apparently complex and difficult shot is exactly like every other slice—a pull with the racquet, a push with the weight. The racquet pulls from high to low (and left to right). The weight moves forward. Most people do not have a sound mental picture of what must be done. They flap the racquet with their wrists and get mediocre results.

Summary

1. The volley is often an inescapable necessity.

2. Do not swing, do not use much wrist. Lift the racquet forward to the ball, with the face closed, and play with a stiff jab. Follow through down across the body to get spin.

3. The technique contrasts sharply with that used for basic drives.

4. Stroke the volley; don't hit it.

5. Squash is less wristy than many believe.

6. Volley grips differ from drive grips when the ball is high.

7. The high backhand volley is a difficult shot.

7

Finesse Shots

Basically the objective of any finesse shot is to make the ball take two bounces in a small space. To achieve this, players use "touch"; i.e., they play the ball softly using great restraint both in the amount of swing and in the amount of force employed. But this is not enough. Spin can be used and is used to influence the behavior of the ball. Backspin will, for instance, go down sharply from the front wall and bounce short rather than rebound farther back towards an opponent striving to get to it. Moreover, there are quite a few fast finesse shots, and these are often markedly improved by the use of heavy spin. The spin that is used is almost always slice, though sometimes chop (a vertical cut) is used on higher setups. In all finesse shots the ball is cut.

Slicing

In most cases, squash players cut across the ball and a little under it. Since slice means to cut across, it is common to say of any cut shot that it was sliced. This, however, is not always true. Undercut means to go forward under the ball. Chop means to cut from above down. Neither of these shots have any sidespin, which is implied by the word "slice." But since most people do not bother with these fine distinctions, the word slice will be used here with its common meaning—to "cut."

In all cut shots the bottom edge of the racquet leads off the ball. The racquet always travels from the outside in, so that the follow-through is always to the left with a forehand and to the right with a backhand. This means that the racquet head starts from a position outside the ball and ends up inside it. It is therefore physically impossible to slice across a ball if the racquet is prepared directly behind or inside the shot's proposed line of flight.

This is why large numbers of comparatively experienced squash players cannot slice. They identify slice with undercut. They prepare behind the ball, go forward to it and cut under it as they play it. This tends to pop the ball up high, which is not desired on a finesse shot. They have also been told (and so has everybody, unfortunately), "Always hit through the ball." It is impossible to hit through the ball and also slice it. The slice spin is created by the action of the racquet head going *off* the ball, so the ball rolls along the strings and spins as it leaves the racquet. The racquet going off the ball creates the spin. If a player takes the racquet through the ball in the direction of the proposed flight of the ball, the ball stays at one spot on the strings while it is on the racquet, and no spin is created. This is hitting "flat," i.e., with no spin. The greatest obstacle to learning finesse for most players is the cliche to hit through the ball. So let's start by saying "The racquet *never* goes through the ball on a well-played finesse shot." (See Figure 7.1.)

Someone will surely ask what makes the ball go if the racquet does not go through the ball? The answer is weight—the weight should always go through the ball. Even on a soft drop shot enough weight is put through the ball to carry it to the front wall.

This gives a good definition of a slice—the racquet crosses from the outside in, almost at a right angle to the proposed flight of the ball, while the weight pushes straight in the direction of the flight. The racquet cuts, the weight glides. The two motions are simultaneous. The weight pushes, the racquet pulls. This composite concept is very strange at first to most people. They have never entertained the mental picture of the racquet and weight moving in sharply contrasting directions—almost at right angles to each other. Think of swinging out and in like a pendulum hanging in front of a moving clock. When they try it they forget to move the weight (like the whole clock) forward, so that the racquet whiffs the ball or just barely touches it with the wood. Then they move the weight but swing back and forth instead of out and in—so no spin results. It takes some fiddling, thinking, and experimenting to get the hang of it, to get the two moves going together. But it is worth a hundred times the needed trouble. It lays the foundation for all finesse shots. There are suggested exercises in the section on drilling which should help you get the feel of slicing with a minimum of

Figure 7.1 Slicing a Backhand Finesse Shot. The first picture stresses a very important detail— the racquet is out to the side rather than back. (Contrast this with the first picture of Figure 4.4.) This is essential. You cannot pull in if you have not first prepared yourself out. Note that the last picture shows that the racquet has been pulled completely across the body so it is now well over on the right side of the player. Meanwhile, the weight has moved directly forward into the shot.

trouble. Actually many people find it intriguing and a pleasure to give a little time to this by themselves in the court at regular intervals. It is strongly recommended to anyone who wishes to improve. It is a must for anyone with high aspirations.

General Finesse

Once you know how to slice you will probably use it throughout your game. A little drag on the ball makes all drives lay down and not come off the back wall. Down drag is what best makes a volley go dead. A little drag, flat down the back of the ball, markedly improves your aim when using a hard service. A great coach, Harry Cowles, once said, "You should not hit the ball. You should caress it." There's great meaning in these words. You get "feel" and accuracy on all your shots as the ability to stroke replaces the tendency to hit.

Footwork and Balance

Positioning the feet with good balance is essential to finesse, for this in large part controls the amount of force applied to the ball as the racquet spins it. In general, a finesse shot should not be attempted unless you have a little time (good players need very little) to address the ball properly with both feet and balance. The front foot should point diagonally forward roughly at the spot where contact will be made between ball and racquet. The rear foot should be braced roughly at a right angle to the proposed line of flight of the shot being attempted. Bending the knees is of extreme importance since a crouched position is the only one that permits the needed slide of the weight into the ball. Handling one's self (as contrasted with handling the racquet) is more fully discussed in the chapter on footwork.

Tight Grip

A very common fault in executing finesse shots is the tendency many players have to relax the grip in an endeavor to achieve delicacy of touch. A loose grip is *not* playing with delicacy—it is weak. Delicacy and weakness have nothing in common. A tight grip on finesse shots is more important than a firm grip on basic drives. The reason is the extreme accuracy required on a fine shot. A player is putting the ball into a very small space. A looser grip and a circular "bolo" swing can be used successfully on a basic drive. A finesse shot must be *exact*. This requires extreme control and this in turn means the racquet must be firmly held and not permitted to waver about even a little bit. This tightness, of course, should not be carried to a rigid extreme that eliminates reasonable fluency of execution. But the surest road to failure is having the mistaken notion that a loose grip leads to delicacy. It is even a good idea to grit your teeth a bit when making a delicate shot. Your aim will be more sure, your restraint in the use of force more perfectly regulated, and the threat of hitting hard that is implied in your apparent tenseness will aid in achieving deception—sometimes you *do* hit hard.

Threading the Needle

Think of doing something *very* exact, for example, threading a needle. Can the thread and the needle be held with a careless looseness and still be brought successfully together? Not at all. The needle must be held firmly and exactly, the thread pushed through the eye with a firm grip that controls it exactly, or one "misses" and tries again. This analogy is frequently used. A player will make fine shots, and a spectator will say, "He's threading needles today—he's really hot."

The comparison is very accurate. The racquet and feet must be arranged with exact correctness so the flight of the ball is accurate within inches, the force applied with the weight just right, and the reaction from the walls produced by the spin is exactly as desired. All this is merely a description of what is meant by total control. There is no place in it for any looseness.

Aiming Finesse Shots

Many players are frustrated in their attempts at achieving a good front-wall game because they make errors in the tin. Various laments are often heard. "Oh *no-o-o!*" "I had him!" "How could I miss such an easy setup?" Their agonizing is always the result of faulty thinking. Players do not realize a great and fundamental truth about the game of squash: *Players hit the tin because they aim at it.* This seems an insulting thing to say. If the answer were as simple as it sounds it would indeed be a slur on anyone's intelligence. But the proof that this is solid truth is quite subtle. Over many years of teaching I have evolved what I hope is an easily understood and clear-cut proof.

The Radius of Error

Take any player, from intermediate to champion, stand him at the T, give him the ball, and let him hit it out of his hand. Pick out one smudge or defect in the front wall that is smaller than the ball. Point to it and say, "Hit that spot." Make him do this four or five times, and keep track of where the ball strikes. The result is always the same. He misses—sometimes to the left, to the right, above, below. Very rarely will anyone hit *precisely* where he aims. This is a concrete and incontrovertible proof that every player has what you might call a "radius of error." When he aims at a precise spot what he is really doing is aiming at a circle drawn around that spot, the circle being defined by his personal radius. A talented, advanced player will have a smaller radius of error than one less experienced or less gifted, but only God has a radius of zero.

Margin for Error

It follows that a player should never aim closer to the telltale than his radius of error. If he always makes this allowance he will get some very low shots when the ball goes lower than his aim, and he will make some shots that are unsatisfactorily high. But only when he misses by more than usual will he make an outright error. He may not make a winner on every good chance, but he will seldom make an outright loser.

A player who is unaware of the necessity of conceding this proof of human fallibility often believes that he should be able to aim the ball an inch from the telltale without missing. Since he believes this is the right thing to do, he does it. If you now draw his radius of error around the spot where he aims, about twenty-five percent or more of the circle will be in the tin. Inevitably he will hit the tin on a considerable percentage of his best opportunities. Why? Because unknowingly he is aiming at the telltale, even though he may swear on a Bible that he isn't.

Cancelling Yourself Out

Champions make winners and almost never make unprovoked losers. They seem to get quite close to the tin and yet hardly ever hit it. Their offense is totally positive. Players who have not learned their own limitations and how to allow for them will often make quite a few winners but will also make a number of errors. The errors tend to cancel out the winners, so the net result of their play, on their very best chances, is close to zero. This is due in considerable part to the faulty concept that setups should be played right next to the tin. They aim at it, they have a good eye, they hit it, they lose.

The most subtle part of all this discussion is that such unsound players actually make a lot of their shots. This reassures them that they are on the right track. You'll often hear them say, "That's what I should do all the time." And so the inexorable percentages pile up. They make many fine shots, but will lose a close match and say, "I thought I was going to beat him, but I made a couple of crucial errors." They do not recognize what is a fact—anyone who believes he can be perfect inevitably falls short. He who has enough humility (not to be confused with timidity) to recognize his imperfection has the best chance of success.

Spin Makes Up the Difference

This brings the discussion back to spin. Using spin to kill the ball enables one to stay reasonably away from the tin, yet still make a good percentage of effective finesse shots. Vic Niederhoffer, when he wishes, makes almost every known shot from all over the court. He makes very few tins. He is a master at the use of spin in controlling the behavior of the ball without undue risk.

The Sliced Corner Shot

This is sometimes referred to as a "roll corner." It is played into the wall the player is facing. The ball should be allowed to drop low and should be heavily sliced so the spin throws it around the corner and quickly to the floor for its first bounce. It will then have room for a second bounce before reaching the third wall (the other sidewall).

Soft and Hard

There are two ways to play this shot. It can be played at low speed with "touch" so it tends to drop quite dead off the front wall. Played in this manner it can be played into the sidewall a little farther back from the front wall and will go dead nearer the front wall on the other side of the court (Fig 7.2a). It can also be played as a very fast finesse shot, with as violent a swing as one used on a hard drive. Most of the violence goes into creating spin, but the ball does go faster, and therefore needs a little more room in which to take two bounces. Therefore it should be aimed nearer the corner (Fig. 7.2b).

The "touch" corner shot puts the ball farther away from an opponent. The fast corner shot gives greater deception. The violent swing causes an opponent to anticipate a hard depth shot, and out comes a corner shot instead, catching him or at least preventing him from making a fast start. Likewise, with exactly the same preparation and the same speed of swing, the attacker can actually make a hard straight or crosscourt shot. Some players prefer the gain in deception to the extra accuracy of the softer shots. This is a matter of personal choice. Perhaps the best of all is a compromise. A quick, snappy slice that has medium speed is made sharply enough to give deception, yet is soft enough and dead enough so it can be placed as far as possible from an opponent.

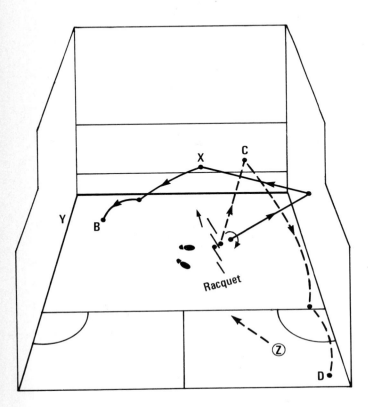

Figure 7.2a A Soft Sliced Corner Shot. (See the solid lines.) Use the maximum amount of sidewall so that the second bounce (B) will be as near the front wall as possible, but will not reach the third wall. Note that the feet, by getting well around for the corner shot are thus perfectly prepared for the deep straight shot (CD) (See the broken line.) Perfect footwork gives perfect deception. This is a combination. Note the slice—the racquet motion is almost at a right angle to the ball direction. Use this shot when your opponent is at Z.

Figure 7.2b A Fast Sliced Corner Shot. The racquet work is the same as in Figure 7.2a, but note the difference in where the two shots strike the sidewall and front wall. This shot, starting from C, has much more room to take two bounces without "coming off" the third wall (C to Y as opposed to X to Y in 7.2a). However, the hard corner comes farther back (compare B in 7.2a with D in 7.2b). Different players have different preferences. Use this when your opponent has just played from Z.

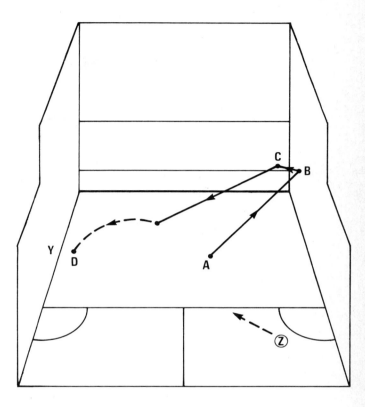

Play Up

A roll corner should never be played unless the ball is allowed to drop low. To take it high means one must play down at the telltale, increasing risk. The ball when played high will also take longer to take two bounces, since when it is played down, it will bounce up more.

If it is taken low, then it must be played up to clear the tin. This is obvious, but many players still hit the tin, because the ball strikes the sidewall and is pulled down by the spin in its rebound from the sidewall. Therefore it must be played up a lot more than most players at first realize or it will still strike the telltale. Playing it quite sharply up into the sidewall, with quite heavy slice, gives the best results.

Where to Aim

A player must learn to aim far enough but not too far down the sidewall. If the ball is played too sharply into the wall it will be halfway across the court before it strikes the front wall. The ball then has very little room to take two bounces without coming off the third wall (which ruins the shot). If it is aimed too close to the corner it will come out into the center instead of going far to the other side. Usually taking three or four feet of sidewall is about right, but each player must experiment for himself.

The Sidewall Drop Shot

This is often called a corner shot, but should not be because it goes nowhere near the corner. It is used as a deceptive variation when two players are hitting down one wall repeatedly. It drops the ball far up front when hopefully an opponent is lingering well back in anticipation of another hard depth shot. This shot requires touch. It must be played from a low ball and be sliced up into the sidewall with just enough force so that it reaches the center of the front wall but is exhausted when it gets there. As it lightly touches the front wall, the spin throws it down so it takes two little bounces far up front. It acts exactly like a soft crosscourt drop shot. The only difference is that it gets there via the sidewall instead of directly from the racquet (Fig. 7.3).

The Reverse Corner Shot

This shot should be sharply distinguished from the roll corner. The roll corner is played into the sidewall several feet back from the front wall so it will carry over near the other wall instead of coming too much to the center. The reverse corner should be played as near the exact corner as a player can aim it without risking hitting the front wall first (the ball then comes to the center and boxes the striker). It should be played quite crisply, with definite backspin but with enough speed so it "squirts" out of the corner and flickers across the court. There is such a thing as a "soft" reverse corner which drops quietly off the front wall like a sidewall drop shot. However, this requires very great touch and deception. A few great players like Henri Salaun have mastered this, but it is not recommended for most. Why? Because a reverse corner puts the ball out in the open up front, and against good competition this is most unwise if the ball lingers there for any length of time—it may well be killed. The crisp corner shot, which leaves the ball exposed for only an instant, is in general a better calculated risk. There is much less chance of a "backfire" (Fig. 7.4).

Figure 7.3 The Sidewall Drop Shot. This is a "touch shot." It must be played just hard enough so it barely reaches the front wall and drops dead. It is usually worthless with a fast "hot" ball, but it can be deadly with a slow ball. Note the slicing motion of the racquet, and the feet, which are equally well-prepared for the "combination" shot—a deep, straight drive to the backhand corner. Use the sidewall drop only when your opponent is lingering behind the T, watching for depth (Z).

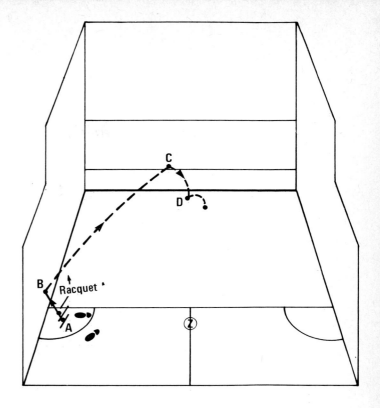

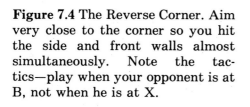

Figure 7.4 The Reverse Corner. Aim very close to the corner so you hit the side and front walls almost simultaneously. Note the tactics—play when your opponent is at B, not when he is at X.

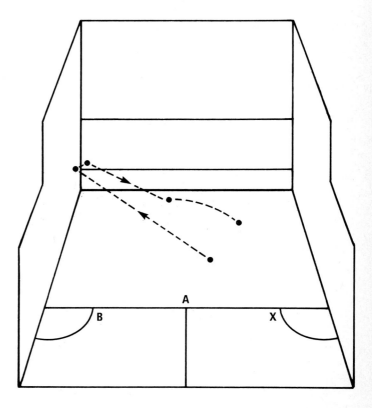

Execution

The secret of successful technique in making a reverse corner is to make it quickly but *lightly*. It should be snapped with a sudden wrist and arm kick (very little arm), but no weight should be added. Any weight will give it length, which will make it come off the third wall (the other sidewall) and it will then be a setup. To avoid putting weight into the shot a player should check his follow-through so it stops just beyond the contact point. Follow-through pulls weight into the shot. Absence of follow-through helps withhold weight. If a player practices striking the ball quite sharply, but severely "checks" his follow-through, he will soon get the feeling of making a sudden crisp but light shot. The suddenness gives deception—it is hard to read the striker's intentions until it's too late. The crispness means the shot will be rather zippy and will take its two bounces in a very short time. Aiming close to the corner insures the ball will strike the front wall close to the sidewall. This gives it the greatest space or width in which to take its two bounces before reaching the third wall. The shot should always carry backspin so it will go down from the front wall and take its first bounce as soon as possible. This leaves a greater width of the court for the second bounce, again reducing the risk of coming off the third wall. The absence of weight in the shot doesn't *make* the ball drop from the front wall, but it *lets* it drop. A player who pounds the ball into the corner merely gives the ball more length—it comes off the third wall. The lightness recommended here allows the ball to drop rather than forcing it to go long.

The Drop Shot

This should always be played from a low ball. It is the softest shot in the game. The delicacy with which it should be sliced is best described by the word "feather." The racquet is prepared so close to the ball that there is literally no backswing at all. The ball almost lands on the racquet before it is played. It is then sliced with a drawing motion (pulling the butt of the racquet through) plus a very gentle push with the weight to cause it to float just barely to the front wall. From the front wall it falls almost directly down (aided by spin) with almost no rebound at all. It can be played either straight or crosscourt (Fig. 7.5).

Masters of the Drop Are Rare

Very few players, including champions, really master the feathery drop shot. There are several basic reasons. First, they try to "hit it gently."

Figure 7.5 The Feathery Straight Drop. Note the slow arching flight of the ball, from A to B. The ball is played *up,* but so gently that it is falling when it touches the front wall. Thus it is literally "a shot that *drops."* Note how snugly it is placed near the sidewall, so that it strikes the sidewall (C) *before* it reaches the floor. This markedly reduces the length of the rebound and bounce, so it takes two bounces (D and E) very far up and quickly. Note the crossing motion of the racquet face—it pulls from the outside in, rather than back and forth. There is *no* wrist action in this shot.

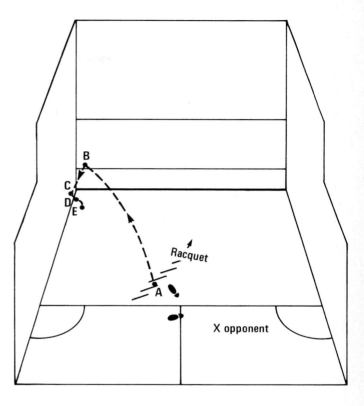

The fact is it will be a poor shot if it is hit *at all.* It must be pressed with the weight only—the racquet merely draws across and under (feathers) the ball. One must get the feel of drawing, pulling, or dragging the strings across the ball from the outside in. A quick hit or strike motion will not give the needed "touch" or "feel," no matter how carefully or gently executed. A no-backswing preparation is essential.

Secondly, most players think of a drop shot as a straight low shot. It is not straight. The flight of the ball should follow an arc. It goes up from the racquet, but so gently that it is going *down* when it meets the front wall. Very simply, it is a shot that *drops.* Think of what it is called—a 'drop' shot. If it is played this way it falls almost straight down from the front wall and is very hard to reach because the rebound is so short.

Thirdly, the importance of using the sidewall is neglected by many who try to acquire this shot. If it is aimed to strike the front wall very close to the sidewall it will graze the sidewall on the way down to the floor. Sometimes this results in a nick that is almost unplayable. With or without the nick the checking effect of contact with the sidewall appreciably shortens the length of the rebound and often makes the difference between success and failure.

Fourthly, few players master the deception which is what really makes the drop shot lethal. If the racquet is prepared with the wrist fully cocked, a player can quite obviously prepare carefully for a drop shot, then at the last second snap the ball deep crosscourt. An opponent who moves up to anticipate the drop shot can often be passed. He soon learns that he had better not anticipate too eagerly.

Fifthly, the drop shot, even if learned correctly, is a "backfire" shot. A bad drop shot is about as fat a setup as one can offer to an eager opponent. There the ball is, sitting in the front of the court, offering many options if it is easy to reach. Therefore many players try it for awhile, then give it up. They'll say, "It just gets me into trouble. I'm better off without it." If executed with less than real excellence, they are right.

So you should not think of the drop shot as the solution to your needs unless you're willing to put a lot of work on it. No one ever acquired a good drop shot without losing many points in the process of perfecting it. It is a great shot but the price of perfecting it is high.

The other side of the coin, however, should be a great incentive to ambitious players. The very greatest players, the champions of champions, have usually been adept at this tantalizing weapon. Harry Cowles, the famous Harvard coach of yore, who once beat the national champion 3–0 and 15–0 in the third game, was an absolute master at feathering the ball to either front corner from anywhere in the court. Hashim Khan, for long the king of the game and still formidable at an advanced age, uses it with fiendish deception. He feathers the ball so delicately it drops incredibly short, but he's always alert and ready to snap the ball past any opponent who dares start a little early to cover it. Germain G. Glidden, (three-time champion from 1936 to 1938, retired undefeated; three-time veterans champion, retired undefeated) was most famous for his fast tempo volleying, but he could always (and often did) vary his ferocious fast game with little dripping drop shots that were the undoing of any opponent who hung back a little to slow the pace. For a time before World War II the principal rivalry in amateur squash was between Harvard and Princeton players. Charlie Brinton (four-time national champion), undoubtedly Princeton's greatest player, was once asked, "What shot bothers you the most in a match?" He replied, "Those damn Harvard drop shots." Brinton, who as a comer had used corner shots almost exclusively, proceded to acquire a very good drop shot of his own, and the shoe often pinched the other foot from then on. This list could go on, but the point has been made. The greatest of the great are usually masters of that nasty little tweak called a drop shot.

Drop versus Corners

The ball can be made to go dead up front with either a corner shot or a drop shot. There have been many fine players who relied solely on corner shots for their finesse shots. But it is generally conceded that the drop shot is slightly superior to the corner shot, for one cogent reason—the corner shot puts the ball out in the open, the drop shot puts the ball on the wall. If an opponent anticipates and reaches a corner shot he can do a lot with it. If he reaches a drop shot he is inhibited by the proximity of the wall and has fewer options. During a tough match this can make that slim difference between a winner and a loser. Harry Cowles and Hashim Khan, probably the two greatest of all time, both spoke in favor of the drop shot for this one reason. If any shot merits the title of the greatest finesse shot in the game, the drop shot should have first claim. Brinton was right—it's the shot that will bother you most.

Nicks

Many times a poor shot will come out into the center but will be too high to offer a good chance at a drop or a corner. Yet the striker has his man boxed behind him and wants to seize the opportunity to run him the length of the court and perhaps get a winner. A standard play in such situations is to try for a nick. This shot is often referred to as a "hard drop shot." It is played quite low into the front wall at an angle calculated to catch the sidewall and floor simultaneously on the rebound. It is usually quite a crisp shot, so if it successfully finds the nick it goes dead very quickly and is reached only by the fastest players in the game, and sometimes not even by them.

Straight Is Best

Usually the straight nick shot is preferred to the crosscourt. The straight shot, if it fails to nick, goes along the wall and is an acceptable continuation of the rally. The crosscourt failure comes right out into the open and is likely to be a disastrous "backfire." While some players have become such masters of the crosscourt nick shot that they gain far more than they lose, percentage dictates that the straight nick is to be preferred. The downside factor is more limited.

Spin Is Important

This shot should be played with an almost vertical swing of the racquet on the forehand, from high to low. The follow-through will go to the left but the racquet acts vertically while on the ball. It is a chop, and heavy backspin markedly improves the results. The ball is thrown down from the front wall by the spin, nicks more often, more quickly, and much nearer the front wall than if played flat, which tends to give a more horizontal rebound. When well-executed with considerable spin, this shot is perhaps the most unanswerable placement in the game. It goes down so quickly into the crack that there is almost no time at all for the retriever (Fig. 7.6). The backhand straight nick is similar, involving heavy "down-drag" so the ball will go down as quickly as possible from the front wall. Both these shots involve a firm wrist and a tight grip. They are not "wristy," tricky shots. To prepare for these, you must line up the racquet and feet with the ball so that a simple quick down-pull on the back of the ball plus a small, sharp push with your weight (these two are simultaneous, not sequential) take the ball to the desired spot on the front wall. Spin does the rest.

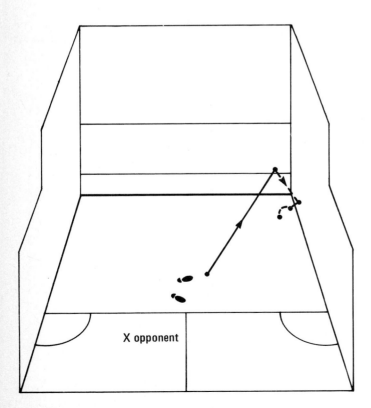

Figure 7.6 The Nick Shot. This is sometimes called a "hard" drop shot. This is possibly the most lethal way to deal with a setup that bounces too high to lend itself to soft drops or corner shots. The nick is a crisp chop, with heavy backspin so that the ball is thrown down from the front wall as vertically as possible. Note the use of the sidewall to aid in killing the ball. This shot is the exact counterpart of a "chip" in tennis. The racquet face cuts from above down the back of the ball. Curling the racquet a little (opening the face a bit on the follow-through) increases spin.

X opponent

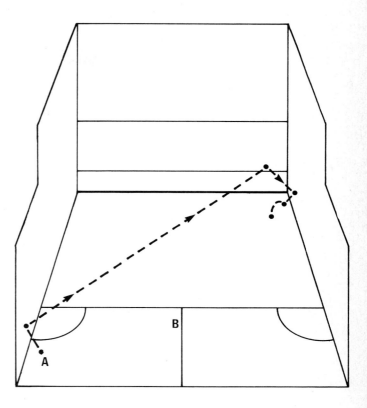

Figure 7.7 The Three-Wall Nick. This is a very valuable shot in a hard-hitting match, particularly when the ball is lively and other finesse shots are less effective. It must be played with real touch, so that when the ball reaches the front wall it is "tired" and drops into the crack instead of roaring out into the center as a stupid setup. Side slice throws the ball sideways from the front wall, increasing chances for a nick. This shot should be crisp, but never bludgeoned.

The Three-Wall Nick

Here is another shot that is markedly improved by the use of spin, in this case sidespin. The objective of the shot is to "catch the crack," i.e., strike the floor and sidewall almost simultaneously. As has been pointed out, a true nick that rolls and is unplayable is extremely rare. What you can actually do is to strike the sidewall very low so the ball almost nicks and takes two very quick bounces that defeat all but the fastest retrievers. If considerable sidespin is put on the ball, it will "reach" for the sidewall in its rebound from the front wall. The spin throws it into the wall. In slicing the ball there is also a backspin component, and this throws the ball down. Thus the ball, if given this treatment, really appears to *try* to nick. Players who use this technique get more "lucky nicks" than those who play flat (Fig. 7.7). Like the slice corner and the sidewall drop, this shot should only be played from a low ball and should be played decisively up into the sidewall. The angle into the wall should be quite sharp, so the ball goes quite close to the corner on the front wall. This betters your chances of catching the sidewall and also means any nick will occur farther forward on the sidewall.

In order to get this angle you should face diagonally backwards so your feet and shoulders are in line with the initial flight of the ball from the racquet to the sidewall. This in no way precludes a hard drive. All that you need to do is pivot if you wish to play the ball straight instead.

Getting Touch on a Three-Wall Nick

Many players fail to understand that this shot is a real finesse shot. They picture it as a slam that will now and then take a lucky low bounce or nick. While the shot is indeed a sharply played ball, it will rarely nick if it is slammed. The extra power causes it to drive horizontally to the sidewall from the front wall, and, striking the sidewall rather high, it will come far out into the center as a perfect setup. Actually the ball should be "tired" when it reaches the front wall. There should be only a little energy left in it, so it drops down and strikes the sidewall low. This requires restraint. The ball should be given just enough sharp impact of racquet and weight to get to the front wall—and that's all. The feeling of playing it crisply, though by no means with full power, is akin to the restrained sharpness of a reverse corner shot. As with that shot, a crisp, quick stroke with a checked follow-through gives the desired neatness. An unrestrained stroke with a more full approach and follow-through seldom results in this feeling of accurate touch.

How to Use the Three-Wall Nick

Basically the three-wall nick is an unsound shot. Whenever it fails to nick it is a sure backfire shot—it comes right out in the center of the court. Many players attempt it only when they must. By this I mean that they are so forced they cannot avoid playing the ball into the sidewall; they feel they have nothing to lose—the ball is going to come out anyway—so why not try for the nick. This policy usually fails. They are so forced and off balance, with the ball somewhat by them, that they seldom have the poise to get anything approaching the needed accuracy. Their aim fails and their opponent gets a nice fat fairly low setup right in the center. They would be better advised to play very high for a lob even if it hits the sidewall first. A high setup for a volley is much more difficult to kill than a low setup that bounces nicely to the striker.

Play It When You Don't Have to Play It

The best player will use the three-wall nick as a surprise. He will play it from behind an opponent off a ball that comes off the back wall. He has plenty of time to get set perfectly, and the threat of another deep drive is bound to be the major preoccupation of his opponent. His chances of surprising his opponent and of actually getting the nick are very good. He doesn't have to play the sidewall. He chooses to play it, as one of several options. Used not too much, but now and then to insert an element of doubt into a long, tough rally, the shot can be really useful. Its value is enhanced by the fact that once an opponent knows a player has the shot he must continually watch for it. He must position himself a little more forward to be able to reach it. He is thus more likely to be passed by deep basic drives. He doesn't dare "lay back" for depth shots, for how can he tell when a player will try that nick shot again? Thus, played from deep in the court the shot should not be used much, but enough to constitute an ever-present nagging threat.

Perhaps the best use of this shot is to play it when your opponent hits straight from behind you but does not get good depth. In stepping sideways to intercept his shot you step right in front of him. For just a second he is pinned in the back corner—he cannot move diagonally directly to the center without getting in your way, and you have the right of way. He is forced to come out of the corner a little along the back wall before moving forward to the T. A three-wall nick may well catch him a good three feet behind the service line when he starts for your ball. An extra three feet is an enormous distance in a game as fast as squash. A decent nick is very likely to be a winner. Additionally, a three-wall nick can be played effectively from quite close to the wall, while most other shots cannot. So if his ball is quite close to the sidewall but lacks depth, so you can take it in front of you, the three-wall nick is one of the best ways to capitalize on the deficiency in his play.

For Advanced Players Only

All the foregoing is very advanced. Beginners and intermediates should forget about the three-wall nick until they have developed a decent basic game. If they try it they will merely develop the bad habit of hitting the sidewall when they don't have to, putting the ball continually out in the center. No green player has the touch to get a decent percentage of nicks or the savvy to use it judiciously or deceptively. By contrast, all advanced players should perfect it on both sides in order to have the double threat of playing long or short anytime from anywhere in the court.

The Boast

This is a truly difficult shot. It must be hit very hard, because when it comes off the first sidewall it gets a large amount of reverse spin. If it strikes the second sidewall softly it will drop into the court without ever reaching the front wall at all, due to this spin. Therefore it must be hit hard enough to force it to slide from the second sidewall to the front wall. "Hard enough" means quite hard indeed—as hard as a good forcing basic drive. Just because a player must hit it so forcefully it is very difficult to get the exact angle required. It takes a lot of practice to get anything approaching percentage results (Fig. 7.8).

If a player can make this shot he can put the ball closer to the front wall than is possible with any other shot. The ball literally drops down only

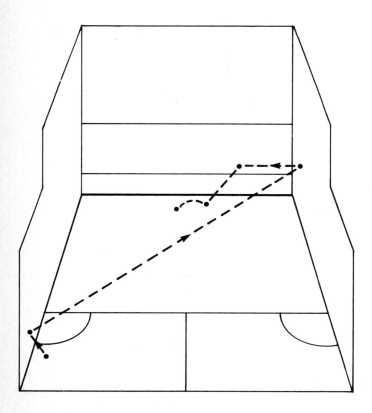

Figure 7.8 The Boast. This shot goes from sidewall to sidewall, then barely touches the front wall before dropping shorter than any other shot in the game. Because of the reverse spin it gets from the first sidewall, it must be hit very hard to force it to skid forward from the second sidewall to the front wall. Otherwise, it will drop to the floor without reaching the front wall at all. This extremely difficult shot is generally frowned on as nonpercentage. However, when once in a while a great player gets it going successfully, it can be a show stopper as the big whack into the first wall dies into a nothing ball up front.

inches in front of the telltale. But when it misses it comes way out in the open and most players feel they are better off without it—the percentage is poor. When it is pulled off successfully it is usually a spectacular winner. There is a hard slam into the sidewall, and there is the ball, only six inches from the front wall. It's a sort of super drop shot that emerges from a hard cracked ball. It is definitely a showstopper.

Volley Finesse Shots

These can be lumped under one heading—nonpercentage. There is no time to get set for sufficient precision, thus many errors and sloppy setups result. The ball is being played from high to low, into the tin, and percentage urges us to play away from the tin, not at it. These shots are only successful against inferior players.

Exceptions

One can never make a one hundred percent blanket statement, however. I recall watching Charlie Brinton defeat a good player with an amazing and continuous stream of drop volleys. But—the court was extraordinarily cold and slow, and the ball was unusually slow. Brinton, who, as a rule, was a model of soundness, quickly perceived that the first player to drop the ball would probably have himself a winner. He therefore dropped the ball from everywhere—high, low, and medium. His opponent was totally confounded. This again points out that rules are made to be broken. Certainly Brinton is to be praised for his quick mental reaction to an almost bizarre situation.

There are other times when it can become a percentage play to depart from orthodoxy. If an opponent is very tired and slowing down, even a mediocre volley drop or corner can keep him running and help finish him off. If a ball comes out exactly right for a volley finesse shot, one sometimes has the feeling, "I *know* I can make a beauty." Why not make it?

The important thing is to learn the rule, and abide by it until it is a habit. The percentage rule is this: Do not try to volley finesse shots. But once you have good habits, you should not let them inhibit your thinking, imagination, or ingenuity in finding a way to win.

The Brinton anecdote seems to favor breaking the rule. Perhaps a couple of others will balance it. I used to have an annual match with another coach who was a fine player. This coach liked to run his boys about using volley corner shots. It was such a habit that he couldn't resist any good chance to do it. I always took pains to lob serve badly, three feet out from the sidewall, so that he would be irresistibly tempted to volley a reverse corner. He always did. But I was always up there quickly and would put it away. He never beat me. The moral is don't volley corner shots, unless your opponent is very slow afoot.

Recently Peter Briggs came to Harvard. He was so talented that he could beat all his prep school and freshman rivals with a lot of tricky plays, featuring all types of strange volley finesse shots, sometimes even from well above his head. I tried hard to talk him out of it. "It won't work with Class A squash," I'd say. Sophomore year he was soundly trounced by every first class opponent he met, including several intercollegiate rivals he was determined to defeat. Junior year, in the fall, he came to me and said, "I see what you mean. From now on I'm tough." He rose, in that one year, to be Intercollegiate Champion and ranked fifth in the U.S. His greatest improvement was to discipline himself into the habit of not trying a tricky shot until he could really make it well. It was not easy. Using trick plays was a strong habit, almost a reflex. He transformed himself from an ineffective, cocky player, riding for a fall, into a real rock capable of challenging the best on even terms.

So the rule is still a good one most of the time.

The Hairy Shot

The unusual is sometimes resorted to in an endeavor to break up an opponent who seems immovably established "in the groove." This shot is really not a shot at all. It merely consists of slugging the ball high into the sidewall so it roars around the court and comes flying out at an opponent's head from the sidewall. It has panicked more than one good player into a silly error and a break in his momentum. When you're losing, it is worth a try simply because it is so wildly sloppy (Fig. 7.9a). It is usually made with the forehand for maximum power. If the angle into the sidewall is sharp and the ball is allowed to go to the back wall, it can be unplayable, since it turns into a four-wall "Philadelphia."

The Philadelphia

This is a spectacular shot from the forecourt. Hit very hard, if not volleyed it will rebound unplayably off the sidewall. The Philadelphia is best played when both players are well up front, so the striker can get the ball past his opponent before the latter can volley.

Ordinarily a Philadelphia is played high. However, a low Philadelphia, hit *very* hard, will go to the second sidewall and rebound so quickly and at such an unexpected forward angle (due to the extreme reverse English) that many players will miss it because of the weird rebound.

Both of these shots are fringe spectaculars, not needed for basic excellence; but they are quite startling when, on rare occasions, a player pulls one out of the hat. They are best played by hard hitters who can put so much speed on the ball that the damage is done before an opponent can adjust and cut the shot off, which is the proper reply (see Figure 7.9b).

Figure 7.9a The "Hairy" Shot. This shot is so called because it is the wildest, apparently most pointless way to play the ball. It should be slugged—as hard as possible—so that it comes flying out into the center, high and from a hopefully unexpected angle. The answer is the volley down the backhand wall. But many good players are so startled they fail to volley and chase it back, where the spin acquired by rolling off the walls makes the bounces at B and C hard to judge. It can be very disconcerting to someone who is "in the groove." It may also be played sidewall first.

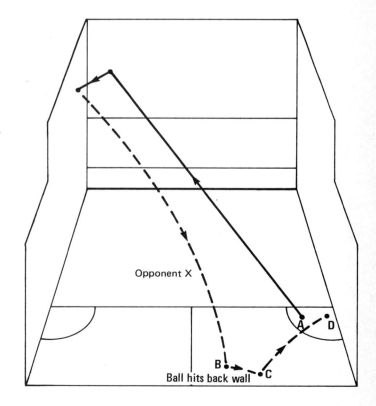

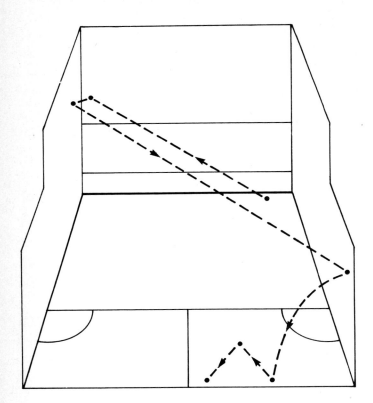

Figure 7.9b The Philadelphia. This shot should be played from far up front so as to get enough angle to go from sidewall to sidewall, then run unplayably along the back wall. The answer is the volley, which catches the attacker far up and may pass him. It's a gamble. The player hopes to hit hard and zip the ball past his startled opponent. Both this and the Hairy Shot are good only as infrequent surprise spectaculars. They are basically unsound, but often win the first time they are played.

Summary

1. Slicing is the key to successful finesse. This involves two simultaneous motions almost at right angles to each other—a pull with the racquet accompanied by a push with the weight. Being able to stroke in this manner helps all one's shots, not merely finesse shots.

2. Good footwork, balance, a tight grip, a restricted backswing and follow-through all are essential to the exactness required by finesse shots.

3. Players hit the tin because they aim at it by not allowing for their radius of error.

4. Errors cancel out aces, so many players have an offense that adds up to little more than zero.

5. Allowing a margin for error and knowing the right use of spin produces a positive offense—a reasonable number of winners but few errors.

6. The sliced corner shot should be taken low and played sharply up into

the sidewall with heavy slice to pull it down and throw it around the corner.

7. The sidewall drop shot is similar but drops softly off the front wall.

8. The reverse corner shot should be small, crisp, and sharp, with backspin to lay it dead.

9. The feathery drop shot is one of the most difficult and most misunderstood shots. It's hard to acquire, but it's possibly the greatest shot in the game. The greatest players use it.

10. Drop shots stay near the wall; therefore they are superior to corner shots that come out.

11. Nicks are best for higher setups.

12. Heavy backspin sharply improves nicks.

13. The three-wall nick benefits from sidespin. It's an unsound shot unless it's used sparingly with a surprise factor. It is a touch shot, not a slam.

14. The boast is spectacular, difficult, and usually against the percentages.

15. Volley finesse shots are against the percentages with rare exceptions.

16. The Hairy Shot and the Philadelphia are good only as unusual surprises.

8

Footwork and Balance

The crouch is fundamental to all good technical execution. Being bent at the knees and the waist, with the weight on the balls of the feet gives a balanced effect besides poise and fluency to what a player is doing. The word fluency is usually thought of in terms of strokes, but it applies equally to the legs. The flow of weight into each shot is achieved by pushing with the legs. You cannot push if your knees are not bent. Also, since you should take most balls only after they get quite low, bending the knees and waist is essential to getting down there where the ball is to be played. If you can be a little feline in the court, stalking the ball like a skulking cat, your technique will be much benefited.

Move the Foot Nearest the Ball

Everyone is taught that the closed stance is correct and the open stance incorrect (see Figure 8.1). This always sounds well and reads well, but it often fails to square with the facts of life in a fast match. One of these facts is tempo. In a fast exchange there is very little time. The talker or writer has all the time he wants, and envisions a person in perfect position. He describes this and advises it for all occasions. The player, however, has only as much time as the ball allows. The ball won't wait. Frequently the player just does not have time to arrange himself in the perfect manner prescribed by orthodoxy. What does he do? He does what he absolutely

Figure 8.1a Closed Stance—Left Foot Advanced. This is the theoretically "correct" stance because it facilitates addressing the ball, weight transfer, and shoulder turn. Both feet have moved to achieve this position.

Figure 8.1b Open Stance—Only the Right Foot Has Moved. Shoulder turn is achieved easily by twisting a little at the waist. Note the economies in motion, time, and effort. Note the additional function of crouching—your entire length becomes "reach."

must do: he gets within reach of the ball. On a forehand he steps toward the ball with his right foot, a sort of sideways sliding motion which gets the hitting arm within reach of the ball. Frequently that is all the time he has. He plays the ball without getting his left foot out front in the "correct" manner. He then slides back to the center. He has used the "incorrect" open stance, because he had insufficient time to do anything more than that. How can we call this wrong when it is unavoidably forced on the player? It is obviously right. It is the quickest possible way to reach the ball, it makes possible the quickest return to position, and it is most economical in the use of energy. The ideal closed stance is impossible due to tempo.

This contrasts sharply with a game like golf. There is no tempo in golf, the ball sits there and awaits your pleasure. There is no problem of regaining position very quickly to be ready for the next shot. Therefore, golfers *always* use the ideal closed stance. In all racquet games tempo frequently forces the compromise described above. One sees it constantly in both tennis and squash. To compare these two games with golf is invalid because of the time factor. The player who thinks like a golfer is often left at the post in the subsequent exchange.

Many times the ball allows more time, the left foot can be moved over and placed out front and the ball can be played in the ideal manner. Most players prefer on such occasions to use the closed stance, particularly on setups in which a correctly addressed ball aids substantially in achieving exact aim. On such occasions the closed stance is to be preferred. A player plans to make a very exact shot that will run his opponent. He must return to position but is not under great pressure to do so. His main concern is to achieve perfection on his shot. The closed stance is best.

The open stance is used less on the backhand because moving the left foot does not get the hitting arm to the ball. As the right shoulder moves toward the ball it is natural for the right leg to go with it. Thus, many fine players will have an open stance forehand and a closed stance backhand. But the foot nearest the ball (the left on a backhand) will still move quickly enough so that when the right shoulder crosses over, the arm can reach the ball.

Perhaps the smoothest example of economical but effective footwork is Henri Salaun. He is small and doesn't have great reach, yet he slides effortlessly from side to side, covers everything, and is almost impossible to pass or dislodge from the center position. Watch him. Always, the foot nearest the ball slides out very quickly so he is within reach. On his forehand he plays from there; on his backhand he crosses the right leg over for the most part. He handles himself beautifully. It is a pleasure, and instructive, to watch him at work.

Keep Moving

A good player is seldom completely still. This is because if you're totally still you become inert. You're "stuck," and it's hard to get started. Good players always bob up and down a little bit, usually timing it so they are down just as their opponent strikes the ball. This facilitates a very fast takeoff, and is a very good habit to develop. It takes the "grunt" out of starting and increases quickness.

Lean Forward a Little

If you lean forward a bit, it increases the crouch and gets the weight on the balls of the feet. Even if you are forced back you can make your move faster from this forward leaning posture. More importantly, moving quickly forward is the greater worry. If an opponent accidentally or purposely makes a very low short shot there is much less time to move to it than if he plays a deeper shot. Many players who stand straight are slow getting up for short balls that they did not foresee, and they are left standing there. A player who is crouched forward will get most of them. It is wise always to be ready to move forward—you can always whirl back with the ball if it goes deep. If you're "on your heels" a short ball is a winner.

Move Both Feet at Once

What you do when you walk or run is move naturally. In so doing, you use sequential footwork—first one foot then the other. This is far too slow for a fast game like squash. If a setup comes out, you should at once take a little hop that takes the weight off your feet for an instant. In this instant they are rearranged so when the weight comes down on them they are in perfect position and everything else is ready. Your racquet is cocked, your shoulders turned, and you are crouched and positioned so that the ball will not be too close or too far away.

It takes some practice to get it all together, to perfect what is a composite thought that includes moving, arranging the feet, the racquet, and the body—all in one quick flicker during which everything is done simultaneously. The best player has perfected this knack, and it gives him great advantages. He has more time to aim, so he is more accurate. And, he is so far ahead of the ball that he can *wait*. This is very disconcerting. It is difficult to tell when or where he will play the ball. His opponent must wait also—until he plays—so he tends to get inert, or "stuck." His takeoff is slower, or he may make a false move. If he started for some shot other than the one intended, he is forced to twist back in a wrenching change of direction—and he still may not get the ball. This is one of the secrets of deception in advanced tactics—to wait before hitting—and it is not possible unless a player has mastered the knack of very quick preparation.

Sidle—Don't Walk

Frequently a player's first move will not be perfect. He is still too close or too far away from the ball, so he must make another adjustment. It is here that the trick of sidling is valuable. If he moves only one foot he has destroyed his poise and stance. He must move one foot, then pull the other along with it the required amount. If he wishes to move forward for a forehand he moves his left foot forward and pulls his right foot up behind it, so they are the same distance apart (for poise) as they were at the beginning of the move. If he wishes to move back, he puts his right foot back and pulls his left foot back after it the same distance. Of course this is done very quickly so it looks like a little hop with both feet moving at once. The quickness makes it look like a jump, but it's really a very fast sidle. The front foot always leads if the move is forward. The back foot always leads if the move is backward. Beginners and intermediates should be taught this as soon as possible so they can shake the natural habit of moving only one foot, and learn to maintain poise and stance in addressing the ball, even when adjustments are necessary.

Keep Your Feet under You

An additional advantage of the sidling habit is that it maintains poise. Whenever you move one foot and leave the other where it was, you lose your balance and the control of your weight. You tend to sprawl. You may at once feel and look awkward, and you actually are momentarily awkward. It is important to bring the other foot along, keep it under you, and keep yourself in one neat package at all times. Tall people with long legs tend to be afflicted more often with this habit of leaving one leg out behind them when they move to the ball. It inevitably impairs their play. They should learn to keep their feet more nearly together by sidling.

The Fast Start

A squash court is small. There is no very long distance. Even when a player is at the back of the court and the ball is played short retrieving it only requires four or five strides. So it is all a matter of how quickly you can get started. How fast you can run after you get going is irrelevant—it's all over by then. Squash players should thus concentrate on the first two or three steps—the takeoff.

The secret of increasing your quickness is to avoid taking big, long-reaching steps. If you do this you may feel that you are straining and stretching—but, not being made of elastic, you don't get there, in spite of mighty efforts. To be more positive, you should train yourself to take several rather small steps in very quick succession, as fast as you can articulate the word "step" three times in a row. Say "step, step, step" as fast as you can. Then, try to take a step each time you say it. You can work up to it.

Use the Legs Only

A track man uses his arms to help him run. It's called "pumping." A squash player should use only his legs, because his arm must prepare the racquet to play the ball when he gets there. Particularly in retrieving a front wall shot the racquet must reach forward towards the ball. This is the opposite of pumping, which takes the arm back. If you think of the body and arms as belonging to a privileged person in a rickshaw, and the legs as belonging to the unfortunate coolie who carries him about, you get a picture of good running in squash. The body maintains poise, the racquet is prepared to play—it is up to the legs to do all the work in getting the racquet to the ball. Therefore, in practicing this "step, step, step" routine, it is a good idea to prepare the racquet before starting, then *don't move it at all* while running. Soon a player learns to make all the effort with the legs. When a player arrives he is perfectly set to play the ball well. If he isn't ready to play, what use is it to get there? Many players "pump" and arrive within reach, but with their racquet somewhere behind them. It then takes too long to move the racquet forward to the ball. *They* got there, but the *racquet* didn't, and the objective is to get the racquet to the ball. These players feel they are slow. Often they are potentially quite fast—their technique is poor. The section on drills will offer specific routines for improving speed to the front wall with proper handling of the racquet. Advanced players can markedly improve their speed and skill on the run with work of this sort.

Flattening Out

This is a knack some gifted athletes have naturally. It can be acquired by others, and it increases a player's reach by quite a bit. It consists of bringing the armpit right down to the forward knee in the final reach for a tough get (Fig. 8.2). This means the entire length of the body and arm are extended horizontally—the greatest possible reach. Some people are not supple enough to do this, but many are supple enough and don't. It certainly adds many inches to a player's last ditch try at staying in the point. Anyone who ever watched Anil Nayar's amazing court coverage will not

Figure 8.2 Flattening Out for a Get. Observe how in one move the racquet has been advanced a very long distance from where the retriever just was (where his left foot still is). By flattening himself out, the player has converted his height and arm length into a horizontal reaching effect. The way to learn this is to advance one foot, bend down and reach forward until your armpit is quite literally on your knee, as in the illustration. Practice slowly then do it in a very quick lunge. Learn to recover instantly (back to where your left foot is). This is not easy, but it is essential if you wish to make a tough get *and* hold your position. It's a very good leg conditioner too!

soon forget his continually incredible ability to flatten out and get his racquet to a ball that looked like a sure winner. He was literally stretched along the floor, yet he still had his feet under him and instantly recovered for the next exchange. Few of us have his unusual physical elasticity, but all of us can imitate his technique, which was unexcelled in this regard.

Retrieving and Scrambling

Staying low and keeping the racquet low increase a player's chances when his opponent is preparing to play a setup. The head of the racquet should be dropped literally to the floor (an inch above it). This is surprisingly important. If the ball is streaked to the forehand side, the racquet moves straight out to the right as the retriever lunges that way. The racquet moves straight out to the left for a backhand. The distance the racquet must move is minimized. If the racquet is carried well off the floor, it must move sideways the same distance also moving down to the ball. This is a longer distance, the hypotenuse. The exchange is often fast enough so this can make the difference between a good try that just fails and a successful get. Carrying the head of the racquet low also tends to force you into the desired crouchy slouch from which the fastest start is possible.

Players too often tend to believe that being adept at scrambling and retrieving is all natural athletic ability, a gift from the gods. This is by no means true. It can be practiced with very perceptible results in the form of increased speed and success. A personal anecdote is pertinent. For various reasons, I was unable to play much over a certain period of time. Then came a match with the state champion. I lost, and lost badly. I was slow, and I couldn't seem to get off the mark. Another match with the same player was due in a couple of weeks. My ego badly bruised, I decided to do something about it. My only available partner was a fairly good but not a champion player. I played him several times, and continually set the ball up in the center, allowing my opponent repeatedly to make every shot he knew. I concentrated only on crouching low, racquet low, and taking off fast to get every shot my delighted opponent made. My opponent had remarked, "I don't know what you think you're doing, but I'm enjoying it." The second match was played, I won 3-0, and my ego was restored. And I did know what I was doing—I was practicing speedy reaction, which was what I had lost. It can be learned as well as restored, by similar practice. See the chapter on "Drills."

Summary

1. Crouching and keeping the weight on the balls of the feet are basic to balance and poise.

2. Starting with the foot nearest the ball is quickest.

3. Always maintaining a little movement and leaning forward a little helps making a quick move to the front wall and speeds the takeoff.

4. Hopping into position with one move is necessary for quick preparations.

5. Sidling and keeping the feet together helps poise and prevents sprawling.

6. Small, quick steps are better than big stretching steps in a fast start.

7. A quiet racquet and fast feet characterize good players.

8. Flattening out maximizes reach.

9. Crouching and carrying the racquet very low enhances speed in retrieving and scrambling. It can be learned. See "Drills."

PART II

Tactics and Match Play

9

Basic Tactics

At this point, I think it would be best to clarify a few definitions:

Technique is how to use the body and the racquet to make a play.
Strategy is the overall plan for the match.
Tactics are the means of implementing the plan.

These words, particularly *tactics* and *strategy,* are constantly confused by being used almost interchangeably. A few examples are in order.

An opponent is a heavy slugger but comparatively slow afoot. My strategy is to avoid slugging with him and to run him up to the front wall whenever possible. My tactics are to lob a lot in the rally and to play finesse shots at every opportunity. Here's another example: my opponent is a deadly shot artist if given a chance. My strategy would be to keep him back almost all the time and rush him as much as possible so he cannot get set to use his beautiful shots. My tactics would be to use hard serves almost exclusively, pound the ball deep, volley a lot, and avoid a front wall crisis except when heavily in my favor. In both of these examples my technique has nothing to do with the governing policy and the ways I apply it.

This chapter will deal with when to use the shots, and will assume the reader can make them.

From Backcourt Play Crosscourt

A player in the backcourt should have one main objective: win the center position (the T) and get there quickly. The crosscourt shot best facilitates this purpose. The opponent must move towards the other side of the court to play the ball. This clears the path to the center. By contrast, a straight shot draws an opponent in front of the striker, and he must take a circuitous route to the center—somewhat along the back wall and then out to the T. If he makes anything short of a very good depth shot he is "boxed" (see Figure 9.1).

Of course there are many exceptions. If the ball is well out from the sidewall there is an opening. The opponent may be forced to stretch to get the straight shot. And some straight shots must be played just to keep him guessing. It is too much of a giveaway always to do the same thing. If he is very strong on one side and weaker on the other, it can be good policy to play every ball to that side during the rally, whether it involves straight or crosscourt shots.

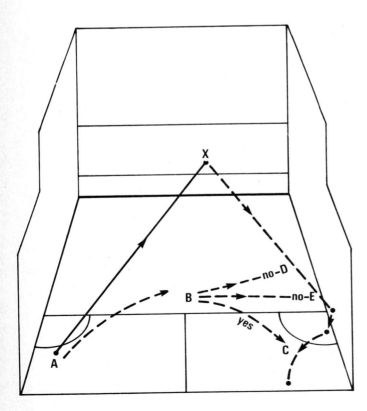

Figure 9.1 The Wide Crosscourt to Win the Center. Note the considerable height above the tin to aid depth. Note the target on the front-wall (X) is quite a bit farther over than the center to give width so that player B (the opponent) cannot intercept at D (the ball is out of reach) or at E (the ball is on the wall). He *must* move over and back (to C) to play the ball. This dog-leg crosscourt, winning both the center and the forward position, is a basic shot all players should learn.

Figure 9.2 From deep near the wall, the crosscourt is a much easier shot. The acceptable target area is much wider. Anything in that whole area will force Player B to move over towards D, opening the path to the center. By contrast, unless the straight shot is very accurate in both width and depth, Player B may be able to move towards E, box Player A behind him, and drop the ball. The moral: Don't hit straight unless you are far enough out from the wall to have a reasonable target area. Otherwise, it is too easy to hit X or Y and box yourself.

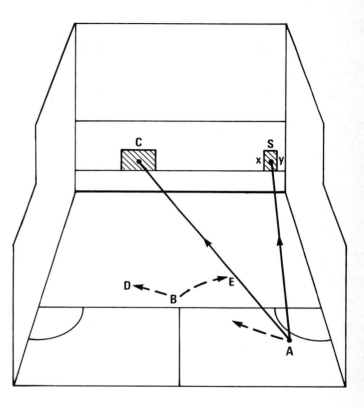

There is one major exception. A crosscourt shot that doesn't have pace can be intercepted before it gets over to the other wall, with bad results. Therefore whenever a player is in trouble, retrieving or hitting weakly for any reason, a high straight shot (frequently a lob) as near the wall as possible is his best play.

Nevertheless, it is a good general rule to play crosscourt from the back corners. It is a much easier shot. If the ball is a foot from the sidewall when played, a player's target for a straight shot is less than a foot wide on the front wall. His crosscourt target is much wider (see Figure 9.2). And the player gets the good habit of clearing the path to proper position.

Play Straight When in Front

There is no fear of being boxed by a straight shot if an opponent must go behind you to play it. Rather, it is advantageous to keep the ball as close to the wall as possible and to force an opponent to cross behind you and dig the ball up to you. The other fellow must worry about getting boxed in, not you. One should not feel at all inhibited about playing to either side as long as the opponent is kept back and cannot cross in front of you to get the ball.

Volley a Lot

The volley is a major weapon in maintaining the forward position. By intercepting at or in front of the red line, a good volleyer can continually frustrate an opponent's efforts and drive him back, keeping him behind until a poor return creates an opportunity for placement.

Don't Let It Go to the Back Wall

If a player volleys the ball it does not go to the back wall. It is a sound policy not to let it go. Many shots that look as though they will come out nicely turn into unfavorable surprises. Some glue to the sidewall as they come out. Some are checked a little by the sidewall on the way back, and don't come out enough to be played effectively or at all. Some go around the corner in an unexpected fashion and get a player in trouble. Some nick and are unplayable. Every time a player lets a ball go to the back wall he runs all these risks.

As with all rules there are exceptions. A high shot that will clearly come far out into the open should always be allowed to do so and to drop low where it can be played with the greatest effectiveness. Here there is a distinct advantage in letting the ball go back and come out, and there is very little risk.

A further advantage of intercepting the ball either on the bounce or volley is that this habit increases quickness. A player cannot volley much if he doesn't react quickly to an opponent's shot. Developing a habit of reacting quickly speeds up his tempo and trains him for the many situations in which quickness is the only means of staying in the point.

Volleying has yet another advantage. It tends to hurry an opponent. It sometimes catches him out of position, still lingering a little at the spot from which he just played the ball. It thus puts continual pressure on him, puts his quickness to the test, and gives him less time to get set and play each shot well.

The volley is very useful as a follow-up shot. If an opponent has been run up to the front wall and his return can be taken on the fly, he is often beaten. He is still up front and has had no time to get back to position. The volley passes him for a winner. This is standard procedure with all advanced players.

Using Finesse Shots

The basic drives and the volley are the ingredients of the rally, which continues until one player is forced into making a poor shot that comes out and sets up. In this situation finesse shots are an absolute necessity. The court is narrow. Merely to hit the ball to the open side will seldom succeed. The distance is easily covered and the rally resumes. An opportunity has come and gone without being exploited.

Think Up and Back

The real answer is to play the ball short to the open side. This runs an opponent the longest distance available in the court—the long diagonal from deep on one side to short on the other. A player should think of running his opponent up and back, not merely from side to side. The only way to do this is to use finesse shots that make the ball go dead near the front wall.

Don't Try for an Ace

Many players realize this and play the short ball, and their thinking stops right there. They think it should be a winner. The fact is it will seldom be a winner. The striker had a setup, yes. But his opponent is still in good position, near the center, ready to run for anything with a high probability of getting anything. The finesse shot is not a winner: it is a court opener.

Follow It Up

When a player runs far up to either front corner and plays, he is *now* out of position. A shot deep to the open side may very well be a winner, particularly if the ball can be taken on the fly before he has much chance to back peddle into a less vulnerable position.

Think Two Shots, Not One

The best player has respect for his opponent's agility and fight. He does not flatter himself that his finesse is so marvellous that, given one good chance at the ball, he can put it away. He thinks in terms of two shots, a shot sequence in which the first shot opens the court and the second exploits that opening. When he plays a finesse shot he is very keen to anticipate where the retriever's ball will go, and very quick to jump on it to slam it deep. It is very much like boxing. When a fighter has an opponent at a disadvantage he does not hit him once then wait for him to topple. He rains as many punches in succession as he possibly can, giving his victim no chance to recover. In squash a setup does not constitute a chance for a one-shot ace. Rather, it is an opportunity to run him, run him again, run him again, and be ready to run him yet again. A good policy is never to expect a shot to be a winner. Always be ready and eager to play the ball again where it will hurt him most. Then when a shot turns out to be a winner it is a pleasant surprise. However, if he gets it back, there is no unpleasant shock or need to question, "What do I do now?" A good player is all set to play again and knows where he will put the ball.

Think One Shot Ahead

Another way of expressing this is to urge players to think one shot ahead. When a player makes a drop shot to the forehand corner he should already know that his next shot, no matter what his opponent does, is going deep to the backhand corner. If his opponent fails to reach his drop shot that's fine, but if he does reach it there is no question about the follow-up. It is thought out and ready.

Press Him, Not Yourself

Thinking in this way not only allows for the inevitable imperfections of your execution in such a fast game, or for the fight and scramble that characterize any worthy opponent. It also has two great advantages in the matter of pressure. If you think you should make a winner on your setup you will probably go very close to the tin, and often you will hit it. You feel your opponent there in the court, crouched and ready to run, and you sense that he is going to dig for the shot and get it. But you may still also think you should make a winner. So you play even lower than you normally would play—and make a dumb error. This is known as putting the pressure on yourself. If you *expect* your opponent to get it, and are pleasantly surprised if he doesn't, this pressure is removed. You'll play the shot as well as you can, with a reasonable margin for error, without putting this fatal extra pressure on yourself. You'll make few stupid tins off fat setups.

The second pressure advantage is that this type of thinking and playing puts all the pressure on your opponent. He is running madly to get the ball, and unless he does something unusually good with it on the dead run, he will be run madly after another one, in an unrelenting fashion. This forces *him* to take chances, to attempt something brilliant while off balance and rushed. Now he is the one who is likely to make an error due to the pressure that makes him try something a little too difficult under the circumstances.

Learning to keep the pressure off yourself and put it on your opponent is the secret of being very aggressive when opportunity offers and at the same time being steady and avoiding that worst of all mistakes—playing giveaway.

Morale

Nothing hurts morale more than to make an unprovoked error. If a player forces me, places the ball beautifully, and beats me on that point, I don't like it—I'd much prefer it the other way—but I am by no means demoralized. Rather, I feel that now I'm going to do it to him, right back. If, however, I play a fine rally, force him to give me a nice fat one out in the open, and then play it into the tin—this really hurts. I beat him, but I *gave* him the point. What could be more stupid, more inexcusable? I tend to be disgusted with myself. I am indeed at least temporarily demoralized. Often fine players, the best, will play grimly and with little show of the emotions and tensions that are undoubtedly within them, until they hit a setup into the tin. Then they may emit almost a wail of anguish. Why? Playing a fat setup into the telltale is the *worst* error a player can make.

This demoralization tends to be true of everyone. Yet players continue to hit the tin on setups, again and again. Basically they don't want to, they hate it just as much as the next fellow, they are hurt as much as the next fellow, but they think they should make an ace—a *perfect* shot—on every setup. Intermittent tins are the inevitable result. If they could learn to think in terms of two shots and the follow-up, taking the pressure off themselves, they could definitely "toughen up" and eliminate most of the errors.

Long Points

Another fault with many players is what might be termed "thinking short." They will run a player expertly for a shot or two, then make an error. This is impatience, and it is fatal against anyone who has any fight or scramble. Again the cure is never to think of a shot as a winner. If the opponent retrieves six, he should make six more. It is wrong for him to take the attitude, after a couple come back that he *will* put it away. Errors inevitably follow. And the opponent is very much heartened. He seems to be saying to himself, "If I stay with this fellow he will miss." This makes him feel energetic, confident, and secure in the knowledge that he doesn't have to take any chances at all. He plays like a rock and the attacker is further frustrated. But if the attacker just keeps running him mercilessly, so he gets little reward for all this hustling except a lot more of the same, he must get discouraged in the long run. This makes him desperate. He must look for other means of winning. Mere retrieving won't do it. He must take chances, and then he's no longer a solid rock: he begins to crumble.

Many matches have been won by a few long rallies. A retriever who is forced to run, and run, and run—with the point going on and on, and the hoped-for error not occuring—must indeed have incredible morale if he remains unshaken and undiscouraged. An anecdote will readily illustrate this. I had occasion to play a well-known professional famous for his retrieving. I had never seen him play. I was astonished; he bounced around the court like the famous superball that almost never stops bouncing. I outplayed him on almost every rally, and I stayed in the center—but back came the ball every time. Finally I would hit the tin from frustration and impatience. He won the first game 15-9, and looked for all the world as though my most clever placements were ordinary plays that didn't bother him a bit. His manner was totally confident. I believe he expected me to hit the tin even sooner in the subsequent games. But it was also clear that I had been beaten on just a few points. I had lost them: he had not won them. So I adopted a new policy at the start of the second game. My plan was to play each point as long as possible, without once going fine enough to risk the tin. If he returned the ball ninety-nine times I was determined to place it one hundred times, with *zero* errors. There followed six of what players often term "eternity points." The rallies lasted minutes each, and the ball was struck innumerable times. But he was doing almost all the running, and I was having all the fun of dishing it out. The score was 3-all after a very long time, and he began to perceive that I was going to keep this up—I was *not* about to make impatient errors. Those six points determined the match, which I won three games to one. The time came when he failed to get balls he had scooped up in the first game. It is hard to continue making an effort when it gets you nowhere. He began to take risks, because he had to do something. After awhile he was making more errors than I. The match gradually swung my way due to the change I made from thinking short to thinking long.

A second anecdote is less favorable to me but equally pertinent to my long point thesis. When Hashim Khan first came to America I had the pleasure of playing him a friendly practice match. I was "over the hill" but still capable of sporadically playing quite well. Hashim politely allowed me to win one game and then won 3-1. There was no question of my winning. When I played a poor point, I lost it quickly. When I played a really good point and performed above myself, the point merely lasted longer. I had the feeling that I was sounding a well that had no bottom. Never once did I feel or think, "If I could play that well *all* the time I could win." I merely had a feeling that if I were twice as good the match would last twice as long, but that it wouldn't bother Hashim at all—he'd enjoy it even more. This is true greatness, and it is based on really good thinking. You do not aim closer or depart in any other way from your fundamentals just because the ball comes back a few times or many times. You stick to your principles through thick and thin—and one test is when the point goes on and on. Hashim Khan is a great athlete in great condition with great speed and great shots. But he is more than that. He is immovably sound in his thinking under any amount or length of pressure; and this has given him the edge over many other greats. At his peak he was as close to an iron curtain as a human being can be, and his greatest essential quality was mental rather than physical. The man has character.

You, Too, Can Be Tough

Perhaps many readers are thinking this has little to do with them. They are not supermen or Khans. This misses the point, which is that at *every* level of excellence good thinking pays off. If you are an average player you are not playing Hashim, you are playing other average players. Being tough and sound in your thinking doesn't mean you can succeed when outclassed, but it does mean you will do your best in your own league. You will either win or get beaten. You will not "blow the match." The basic idea is pertinent to players at all levels of talent and skill.

Summary

1. Technique is how to execute a play.

2. Strategy is the overall plan.

3. Tactics are the means whereby the plan is implemented.

4. From backcourt play crosscourt a lot.

5. Play straight when in front.

6. Volley whenever possible to stay in front and press your opponent.

7. Follow up finesse shots with the volley.

8. Use finesse shots on setups that block your opponent into the back of the court.

9. Think up and back, not side to side.

10. Don't try for an ace. Instead, follow up each shot with another and let the point come by itself.

11. Think two shots, not one.

12. Press your opponent. Avoid pressing yourself.

13. Unprovoked errors are the worst mistakes and are very damaging to morale.

14. Think long and play long points.

15. Anyone can be "tough" at his own level of excellence.

10

The Psychology of Match Play

Psychology is a vast subject that cannot be approached in its entirety except by professionals in the field. In this chapter, my purpose is to explore the mental attitude of players under the stress of competition, emphasizing the most common reactions and how they influence performance. A much more thorough probe of what goes on in the mind under competitive pressure can be found in Tim Gallwey's excellent book, *Inner Tennis.*[1] Competitively, squash is exactly like tennis. It is played one against one, with a racquet and a ball, and with the same demands for quarterbacking, anticipation, endurance, and mental fortitude. For four years Gallwey played for me at Harvard and was a consistent winner. It is my understanding that he studied psychology. The man knows whereof he speaks.

Thinking Pays—Emotion Loses

If things go badly at first, it is important to keep cool and to try to assess the situation. Are you playing too many balls to his strength rather than his weakness? Are you playing a style he likes, such as slugging with a slugger? Are there any patterns of play which repeat themselves, usually to your disadvantage? Are you pressing, trying too hard, overplaying the ball so it always comes off the back wall? Is your service or return of ser-

[1] Timothy W. Gallwey, *Inner Tennis: Playing the Game* (New York: Random House, 1976).

131

vice getting you in trouble? In sum, what is going on? If what is occurring can be identified, it is quite possible that a constructive alteration in your play can effect a favorable change in the percentage of the results.

Many players become very angry while losing and rage at themselves. Emoting does not get a player anywhere. If the result of his efforts is unfavorable, what good does it do to cry about it? (Raging is a form of crying.) Wouldn't it be better to try to identify causes and effects and to take action to bring about a change? The worst aspect of emoting is that it eliminates thinking. Any player who allows his emotions to control him has, as a rule, lost the power to think. He may be a very intelligent person, but of what use is an intelligence that is suffocated and beclouded by uncontrolled emotion? A good player realizes that he can't afford to get mad.

Many matches have been decided by some small event which has triggered an emotional breakdown by one of the contestants. He "cracked," as they say, and a tight, unpredictable battle swung inevitably towards the fellow who kept his cool. On one occasion, in the finals of a championship, a terrific hitter was playing a superb shot artist. Each played his game very well. The games were one-all, the result clearly in doubt. The hard hitter played a bullet service down the center, directly at the receiver. The receiver ducked, intending to play it off the back wall, but he was a fraction of a second too slow. The ball hit the top of his head, soared high in the air, and fell into the middle of the court. The entire audience giggled and chortled, and the receiver's face became black as thunder. He fumed. He had been beaned and made to look silly, and it was too much for him. His play fell off, his choice of shots became less astute, and his assurance was shaken. He lost 3-1 as the hard hitter pressed his advantage with all the fury at his command. It was a small thing, it cost him only one point, yet because he let it "get to him" his chances were ruined. His play began to be emotional rather than cleverly calculating as it had been up to that point. As emotion intruded, his thinking deteriorated. The result was no longer in doubt.

Someone may argue that it was a tough break, that if it had happened to the other fellow he too might have cracked. Not so. On numerous occasions in the first two games, when the match was even, the shot maker had totally deceived his opponent, leading him up the garden path so he ran exactly the wrong way and was made to look foolish indeed. But the hitter merely smiled a little, said, "Too good," and attacked him on the next point with renewed ferocity. He had many excuses to become shaken, to fume angrily about being foxed, to lose his mental balance. The difference was that he didn't. He lost many points but he never lost his cool, so he won the match.

Respect Your Opponent

In a match two players are constantly trying to fool each other, to catch each other unawares, to force poor returns or induce errors. If the two are evenly matched, it's to be expected that each will get the better of the other about half the time. If a player has the proper respect for his opponent he will not like it on those occasions when his opponent does him in, but it will not shake his confidence in himself or upset him. He will go into the court fully aware that he is going to get the short end of the stick, on not just a few, but many, occasions. Any player who thinks he can take the court against a first class opponent and look smoothly in command throughout the contest is guilty of supreme arrogance. Such pride is a balloon that is always pricked under pressure. A real winner is a person who has enough humility to know that he has to take a lot of dirt in a tough match as well as dish it out. This is what good players mean when they say, "You have to learn to take it." Respect for an opponent is one of the basic essentials in what is generally referred to as "toughness."

Letting Up

Perhaps the most common fault in match play is the phenomenon known as "letting up." It is frequently at the bottom of that bitter feeling, "I should have won. I had him." All sorts of excuses and rationalizations are indulged in by losers to explain away a defeat which might have been a victory. An exploration of what can and frequently does occur in players' minds may be of profit to anyone who suffers from this prevalent malady.

Tension

One frequent cause of a letdown is a purely physical result—temporary fatigue—brought on by tension. Situations are tense at almost any time in a tough match. If this mental tightness is allowed to control a player's muscles it can definitely interfere with his breathing. His breath is shallow, he runs out of oxygen, and he cannot "stay with it." Henri Salaun, a great champion, tells a story of himself that clearly illustrates this. He was in the finals of the Boston Open and was playing against a great player (Ed Reid, many times pro champion). Salaun recalls that he was a comer then. This was his great chance and he was all keyed up. He played like a demon at the start and was leading about 8-3. But then suddenly he was so exhausted he couldn't run hard any more. He became literally helpless, and he lost 3–0. That game taught him that a player *must* relax his muscles and allow himself to breathe deeply no matter what the situation. This tension is particularly characteristic of less experienced players. It is not a matter of being out of condition: Salaun was in excellent condition. It is the tendency to hold your breath in the excitement of a point, and it is comparable to being partially strangled. Usually experience overcomes this. Until it is overcome, however, no player can "go hard," except sporadically, since after all he does have to stop to breathe now and again!

Fear

A green player tends to lack faith in himself. He has practiced, he is good, but his excellence has yet to pass that test we call "playing under pressure." He is very afraid he will do something wrong. He is more concerned with the negative concept of avoiding a mistake than he is with the positive idea of doing something well. This tends to tighten him up, to inhibit him, to hold him back. As has been pointed out, it can even reduce his breathing and bring about exhaustion. This indicates he is being dominated by fear—the fear of losing, the fear of hitting the tin, the fear of making a short shot at the wrong time. The net result is that he hardly does anything at all, either good or bad. The word for this is that he "clutches." Also, the expression, "I froze," is a very accurate description of what happens.

Trust Yourself

A player must trust himself. He has practiced and his body can do many things. He must allow his body to function, not only to breathe but to play the ball with fluency of limb and racquet. One's physique is prevented from functioning, and likewise one's mind is atrophied if fear is allowed to predominate. No one has explored this area of psychology in racquet games better than Tim Gallwey in *Inner Tennis*. He very clearly points out that a player will be unable to do well unless he "let's it happen," and he describes the paralyzing effect of fear, which takes the form of worry and doubt and jerky hesitancy.

Don't Worry—Play

There is no truer saying than the very common one, "God only knows who will win this one." Putting the emphasis on *only* can lead to important reasoning; i.e., that nobody else does know or can know. Certainly neither of the players can know. If, by some magic, a player could know with absolute certainty that he was about to win or lose, what would be the point of playing the match? The most essential ingredient in any good match is doubt. Without a solid element of doubt, it is a mismatch—a very dull affair in which few people would take any interest.

It is thus a waste of time to worry about who is going to win. You won't know and can't know until it happens. What can you do? You can determine to take the court and do your best. If that won't win, what else can you do except lose faster? Worrying is not only totally futile—it diverts you, hurts you, and literally "freezes" you.

Be True to Yourself

In forty-three years of coaching at Harvard I have never told a boy, except in jest, "You've *got* to win." There is no surer way of putting intolerable pressure on a player. It is telling him, "You must be God, and *know* you are going to win." It is a psychological burden that will crush even the best. I prefer always to tell them, "You must be true to yourself, and that means do your best. If you do that, I'll congratulate you at the finish, whether you win or lose. Don't worry about winning. Keep your head down, run like mad, play as you think best all the way, and keep thinking." This encourages him to put forth his best effort, and what more can a coach ask of any player?

On one occasion, the intercollegiate season culminated in a match between Harvard and one other very strong team. Both teams were undefeated and had proved they were formidable. The day of the match a spectator asked one of my players, "Are you going to beat them?" He replied, "I don't know about that, but they're in for an awful lot of trouble." I remember thinking, "I hope all nine of them feel the same way." They did, and Harvard won 7–2. The boy who made that perfect answer to the question, "Will you win?" played a veritable hurricane of a match and won 15–4, 15–6, and 15–5, against a highly regarded opponent.

Having a good attitude does not ensure victory. Harvard was once the underdog against a fine Princeton tennis team. We thought we might beat them in doubles if we weren't wiped out in the singles. The attitude was to hit them as hard as we could in the singles, then, if we still were in the match, hit them harder in the doubles. We played excellent singles, but Princeton got us down 4–2. Then we won the third doubles, then the second doubles. The score was 4-all. Anything could happen. We took the first set in the first doubles, reached a tie breaker in the second, lost it, and lost in three sets. A reporter asked me what I thought of the match. I replied that I liked everything about it except the score. This was the truth: my team could not have played better. I was then and still am quite proud of that team, even though the loss, being so very close, was a heartbreaker. However, underneath my disappointment at the loss was a solid feeling that in relationship to its talent and potential the team had played a great match. How can a coach be displeased with a team that plays like that, just because another team has been even better?

A player who plays his best is true to himself. He realizes his full potential and has cause for pride even if he loses. I'm not trying to be hypocritical: no one likes to lose, everyone prefers to win. But there are differences in losing. If a player tightens up, is afraid to hit the ball, and plays a mediocre match, he hates to think of it afterwards. He hates himself, too. Why? It's because he was not true to himself, he did not trust himself, he did not "let go" and do his best. This is a much worse feeling than the disappointment felt in losing the match. Listen to Tim Gallwey and "let it happen," win or lose.

Fight

Even among those who have overcome tension, worry, doubt, and other forms of fear there is a tendency to fight for awhile and then let up. Anyone worth his salt will fight when he is behind, because defeat looms before him. He *must* fight. Most players also tend to be good fighters when they are about even, because of the imminent danger of getting behind. It is when a player is leading—in points in a game or in games in a match—that the fatal letup occurs. Momentum is lost to the opponent, and the pendulum of percentages swings from above fifty to below it, often beyond recall. "I let him get away!" laments the loser. Why does this letup occur, even on the part of top-ranking players in big matches? Because there is no immediate threat of defeat, there is nothing forcing the player to keep on fighting. Without this spur his mental discipline relaxes. He may serve a little carelessly, or try a too risky shot here and there. He is still a good player, but he has lost that all-important quality known as toughness. He is like a generous fellow with a fat wallet: a point here or there is no longer of serious importance. His concentration wanders. "After I win this I'll be playing so-and-so, and I think I'll play this way or that against him. . ." "All I need is five more points." Such day dreaming, just when the other fellow is fighting for his life, is a sure way to allow the line to go slack letting the fish off the hook.

To be successful in matches you must learn to fight at least as hard when you're ahead as when you're behind or even. Since the compulsion to play your best no longer comes automatically from outside, it must come from within. You must discipline yourself so that a favorable score does not cause all these subtle changes in attitude. It is very easy to write this. Ask any seasoned player if it is easy to practice.

The Reverse Letup

Some players become conscious of this tendency to let a match escape after victory is in sight; so they scold themselves the next time, saying, "Now that you're ahead, don't let up. Don't make any mistakes. Don't blow it." This totally negative attitude results in such conservative play that it removes a considerable amount of the pressure that was defeating and frustrating an opponent. Much relieved, he seizes his chance to make a come-back. This type of letup in reverse can be just as bad as the overconfident kind. In each case pressure is relaxed, and the opponent rebounds.

Don't Play by the Score

What happens in most letups is that a player allows his attitude to be affected by the score. The fact is that the best way to play any point has no relationship whatever to the score. If a player should play one way at 10-12 and another way at 12-10, then this is indeed a complex game. There are no crucial points. If a player is behind 2-0 set 3, what is more crucial about the third point than the first two which put him in such peril? The scoring system clearly shows that each point is equally valuable. It counts one, no more and no less. Saying "this is a crucial point" is total rot. No point is more important than any of those that preceded and created the situation. The point *appears* to be more important because it is a culmination. If two players reach 4-all set 5 in the fifth game, one cannot help but feel that the ninth point is more important. It is not. Change *any one* of the preceding eight points and there would have been a winner 5-3.

Any variation in your evaluation of any point must be downwards. If one player considers every point worth his maximum effort, and plays that way, against an equal opponent who does his best only on "crucial points," who will be the better fighter?

The Solution: Win _this_ Point

At any instant throughout a match a player has one task and one task only—to win the particular point he is now playing. A player who can focus his concentration on this job to the exclusion of every other consideration, and maintain this focus throughout the match, is really playing his best. He must _forget_ the score, both in points and games, and behave as though the future of the universe were dependent on this particular point. Actually, this makes a lot of sense. It is the _only_ way a player can, at that moment, influence the outcome. Addressing his mind to other things is diversionary, wasteful, and impairs play.

Concentration

There is a well-known phrase, "I lost my concentration." This is absolutely not true. No one ever loses his concentration until he is asleep or dead. We have learned that even in sleep the mind continues to be very busy. Therefore, it may be said that no player loses his concentration unless he is knocked cold by a blow from the racquet or passes out from fatigue or illness. The phrase, "I lost my concentration," implies that concentration ceased to occur or by some magic disappeared. It never does. What really happens?

The mind will only focus on one thought at a time. It is like a flashlight with a narrow beam. It will illuminate only one object at a time in a darkened area. If it is moved to another object that object is at once lit up, and the first is as quickly lost again in the dark. Your thoughts in a match are subject to the same limitations: you can only focus your mind's light on one objective or consideration at a time. The moment you think of something else you're no longer concentrating on the point being played.

To "concentrate," after all, as applied to an activity such as squash, simply means to "pay attention to what you are doing." As soon as you allow your mind, i.e., your attention or concentration, to wander to anything other than the particular point you are playing, the quality of your play deteriorates. You have not stopped concentrating: you've shifted your concentration to something other than this point, and since all other subjects are irrelevant, you suffer a loss in results. You don't "lose" your concentration: you allow it to wander about. You lose _control_ of it.

This makes it simple: think only of the point and concentration will be perfect. This is true but it is not easy. It requires tremendous mental discipline. The prospect of a shining victory near at hand is a very tempting subject on which to focus the mind. The next game, after this one is finished off, is indeed very important. It's not easy to shut it out of the mind. The temptation is strong to polish your opponent off quickly and brilliantly by taking a few extra chances. The lure of the gallery has its effect: we all like to bask in the admiration of the spectators. There is a little "ham" in everyone. These and many other intrusions continually threaten to divert your concentration from *the point you are playing*. As soon as it is diverted, you begin to lose points. The job is simple, but it is far from easy. Probably the best approach is to go into the court planning to play each and every point as though it were match point for the other fellow. If you can stick to that right to the end you will win unless you are beaten—you will never let a match slip away. Such control of the mind must be developed. No one is born with it.

When one plays with total intensity this unswerving concentration is not only possible, it is unavoidable. When Germain Glidden was peaking to win his first Nationals in 1936, we played each other several times a week in a rivalry I have always cherished. We usually began in a friendly way, but it always quickly developed into a serious match. So totally did we focus on each point that we continually forgot the score. At the end of a prolonged exchange neither of us could remember it. We developed the habit of asking a spectator to keep track. Each separate point was a match in itself, requiring every atom of our attention and effort. At the end of each of these practice matches, I always felt fatigued mentally as well as physically. To play a truly concentrated match is as much a constant test of the mind as it is of the body and your skill. Your mind must therefore be trained and conditioned as much as your body.

Never Stop Thinking

Many matches are lost or reversed in trend because one player, having played with mental keenness to build a commanding lead, begins to assume that things are well in hand, stops thinking, and also stops winning the majority of the points. Often the change in the number of points won and lost is amazing. I once witnessed a tough class A match in which one player (a state champion) led 2-0, 12-3. He lost. Any experienced player could remember a dozen similar cases. Some of them like the one noted above seem outside the bounds of any reasonable probability. How can such things happen?

Subtle Scoring

There is a subtle thing about scoring in squash racquets. The play may be extremely close and hard fought, but the final result—one point—goes entirely to the winner. The loser gets nothing. If one player is gaining the upper hand by an infinitesimal margin in the actual play, he may win almost all the points. But a very small deterioration in his play can easily mean his opponent will win almost all the points. Thus a slight letup in concentration, toughness, keen thinking, and unrelenting pressure can have a drastic and catastrophic effect. Suddenly, the opponent may win an avalanche of points and the entire match may be reversed. It is a classic case of leverage, and, as Archimedes remarked, it can move the world.

A seasoned player has always experienced at least once this sudden and demoralizing reversal. "I was winning everything—now I'm winning nothing. What happened?" It can be expressed numerically by saying that a player playing to 100% of his best may be good enough to win 15–5, while the same player playing to 95% of his best may lose 5–15 to the same opponent. The play in squash is frequently just as close as those figures. That is why it is such a marvellous game to play and watch. The scales are often so finely balanced that a tiny shift can have vast results. If either player stops thinking and anticipating and planning even a little bit he may well be lost. The spectators feel this. The atmosphere is electric. If both players strain with all they've got to the very last it is a great match. Players and spectators alike are drained at the finish.

Another Subtlety—The Context of the Match and Momentum

One may well ask (and many have), "Why is it so very hard to get going again and regain the initiative once it is lost by a letup?" It is a fact that once a player has slacked off he seldom gets rolling again and loses in spite of herculean efforts to regain the stride that originally put him in command. This is particularly true if his opponent does *not*, in his turn, let up. One would think that concentration could be regained rather quickly once a player realizes that he has permitted his attention to wander a bit. It is not so.

Concentration on the point does not mean merely to watch the ball and to play it as well as one can. It means to be keenly aware of what has happened in previous points, aware of an opponent's favorite options, his favorite shots, his vulnerabilities as revealed in previous play, and his particular strengths as similarly revealed. It means being in tune with the total flow of what is occurring and what has led up to it. It is having a "feel" for the context of the match. Without it, a player's anticipation is more often faulty, his deception fails to deceive, and his plans don't come to fruition. Therefore, although he again plays the ball just as forcefully and fights just as grimly, he usually has great difficulty in wresting control of the play from his opponent. This is often referred to by the rather vague word "momentum." His opponent now has this momentum with all its subtle implications and to get it away from him is like trying to reverse the direction of a freight train. It is often irresistible if sustained. Players are often heard to say, "He got going and I never could get back into the match." They do not say, "I couldn't play the ball well any more, or execute my shots." It is that feeling of initiative which is a priceless asset and, once lost, is perhaps permanently gone. With it goes the match.

One Thought Ahead

The winning player frequently does not play the ball technically any better than his opponent. But he is one thought ahead of his opponent and constantly maintains the initiative. The moment he loses this ascendency in the thinking contest he has lost his apparent advantage and the match sways toward his opponent. This is all in a way a repeat of the advice already given: "Fight when you are ahead." It means a player must fight when he is ahead with his mind as much as with his racquet and feet. A mental letdown is as fatal as a physical slow down. In fact, in most cases a physical relaxation merely reflects what has happened in the mind.

False Psychology

Players who are erratic frequently attribute their shortcomings to psychological causes. In the majority of cases this is not the true cause. Much more commonly what is at the bottom of the trouble is bad technique or bad thinking. They are playing either against technical percentages or against tactical percentages. Errors are inevitable. They say, "I did not concentrate hard enough." "This game is all concentration and I don't do it consistently enough." Analysis usually shows that most of their errors occur repeatedly in the same context. It is always their forehand that hits the tin, seldom their backhand. Is their concentration weaker on their forehand? No. They roll it over, thus every so often it inevitably strikes the tin. Or, they think high floaters can be volleyed for aces into the front corners. They play right down at the tin and inevitably hit it occasionally. This has nothing to do with concentration. It is a matter of playing with or against the percentages.

Getting Psyched

The most common rationalization by losing players is to say, "I got psyched." This implies they lost for psychological reasons. It is almost never true. "Getting psyched" is simply a modern way to say, "I became discouraged." If your play is unsound technically or tactically, you lose a majority of the points played. After this goes on for awhile it is natural to become discouraged. Who doesn't when defeat looms and appears ever more unavoidable? The point is that getting psyched is almost always a result, not a cause. Some players who continually lose actually refer to themselves as "psychos." If they would analyze their technique and tactics they might well effect a great improvement. Dwelling on the psychological effects of poor play gets nobody anywhere. They should recognize that to say, "I lost because I got psyched," is bunk—a rationalization that fails entirely to get at the real reasons why their play was unsuccessful.

"Psychology" connotes something tricky, esoteric, interesting, and special. It's fun to talk about it. It makes people feel very knowing. But everyone should realize that beyond the pleasure it gives us to observe and note the attitudes and emotions of players it is really of no significance. We are discussing effects, not causes, and it is the word "cause" meaning 'to make something happen' that is important. "Effect" (the noun) simply describes a result. It has nothing to do with bringing it about or changing it for better or worse. Thus, most talk about psychology is amusing but profitless.

A single example will illustrate. A somewhat crude slugger was playing a touch artist. For a while the softer player hit with the slugger, who did very well, was very much "in the groove," and won the first game. Then the clever player changed his game to lobs and drop shots—high floaters that gave the power player nothing to hit, and the front wall shots that ran him up and back a lot. He became baffled and confused and lost 3-1. He emerged and said, "I was doing all right until I got psyched." The fact was that he did not know how to volley lobs at all well, nor did he know what to do with a drop shot when he reached it. His technique and tactics were both inadequate to deal with the situation. This is a very obvious case of identifying effect with cause. In most cases the cause is more subtle and less easily perceived. The underlying cause is always there though, and it is almost always technical or tactical, not psychological. All players may truthfully say when they lose, "I got psyched." But then they should follow it up with the question "Why?" If they don't, they may well spend the balance of their squash careers going through that same unpleasant experience over and over again. This is hardly a happy prospect. Using "psychology" as a crutch is the poorest and least rewarding kind of self-criticism.

Human Nature

The real value in considering the psychological aspects of the game lies in achieving an understanding of the strengths and weaknesses that tend to be common qualities in all people, or, one might say, basic to human nature. Each of us is a microcosm of the whole human race. Humanity has on many occasions demonstrated almost unbelievable fortitude and determination during great adversity. The defiance of England against the mighty Hitler blitz, the defense of Leningrad, the U.S. Marines on Guadalcanal when the Japanese had superior numbers and complete command of the air and the sea—these are some recent occasions when the strengths of humanity have proven to be immeasurable. The other side of the coin is, unfortunately, no less impressive. The blindness of England to the impending disaster foreseen by Churchill, repeatedly derided and defeated during the thirties, was equalled only by the stupidity of Russia in making pacts with Hitler and the ostrich-like insistance by the United States that it was none of our affair. These examples from history demonstrate an admittedly oversimplified pattern of human nature, but it is nonetheless valid for our purposes. We are often great when in trouble but with equal frequency we seem to be short-sighted and blind to danger when things are going well.

Individuals tend to play matches in much the same manner that society has governed itself through history. Our best qualities come to the fore when disaster is imminent and glaringly obvious, but success tends to lull us into a feeling of security and our guard goes down. We build a lead, then squander it—even as vast numbers of people become big spenders and blow their wads in periods of economic prosperity. And so we swing and sway, from boom to depression, in cycles that seem to be inevitably based on the nature of man.

A competitor, who sees this clearly and recognizes that he has in him both the strength and the weakness of human nature, can discipline himself to encourage the positive qualities and suppress the tendency to relapse into a negative phase when success is coming his way.

See the Real Goal—Stay Hungry

The objective is to win the match. If a player wins the first game, he has not achieved his aim. If he wins the second game, he is not yet home. If he leads 14–10 in the third he has still done nothing unless he wins one more point. To sustain an effort all the way before allowing yourself any luxuries such as self-congratulation, elation, or overconfidence—this is the requirement for successful match play. If a player sees clearly that the achievement of partial goals means nothing if not crowned by the final victory, he is much less likely to let down and permit a resurgence by his opponent. If he allows his mind to dwell on how well he has done up to now, instead of concentrating on continuing to win, he is wide open to the in-inevitable comeback that will be staged by any fighting opponent. If, instead, he appreciates that his opponent, being also human, will now play his absolute best since he is spurred by the pressure of adversity, he will tend to be more alert to meet any last-ditch stand.

The goal is the match. If you are ahead, this is your chance to achieve the goal. Fight your hardest to make the most of the opportunity. Don't be "human" and treat prosperity carelessly. If you do, you will receive the reward that has, so far, been the lot of the vast majority of human beings—a lot of grief. The only way to be a winner is to discipline yourself to stay hungry not only until you get well ahead, but until you finish the job you entered the court to do.

Working Up to It

One of the best concentrators the game has known was Charlie Brinton. He had the ability to focus himself on each point in a sustained effort which, coupled with the excellence of his play, was at times well-nigh unstoppable. One of his chief qualities was timing. Early in the season he was often defeated or carried to five games by players who were good but not really in his class when at his best. But each year, as the Nationals came closer, his play and his consistency peaked so that he swept the field in the big one. This was quite conscious on Charlie's part. He did not wish to peak in December or January. He appreciated that he could not get up there and hold himself there over a long period. He understood that to do so would be almost impossible, and it is a tribute both to his perception and modesty that he shunned such an unattainable goal. He looked upon the season as a ramp that led to the top of the mountain—the National Championship. In that event his sharpness of execution and keenness of concentration were beautiful to watch. That this culmination of his abilities always occurred at exactly the right time shows that Brinton really understood himself, not only as to what he could do but also as to what he couldn't do. There is always a component of humility in complete understanding, or perhaps one should call it an absense of false pride. A champion is usually a very level thinker, about himself as well as about the game.

Practice Mental Discipline

A champion like Brinton plays a mature game. His problem is to peak his abilities when he wants them peaked. Most players are striving to improve attitudes that at present are less than ideal. This can be practiced by consciously varying the match conditions. Players too often think—one hears it constantly—that the way to improve is to play someone better than themselves. This is only partially true. A player must learn to play down as well as up. Few players give up when behind. Most players are prone to ease up when ahead. A very good training is to play a superior player and fight up, then the next time play someone almost but not quite as good as yourself—and try to beat him 15-0. This is specific training in the habit of fighting when you don't have to—when you are ahead. It is extremely difficult, psychologically, to strive with might and main when the score is 1-0, 12-5, in your favor. But this is the habit that must be cultivated if one wishes to be a winner. It is often called "the killer instinct," but it is very seldom an instinct because it goes against human nature. It usually must be learned, often through bitter experience and much striving to achieve the discipline involved. If you are at all ambitious about your game it is an essential.

Summary

1. Players tend to relax when doing well, and to fight only when they are behind. They must learn to keep fighting and thinking when they are ahead.

2. Emotion suffocates thought and hurts play.

3. Tension can cause fatigue.

4. Fear can cause tension and a negative attitude.

5. Worrying about winning is futile. A player must trust himself and "let go" so he can play his best.

6. Playing by the score is invalid.

7. Concentration is never "lost"—it wanders.

8. Scoring is subtle: it can fool you.

9. The mind can focus on only one thing at a time. This one thing should be the point presently being played. All else is irrelevant and detrimental.

10. The context of the match, once lost, is hard to regain. It controls momentum. That is why a letup often causes an irreversible change.

11. Psychology should not be used as a crutch to explain away tactical and technical deficiencies.

12. "Getting psyched" is an effect, not a cause.

13. Mental discipline can be practiced profitably by varying the calibre of one's opposition.

11

Advanced Tactics

Mature players are sure of their shots. They know the basic tactics so well they have become almost instinctive, are quite percentage conscious, and are usually in good condition. When two such players meet, you will frequently be privileged to witness a fascinating battle of wills and minds. Each player has his preferred manner of playing. He likes to hit, or he likes shots, or he likes a mixed game. He endeavors first of all to impose his game on the other fellow. If this is not successful, he will use other ploys in an attempt to arrest and change an unfavorable flow of events. The very best matches are those in which the flow is quite even and each player attempts to set up a plot whereby he can gain a slight edge at the finish.

Holding Back a Little

A seasoned tournament player usually doesn't wear his heart on his sleeve. He will often try very hard to stay with his opponent, fighting for each point, but holding back a little of his best so that, when the score near the end of a game has reached ten or eleven points, he can mount a spurt by playing harder, sharper, and a little lower. It is often like a poker game. The hand starts rather quietly, with each player holding his cards close to his vest and advancing his chips with some caution. Then there is a buildup to the climax where one player says, "I raise," and another quickly looks him in the eye and says, "I call" or "I raise you." In squash this can take quite

147

a few forms. A player may suddenly switch from a soft to a very hard service, or he may, after playing consistently deep, burst out with a rash of finesse shots from all over the court. Or he may step up the pace, suddenly playing far more ferociously than before. A close game often slopes upward to a furious climax with both players pulling out all the stops near the end.

Getting the Jump

Many matches have been determined at the start. One player will play all out starting with the very first point, hoping to rush into a commanding lead right from the gun. This tactic can have two results. The attacker may rush his opponent off the court and win decisively. He also may find himself in an even match with no reserves—like a general having committed all his troops to the initial encounter. Thus his plan may backfire. He has started at his peak and has nowhere to go except down. Seasoned players are well aware of this danger, so if they adopt this manner of playing a match they usually have special reasons that relate to their opponent's style. If he is in their opinion slightly favored, their judgment may be that their only hope is to go at once for the throat. If the opponent is a shot artist, with a dead eye for placements when given time to set up, a policy of rushing the opponent from the start and keeping it up may be a very sound way to play the particular match. The clever player is suppressed and inhibited and never builds momentum.

The Wave Player

Some players seem to go in great surges. They may win the first game but lose the second. Then they will mount another irresistible drive that wins the third. This approach to match play is not recommended. It is all right if a player is definitely superior to his opponent. But if he is not, and one of his waves breaks against the opposition, he is in real trouble. It is better to try for all five games, so that even if two are disastrous one may still win three. Giving away games is a luxury few can afford.

Attack with Every Shot

The best of players is a master at seizing the initiative. He seldom merely gets the ball back. Even when running full out he often manages to place the ball in the least convenient spot for his opponent, so he in turn must hustle as hard. This policy is not merely aggression. It is also a condition of survival. A good player can beat you if you give him the chance. If you merely get the ball back he will do exactly that, no matter how fast you are in the court or how superbly conditioned you may be. A good example of this was Anil Nayar, who, after being twice champion of India, came to Harvard and was suddenly placed in championship American tournaments. The English game is quite different from ours. Nayar was beautifully conditioned and so fleet it had to be witnessed to be believed. He seemed to get everything, no matter how well placed. But he did not know what to do with it when he got there. Our game was strange to him. The three times he met that superb shot artist, American champion Sam Howe, Nayar could not win even a game. Three times he lost 3–0. His spectacular retrieving merely meant that it took Howe longer to beat him. Only after Nayar learned the right answers and attacked in his turn was he able to capitalize on his superathleticism and win the championship. What are these answers, which, to quote Churchill, may be called "the apparatus of counterattack"?

Drop the Drop

When the ball is dropped up front (with any finesse shot, not just a drop shot) a player hopes to pass the retriever on the next shot by playing hard and deep. The worst answer to a front wall shot is to rush up and whack it crosscourt. A crosscourt, in going across the court, travels through the open area of the court. A good attacker will instantly intercept this, often for a winner. A player who returns a drop crosscourt is playing into the hands of the enemy. The attacker has said, "I shall drop the ball and run you up, and when you hit the ball back to me I shall pass you and run you back." By hitting out into the open you have accommodated him nicely and he carries out his plan. The best answer is to drop it back on him, as though you have said, "Now the tables are turned. I am going to pass *you* on the next shot." The feathery drop is the best answer to short shots.

Keep the Ball on the Wall

If he then runs up he should not now drop again, because you are already up there. He should hit, but again he should not hit out into the open. He should play the ball deep down the wall, so it is on the wall all the time and never in the open subject to easy interception. If he is desperate he should lob, but again along the wall.

Few Players Do It

The foregoing reasoning is fairly simple, yet few players actually do it. Why? It is difficult. When running to a ball up front a player tends to think only of getting it. He swings at it in the easiest and most natural manner without thought. He does not *choose* to hit it crosscourt, but his natural swing always goes crosscourt, so without thinking one way or the other he plays into the trap and is at once passed down the other side. A top player knows of the high probability of a crosscourt return. He watches for it, anticipates it, jumps on it every time. So just as a player thinks with pleasure, "I got it!" he is left sprawled near the front wall by the instant follow-up. The ability to drop again or keep the ball on the wall when running up front is one of the tests of class. It behooves every ambitious player to become expert at it or astute tacticians will make a monkey of him at every opportunity. You must learn to lay the wrist far back so that, even when playing a ball at full reach in front of you, you can still make it drop or hit straight, not crosscourt. The chapter on "Drills" is recommended to any who are less than adept at this fast and difficult maneuver.

Advanced players, whenever pressed to the point where they cannot make a telling return, always resort to the lob. They never consciously provide a short ball that sets up. Even when they are digging a ball out of the back corner (when it only comes a bit off the back wall or is going dead as it arrives), they will snap around it with the wrist and often achieve a high floater, close to the wall from where it cannot be put away. A player who is clever but not very powerful must be adept at this trick on both sides, since a hard hitter will have him in this predicament on many occasions. With this skill he can "stay with it" until a less accurate drive by the hitter enables him to do something more constructive. Without it he is overwhelmed in short order.

Finesse from the Backcourt

A touch artist may often be unable to get a powerful opponent out of the center by trading drives and forcing him back. The hitter dominates such exchanges and has all the better of it. But it is possible to move an opponent out of the center by making him go forward as well as by making him go back. The greatest player of this type was the original Harvard coach, Harry Cowles. He was very quick, so quick that he could position himself to get good touch even when his opponent was slugging the ball. He had so mastered sidewall drops, three-wall nicks, reverse corners, and feathery drops that he could make them, not just well but superbly, from the back of the court as well as from out front. His quickness and his great anticipation then enabled him to follow up these front wall shots with sharp accurate passing shots. He would constantly break up a long exchange by dropping the ball from behind his opponent, precipitating a crisis that usually ended in his favor. It began with moving his opponent up out of the center rather than first getting him back. Needless to say, such tactics require extreme finesse or they merely set the ball up out front for the other fellow. Most players must stick to the more patient, orthodox tactic of rallying until the other fellow is behind you when you play short.

All top players, however, use the tactic occasionally. The three-wall nick is the usual ploy, dropping the ball suddenly up front as a surprise from behind an opponent. This is done sparingly, seldom enough so that it is indeed a surprise rather than unsound policy. Good players are cautious about giving the other fellow a front wall ball when he is already halfway up there. It can easily backfire.

Brainwashing: The Most Advanced Tactic

An astute player will sometimes go to great pains to set up a play that will catch an opponent just that hair out of position which can make the difference, or a play that will achieve the advantage of being one thought ahead; thus impairing the opponent's anticipation, quick start, and initiative. He may want to hit crosscourt to gain the center, but you are alertly watching for this, and cut them off. What to do? It is possible sometimes to set up the crosscourt by playing five or six consecutive straight shots, then by suddenly playing very hard crosscourt. The opponent is keenly observing your tactics, and hopefully concludes that you decided to play straight. He begins to place himself a trifle nearer that straight shot, and the opening is created. The crosscourt gets around him, he is dislodged from the center and must dig it out of the corner. This brainwashing process, it will be noted, was all merely to gain the dominant position, not to win the point.

Use Your Fanny

This power of suggestion is frequently carried to extremes. Tiny movements of the body to suggest the possibility of some shot other than the one intended may lead even a keen opponent astray. The author actually won a match with his fanny. Playing a former pro champion in the Boston Open, I had been winning with shots. He had then bottled me up in the backhand corner, playing with relentless depth. But I had answered with three-wall nicks. The score was in my favor 2–1, 13–11. How could I get two more points? I decided to hit six shots down the wall with him, then at the first good opportunity fake (but not make) a three-wall nick. We hit the six in an even exchange of good depth, and his ball came off the back wall at about the eighth exchange. I prepared in the usual manner, but just before I played I twisted my fanny around about two or three inches extra as though I had a secret plan to hit the sidewall. He took off forward for the suspected three-waller and my straight drive, the ninth in a row, a foot over the tin, was a clean ace. I needed one more. We exchanged again, again after five or six, I made my tiny fanny move, and hit a hard wide crosscourt. It was an ordinary depth shot but it was an ace for the match. Brainwashing can really pay off even against the best in top play.

They All Do It

Anecdotes like the foregoing must be personal. How can a writer read the mind and record every little thought of any player except himself? But they all do it. Charlie Brinton used to wait, and hit, wait, and hit, then wait—and flick a corner shot. It you watched for that corner a bit you were likely to be passed. If you didn't, that was the time the rascal made it. Germain Glidden used to play a bang-bang-bang volley game, and just when you were in tune with it and congratulating yourself that you were staying handily with his best there came a total change of choice that was often totally upsetting. He could have done it any time, but he was waiting until you were "ready," i.e., brainwashed. Niederhoffer is famous for his great variety of shots. His opponents know this. They enter the court determined to "watch for those shots." But Niederhoffer is always in tune with the context of the match. He senses it, and though he gets ready each time as though he might make a shot, he plays deep instead. I have seen him play the whole first game with no shots at all, as though he were a dull player whose imagination was limited to playing straight and crosscourt for depth. In reality, he is very patient when it is called for, withholding his shots until his opponent becomes so preoccupied with depth that the shots will take effect. All of a sudden, out come the shots, and they win.

The Double Threat

Basically, every player who gets far in the game does so because he always carries a double threat. Diehl Mateer achieved great skill at an early age. He totally dominated the Intercollegiates and it was generally forecast that he would hit the top at once. Not so. He was very powerful, with the strongest basic drives in the game, but it took him a year or so to learn that any one asset is by itself insufficient. He found that only when he mixed in a shot here and there, thus inserting an element of doubt into his offense, could he overcome the best of his rivals. The court is quite small. An alert defender will return *all* your shots if he must worry only about your depth. He will return all your shots if he must worry only about the front wall. The contrast of the two, the double threat, is the basis of advanced tactics. Mateer eventually came to know just when, after a series of streaking drives, to insert that final straw which broke his opponent's back—a little drop or corner shot.

Combinations

The best players relate two shots with each other. The two shots always consist of a finesse shot that goes short to one side and a drive that goes deep to the other side. The reverse corner and straight drop can each be combined with the crosscourt drive; the slice corner can combine with the straight drive; and the three-wall nick with the straight drive. The combinations can work either way: a series of crosscourt drives may set the stage for a reverse corner. Likewise, if a player has been using reverse corners on his best chances he may well profit by using the other end of the needle as a change—a hard crosscourt.

The Context Governs

Green players often think that change is good in itself, that a player should play a shot once, and then the appropriate combination shot on his next opportunity. This is not sophisticated tactics. Change for the sake of change accomplishes nothing beyond showing the gallery, *and* your opponent, all the different things you can do. If a shot works, play it again. If it still works, play it again. Keep playing it until an opponent anticipates and handles it well. When he does this, then and only then is the combination shot open, and the switch will perhaps catch him moving the wrong way. The context of the match—what has happened in similar situations up to now—is what should govern your thinking and dictate any changes.

The author used to have a pet combination on the forehand—the slice corner combined with the straight drive. If I had a good chance out in the open on my forehand I would play a rip corner. Often an opponent would be caught the first time. The second or third time he would be watching for it and would reach it, but if I was able to defeat him with follow up volleys and drives I would still keep playing it. I wanted to keep my other blue chip—the straight drive—up my sleeve as long as I could. Only when he reached my corner early and did a lot with it, getting me in trouble, would I decide to switch on the next similar opening. Never change until the context of the match suggests it.

One does not get a setup on the forehand every point. What was happening was spread over a considerable period, perhaps more than an entire game. Situations repeat themselves but only at scattered intervals. Simultaneously, other situations requiring the use of other patterns were occurring on the backhand and in the back of the court. Simultaneously, the opponent was not idle, but was also using his own pet combinations. A player must be thinking defensively as well as offensively, in terms of meeting and counterattacking against the other fellow's combinations. "He got me with that three-wall nick. Next time I'll be up there and drop it on him." "He likes that reverse corner when he's way up there. I'll watch for it and pass him down the line." An astute player not only uses his own combinations but tries to turn the other fellow's pet plays into winners for himself, or at least into turnovers, like intercepted passes in football, which reverse the flow of the action. In this sense defensive play is also offensive. Squash when well played is a very lethal game, with many almost invisible subtleties arising out of the context of the play.

Drastic Changes

Often a fundamental change in the use of options is needed to turn the flow. Many times I would start out using a lot of shots (the front wall options) on good chances, and be quite successful at first, winning the first game. Then success would become more and more elusive. My opponent was positioning himself a foot in front of the red line. My best shots were covered every time. If I stubbornly kept making them, the match would turn my opponent's way or I would hit the tin trying to improve my shots, which again would turn things his way. If I was alert and sensed the fact that he was right with me and covering everything, I would decide not to play any more shots for a while, thinking, "I must establish my depth. He's onto me." I would try to do this as subtly as possible, preparing for each opening in such a way as to threaten that I was all set, and that I *might* make that shot again. But I would hit instead, almost every time, hoping to capitalize, by playing deep "streakers," on the fact that he was anticipating a little extra toward the front. This would usually bring some additional success, but soon he would adjust to that too and begin to cover all my deep ones. I would then have to revert to the shots.

This reads as though I were doing all the thinking and he were doing all the reacting. Not so. He would simultaneously be giving me an equal going over whenever I gave him an opportunity by making a less than first class stroke. Each player is thinking all the time, striving to get one thought ahead of his opponent in this unending battle of wits.

Letting Up

In the chapter, "The Psychology of Match Play," there is a lengthy exploration of the problem of letting up. The passages here merely reinforce what was said, and perhaps further illuminate the apparently puzzling question: "Why can't a player get going again once he has let up?" It is because once his alertness drops off he loses touch with all these threads that go to make up the context of the match. He has not just let go of the steering wheel—he has let go of a dozen steering wheels. He may succeed in regaining control of some of them, but he is lucky if he ever again gets the whole situation in hand. While he is trying to, his opponent is winning, building momentum, gaining confidence. Panic seriously threatens, and this again inhibits his ability to reestablish a good grasp of the tactical situation. This is why we frequently hear the doleful sentence, "I eased up a little and I couldn't seem to get going again."

Overconfidence

Most players learn through bitter experience the heavy penalty usually exacted for letting up. It is so easy, after winning 15–5, to think, "All I have to do is keep playing those shots—I'm killing this guy." Instead you should think, "My shots are getting him, but he may at any time start covering them. I have to watch out or I'll no longer be winning." Overconfidence consists in identifying temporary success with a total solution, which it very seldom is against a thinking opponent. Overconfidence is the greatest source of fatal letups.

Keep Thinking

A player's attitude should be constructive. You should not dwell on the negative concepts: "Don't let up." "Don't emote." "Don't be over-confident." The road to success is to adopt the positive approach—"I *will* keep thinking all the way." Some players go to great lengths to keep themselves up to the mark. Henri Salaun frequently assumed a doleful facial expression and a general manner that indicated he was in the last stages of fatigue and discouragement. It was obvious he was all through. But then he would run like a deer, play with masterly touch, and win another point. When asked why he indulged in this mannerism he replied, "I *must* convince myself that I am in trouble or I can't keep playing." It was Henri's way of guarding against a letdown. On one occasion it backfired. Henri was actually sick and running a temperature, but was gamely play-ing out the tournament. He deserved sympathy but didn't get any at all. The gallery jumped to the conclusion that Henri was putting on his "in ex-tremis" act again, so they cheered his opponent madly as the great Salaun was upset and defeated. He had cried wolf too often, and his condition, which was truly pitiable on this particular occasion, met with total cynicism.

It is usually not necessary to be quite so dramatic in combating one's tendency to play less keenly when ahead, but some means of achieving discipline must be found. Dick Dorson, a person with a quite sunny disposi-tion, much given to having fun with people, used to concentrate with such ferocity that the corners of his mouth would go straight down and a heavy frown would dominate his features throughout the play. He won the Inter-colleges for Harvard in 1937 against a favored opponent. He looked like a harbinger of doom, a judge who has just steeled himself to announce, "The sentence is death!" Several people have asked me, "What sort of a person *is* this guy Dorson?" I had to tell each of them, "He's a very cheerful fellow—he's just concentrating."

All of this goes to show that while human imperfections can be over-come and are surmounted by the best, it requires a truly mammoth effort and an iron hand. Top play requires character as well as excellence.

Playing a Weakness

In a golf match a player cannot do anything to affect the play of his opponent. In a squash match he can. Victory depends not on merit, but on relative merit. If I can succeed in opposing my best to your worst I may defeat you even though overall you are the superior player in general skill and versatility. This sounds very simple: if his backhand is weaker, play it. Yet most players do not understand what this means. They play his backhand, receive a weak return, and decide to run him to the other side. Alas, it is to a very strong forehand, he takes over and wins the point from there.

Play It One Hundred Percent

Playing a weakness means playing it not just with a majority of your shots, or most of your shots, but with every shot throughout the match with no exceptions. In the rally, play the ball straight to his backhand with your backhand, crosscourt with every forehand. The same applies to all volleys. When you get a setup, drop your backhand straight, play a slice corner with your forehand: the ball always goes to his backhand. When you serve, serve to the corner from the right court, serve crisscross or straight down the center from the left court. Thus you will vary your play, run him up and back, change services, and play an apparently well-rounded game, *but:* every shot you make goes to the weakness. Ideally he never hits a forehand after the warm-up, not even one.

This takes great concentration but it can be done at all levels of play. Harvard once had a tough team match coming up. The opponent's number three man was fast, shifty, an all-round good athlete. I had seen him play, and saw only one weakness, a backhand that was steady but had little severity. His forehand was strong. The Harvard player was much slower, not nearly as good an athlete, but an intelligent player. He began the game at Harvard and was far from polished, but he could concentrate. He played exactly as I have described above and defeated his superior all-court opponent 3–1 by sticking relentlessly to the plan. The old saying comes to mind: a chain is no stronger than its weakest link. Another way of looking at it is to point out that there are always many ways to lose. Find *one* way to win, get a bull-dog grip on it, and never let go.

Twist Him: The Most Subtle Tactic

The most subtle of the top players can sometimes persuade an opponent to run a greater distance than the long diagonal. He fools his opponent so well that he starts for one shot only to find he must twist around in a circle and go back where he started. This not only increases the distance he runs but is very punishing physically because he must fight his own momentum.

This ploy is the funniest thing to watch in the court, the most maddening to the victim, but also the most difficult to execute. If it is done poorly it is a stupid shot—the opponent is not deceived, stays where he is, and the ball goes right to him. It requires perfect technique. A player must be quick enough to set up instantly and threaten one shot (the one that goes farthest from him) so persuasively that the opponent will take off after it—but at the last instant flick his wrist to make the other shot that goes back to where he just was.

No one ever did this as well as my coach Harry Cowles. He used a very loosely strung racquet so the ball would seem to sink into the strings and stay there for an appreciable length of time. He created the illusion that the ball had already started one way, but just as his opponent took off to chase it, he would turn it the other way. When as coach he played us (we took turns being alternately victims and audience), we enjoyed many a belly laugh as a teammate ran in a distraught circle to retrieve a simple crosscourt that was four feet over the tin and only half speed. He had started for that straight drop because he saw the ball start to go there. Playing Harry was most humbling! While watching one of the players with Harry, you could not help thinking of the old saying: "He ran around like a chicken with its head cut off." Inflated egos never survived a lesson with Harry if the lesson involved actual play.

The Up-and-Back Twist

This is the most wrenching twist of all. Against a player who is very fleet it can be devastating. If he is run up to the forehand corner for a drop, and retrieves it crosscourt, you should at once threaten to play deep to his backhand. He starts back to the backhand at full speed, and you play crosscourt around him to the deep forehand. He must now continue back, but must twist around to play a forehand instead of a backhand. The faster he started back for the backhand the more violently he is twisted (see Figure 11.1). His own quickness is used against him, causing him to fight himself.

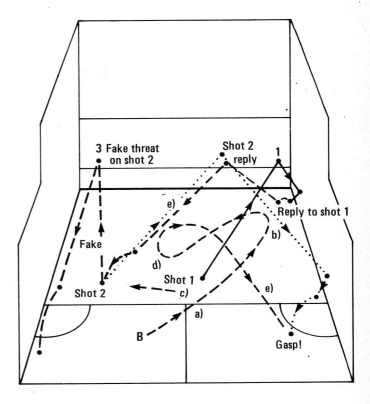

Figure 11.1 The Up-and-Back Twist. This is the most punishing tactic in the game. To help readers to unravel the diagram: Player A plays a straight drop (1). Player B runs path a to get it, and replies crosscourt. Player A fakes (3), causing Player B to twist via b and c to d. Player A snaps a wide crosscourt, (shot 2), forcing B to twist again at d, all the way back via 2—if he gets the ball at all! This is great fun, provided you are dishing it out rather than taking it. The moral: Don't hit into the open (crosscourt) when someone runs you up front. Play Straight.

The Subtle Effects of Twisting

There is no one more difficult to play against than a master of the various twisting plays. It has an unbalancing effect, so that after a game or so the victim can't seem to play well even when he gets a clean crack at the ball. The continual wrenching effects are mental as well as physical. Sometimes, they break up a player's entire game so that he plays beneath what he and everyone else expected of him. It has frequently occurred that the defeated player is unaware of what happened to him. He emerges in a black rage and comments, "I stank!" Everyone is too tactful to ask why.

One of Harvard's rival institutions had a player of great talent and exceptional speed. He was all over the court like a whirlwind. He was cleaning up the intercollegiate circuit. The ordinary up and back play merely gave him a chance to show his speed. But he was comparatively green and had not had great experience with subtle players. Harvard's number one was Henry Foster, a master at the flicking twisting game. He almost turned this fellow into a pretzel so that he actually injured one of his ankles in a violent reversal of direction. The next year the same thing happened again. The third time the poor fellow requested that he be allowed to use some other court. He felt that every time he played in that court something awful happened to him, and he was right! He later matured to become the third ranking player in the country, but at the time he didn't know what was going on. He only knew that he was continually forced to whirl and twist and play off balance and couldn't "get going."

Niederhoffer is very astute in using this play. Again and again he threatens to play short—and hits long—until his opponent is convinced that he doesn't really mean it. Then he threatens to play short—and plays short. The obvious becomes deceptive. In between he twists you.

What is the answer? Get him before he gets you! If you let him retain the initiative, he will give you a terrific going over until you can't stay with it any longer or just miss. You can't prevent the best players from beating you—you must beat them first, in every possible point. That is why championship squash is so lethal and so exciting to watch. What can go on within the limited dimensions of that small court is quite extraordinary. And it's remarkable how the power of suggestion can be used with such a devastating effect. All the very best know all about it. They aren't among the very best if they don't.

Summary

1. The mind dominates most matches.

2. Players may hold back a little, start with a rush or play in waves.

3. The best of players tries to attack with every shot, answering shot with shot, and lobbing high on the wall when he can't be aggressive. He uses finesse shots from the backcourt, brainwashes his opponent by setting up a pattern of play and then changing suddenly, faking and deceiving in every possible way. Above all he uses combinations—two shots that are as far apart as possible (the long diagonal). This presents the opponent with a double threat on almost every play. Sometimes he will make drastic changes, such as from a predominantly hitting game to a rash of short shots.

4. He is always in tune with the total context of the match.

5. Letting up is fatal because you lose touch with the context and cannot regain it.

6. Playing a weakness means to do it one hundred percent, and most players do not understand this.

7. Twisting an opponent is the most difficult and most effective tactic of all.

PART III

Teaching and Learning

12

General Principals

This section applies equally to teachers and to anyone wishing to learn who does not have access to a teaching professional. In either case the generalizations that follow are applicable, and will perhaps help both teachers and players to understand what is involved, the procedures that will bring results, and some pitfalls to be avoided.

Mental Knowledge and Muscle Knowledge

Mental knowledge is easy. A person's mind will quickly grasp a tactical concept if it is explained clearly. A basic tactic, such as hitting crosscourt from behind an opponent to open the path to the center, can be taught in a single session or learned in a single reading. It only takes a few moments. Mental habits take longer to create, yet are rather quickly acquired. A good example is the habit of intercepting the ball with the volley. It does not take long to learn to cut the ball off rather than allow it to carry one back into the corner before playing it.

Muscle knowledge is what takes time. The technique of playing the ball off the back wall crosscourt around an opponent involves preparation of the racquet, good timing, crouching, footwork, pivot, and the proper follow-through. It may well require hours of practice before all the physical actions begin to approach consistent excellence, and many hours of play before the actions become physical habits; i.e., actions that happen without thought, like walking without concentrating on it. Only when the actions reach this reflexive stage and happen by themselves, so that we are able to think of other things (such as tactics), can we call this "muscle knowledge."

Consider walking. It involves a lot of technique. The weight is controlled, shifted from leg to leg. Each leg is swung forward in perfect timing, balance is maintained at all times, the knees and ankles are properly flexed, etc. Yet anyone can walk and simultaneously think of anything else that may concern him. The walking is true muscle knowledge: it requires no concentration at all. Watch a baby learning to walk. He holds his arms out to help with that awful problem of balance. He staggers awkwardly from leg to leg, often in a jerky fashion because his timing is not yet smooth, and often topples over when he gets mixed up and is overcome by all these tremendous problems of technique. He is obviously concentrating on it, thinking of nothing else. Only after a considerable learning period does he reach that point where he can rush about, turn, walk, run, even jump when he wishes, without loss of coordination and balance. He quickly acquired the concept of walking, but the technique took many weeks of practice.

People Are Single-Minded

It has already been pointed out that the mind will focus on only one concept at a time, like a narrow-beam flashlight that will illuminate one object but no other in a dark room. It follows that so long as you must worry about getting your racquet and your feet right, you cannot simultaneously be thinking tactically or strategically. Therefore, technique is a bother and often causes you to play unintelligently without deception or good tactical thinking until it is so mastered that you don't have to worry about it any more. Technique must be muscle knowledge to be really useful in competition. It must happen by itself so your mind can be wholly on the competitive aspects of the contest. What good does it do to play the ball nicely if it is played frequently to the wrong spot and an opponent can see it coming?

Muscles Are Obstinate

Your mind is agile and much more instantly adaptable than your muscles. The latter are total conservatives if conservatism is defined as resistance to change. If you have been hitting straight, and become persuaded that the crosscourt is better, the mental switch is easy. But if you have been preparing your stroke with a close-faced racquet, it takes a long time to change the habit so that you automatically prepare the racquet with an open face every time that situation occurs. Your muscles just won't do it without a lot of mental concentration on your part.

This obstinacy is in the end a good thing. It is just as hard to change a good stroke as a bad one. Once you have acquired good muscle habits this tendency of your muscles to stay in their groove means that they will be just as unwilling to switch to something bad. A person with a good backhand seldom if ever loses it. The problem is to acquire it. You must expect to have to go through a technique-learning stage which may mar your competitive performance for awhile.

The Function of Drilling

There is only one way to acquire a muscle habit, and that is to repeat the physical act many, many times. A drill consists of repeating one particular act over and over again until it becomes habitual, or a reflex action. A drill permits us to focus on creating this habit without constant diversion and interference. Playing the game will not build good technique. Playing involves using whatever technique a player has already acquired. Playing will improve your ability to use your technique to better advantage, but it will not improve your skills. Anyone wishing to effect a change in his stroke, or to add a new shot to his repertoire, will progress with extreme slowness unless he resorts to drills. You can't learn to play a musical instrument merely by playing pieces. You have to do your exercises.

Constructive Practice

Anyone wishing to improve always practices, but many players have only a vague idea of how to practice constructively. "I play five times a week," he may say, implying that no busy person can improve on that. He does not appreciate that mere playing will improve him tactically but ignores the need to improve technically. Another player may say righteously, "Oh, I go in the court by myself and play some drives, some corners, and then some drops. I work on all my shots." This again is a very vague and dispersed use of practice time.

The best practice is very definite. A player should plan to play, but should plan to be there a half hour early, and spend that half hour on one (and only one) particular thing. If he wishes to learn a drop shot, he should set the ball up and make the shot a hundred times in succession, trying to do it exactly right each time. In this way (and there is no other way) he builds a habit, so that if in the middle of a game the ball pops out and offers a chance for a drop he will automatically do it correctly.

Get the Concept Right First

Much time and determined effort are wasted by players who practice assiduously but incorrectly. Their concept of how to play the shot they are after is vague or simply just wrong. "I've worked on that shot a lot but I just can't seem to get it." The fault here is in the mind, in the mental picture of what their racquet, feet, etc. should be doing. The best they can achieve is mediocrity. It is of extreme importance to be keen to understand exactly what the best procedure is. Any determined person can climb a mountain if he can find the path. If he misses the path, his best efforts may lead him up against a cliff or mired in a swamp. He may be farther from the top than ever, if he must retrace his steps. In squash he must undo what he has done, for he has created a bad habit.

Rationalization

Many players do not understand that muscle knowledge takes time, since the muscles must become accustomed to their new actions. They will try a new method a few times and then state flatly, "I can't play the ball that way." "I don't like it." "I'll never be able to do that." All these remarks are merely a verbalization of the tendency of their muscles to resist change. Of course it feels awkward and strange, and they don't like it. If a player doesn't understand this, all of which is quite natural and common for everybody, it is logical for him to chuck the idea and resign himself to his old ways even though he recognizes their inadequacy.

Mind over Muscle

The most difficult and fundamental task for any player is to learn to dominate his muscles. It is quite astounding that it is so hard to control your muscles. Establishing effective communication between your mind and your muscles is a new experience for most people. Their muscle actions are habitual, as in walking. Their conscious mind is not accustomed to con-

trolling their muscles and the muscles are not accustomed to being in-
structed by the mind. There is obstinate resistance at first both ways.
Establishing mental dominance is a gradual process that requires persistence and determination. Anyone who is impatient about it merely gets
angry and frustrated. Teachers who are not patient and persistent throw up
their hands and excuse themselves saying that they told the player how to
do it but he won't.

The easiest person I ever taught was Vic Niederhoffer. I would spend
ten or fifteen minutes with him on a certain shot, then he would say he had
the concept. I would leave him in the court, knowing he would drill it
endlessly by himself until it was a reflex that would just happen, and happen right, in the course of play. Niederhoffer began at Harvard, was Junior
Champion his sophomore year, Intercollegiate Champion his senior year,
and has since won many National Championships. Vic was very young when
he came to Harvard, but he learned the technical aspects of squash racquets
faster than anyone I ever taught. His approach was as described
above—get the concept clear, then drill it until it is grooved so you can "let
it happen."

Racquet Skill Is the Key

Any player taking up squash or making an effort to improve is always
far more advanced in handling himself (footwork, balance, moving) than he
is in handling his racquet. He has had to learn to handle himself throughout
his life in every activity involving moving: walking, running, climbing the
stairs, and playing games like tag. Therefore the area where most of his
work must be concentrated is the racquet skills: preparation, stroking,
spin, follow-through. These are totally new concepts to his muscles. It is no
exaggeration to say they involve ninety percent of the work in acquiring
technique. The player may be an adult and a good athlete, but when he first
picks up that racquet he is like a baby learning to walk.

Learn to Handle the Racquet

When we watch an accomplished squash player we say, "He handles
his racquet beautifully." The words "to handle" mean "to manipulate with
the hand." This is a very accurate description of what distinguishes
athletes who are fair players from athletes who are fine players. Both move
well, compete well, fight well. But the better player has more resources,

more exact execution, and wins with ease because he knows how to handle his racquet. Every aspiring player should understand that he cannot realize his athletic potential unless he can execute his thoughts in the court and execute them with precision. Too many players talk of "concentration" and "moving well" and "the killer instinct." All these are fine, but these players might consider this: do they have much chance in a wood-chopping contest against other equally determined contestants if their ax is dull? It is a perfect analogy that is all too often unappreciated. A good chopper spends a lot of time honing his ax to a razor edge. The blade of a squash player's ax is his technique.

Summary

1. Muscle knowledge comes only through patient drilling.

2. Muscle knowledge is essential because a player's mind must be on competitive considerations such as tactics and strategy.

3. A player learning a new stroke is like a baby learning to walk—his muscles have never done it before. He should accept this as a fact, however unflattering it may be, and not give up easily.

4. A player should realize that it is a time-consuming job to establish mental dominance over his muscles in order to discipline them to perform correctly.

5. Nine-tenths of the job is learning to manipulate the racquet with the hand.

6. One must sharpen one's technique just as a woodsman must sharpen his ax.

13

Successful Teaching

A short time after a teacher starts helping a new pupil a feeling develops between them. The pupil feels positively or negatively about it. He feels that his teacher believes in him and is really helping him. Or, he senses that the teacher doesn't get through to him. He doesn't know if he can learn much from the teacher. A teacher's first consideration should be to establish good rapport with the pupil. A person teaching himself must likewise establish a positive relationship with himself. Haven't we all seen people raging at themselves? How can a person teach himself that way, any more than a teacher could help him by storming at him? So the principle is equally applicable in each case.

Understanding

The basis of rapport is understanding. If a teacher comprehends the difficulties of learning as outlined in the preceding chapter, he will be patient and determined. He will also go slowly, staying on one thing until it is somewhat mastered. He will expect a pupil to miss many times before he begins to get it right. He will be as positive as possible, making few demands and encouraging the pupil constantly. This gives a pupil the feeling that the teacher thinks he can do it, and that maybe he can. He'll begin to like this teacher because he doesn't rush or press him by telling him too much all at once.

Lessons Are for Missing

It is very helpful to point out to players that lessons are literally for missing. A lot of the tension that develops in a player taking a lesson is due to the fear of missing. Tell him, "I expect you to miss. The reason you are here for a lesson is because you *can't* make this shot. If you get it right three times in the first twenty tries I'll be delighted. Personally, I missed eighteen of the first twenty when I learned it." This usually has a very relaxing and beneficial effect. Figuratively speaking, it removes the feeling that the teacher's ruler is going to whack his knuckles after each failure. Putting yourself on an equal footing by admitting your own early difficulties consoles him. Kid him some. "If you could make that shot every time, you'd be giving the lesson, not taking it." "As soon as you get this shot I'll find something else you can't do—and you'll be missing again." This approach substitutes persuasion for compulsion, sympathetic patience for demanding intolerance. Things go much better and progress is speeded.

Success Is Built on Failure

Most success crowns a heap of failure. Edison tried hundreds of materials in his light bulb. Every one burned out—a failure. Finally, he found *one* that worked, and he became forever famous. If a player tries a shot twenty, thirty, forty times, and finally finds the way—what does he care about those failures? They mean nothing. Now he's *got* it, and that was the objective. This also can be pointed out to nervous, tense pupils to relax them.

One Thing at a Time

A teacher is dealing with a mind. The conscious mind can focus on only one concept at a time. If it is asked to concentrate on several ideas simultaneously, it will fail to do it. A good lesson teaches one thing only, but teaches it thoroughly. If a pupil asks for help on a forehand and gets it going after a bit, then asks, "How about the backhand?" the teacher should refuse to switch and insist that he hit a lot more forehands. He should explain about muscle knowledge and urge the pupil to get that forehand, which is still mostly in his head, right down into his hand by repeating it another hundred times. Leave the backhand for another day.

Sequential Teaching

If the mind can only hold one concept at a time, how can a player think of a whole stroke which involves several concepts: preparation, timing, follow-through? The mind can think of them sequentially, one following upon the other. A very good method for every shot is to think in terms of the racquet—Racquet ready, wait, play. The racquet prepares, high or low, open or closed, as the shot may demand. It then waits until the ball arrives, then plays. While the racquet is waiting, you move your feet, crouch, and line up the ball. This sequence allows the mind to dwell on each essential separately. After awhile the player may feel that he is doing one thing, because with usage the actions tend to flow together and the sense of separation disappears. But it is much easier to learn a series of individual concepts rather than a composite thought that one can't quite get hold of in its entirety. It is quite possible to teach using a more composite method. The contention here is that the sequential method is the easiest and fastest path to the objective because it takes into account the abilities and limitations of the mind in its natural functioning.

Rhythm Will Come Later

Many players and teachers worry about rhythm and smooth coordination. This is to a considerable extent a waste of time. Trying to control the muscles and make them do a series of acts, some or all of which are unfamiliar, inevitably produces tension which precludes rhythm. A player learning something new must *make* himself do it that way, no matter how funny it feels. He is fighting his muscles, and frequently his muscles fight back quite vigorously. He must often grit his teeth and be tense and not trust himself at all if he is to win the battle against his muscles. Until he wins this battle the relaxation necessary for rhythm and easy flow is impossible. If he sticks to it, the muscles begin to yield. It is as though they said, "I guess maybe I can do that after all." After more drilling they may seem to say, "I like it." The player, who at first felt it was a major battle to do it at all, now feels that it isn't so hard to do. As this feeling gains, he will automatically relax and let go and do it more smoothly and with rhythm. If he doesn't, he should be told to, but only after he has pretty much mastered it.

Power Will Come Later

People tend to aspire to perfection. Therefore they think in terms of perfection. They try to learn a backhand like Charlie Brinton's right at the start, with all its smooth action, sharp kick at the instant of contact, and good use of weight. This resembles sitting down at the piano for the first lesson and saying, "I want to start with a Beethoven sonata." Again, as with rhythm, power should be ignored and good execution stressed. Once the stroke is mastered and is consistently correct, then (and not until then) is it good to instruct a player, "Play it the same way but just as you meet the ball, STING IT." The power, like the rhythm, is the cream that will, almost by itself, come to the top after the bottle has been filled with milk and allowed to sit there for awhile. Don't try to hurry it.

Teach Finesse Early

Conventional thinking—and it seems quite logical—dictates that players should pretty well master basic drives, volleys, and serve and return before they attempt finer shots like drops and corners. Almost the opposite sequence is the fastest way to learn a well-rounded game. The finesse shots require the most exactness, the most spin (ability to stroke rather than hit), the most perfect balance and footwork. Therefore they take the longest to master. Moreover, in actual play most of the action consists in serve, return of serve, and drives, with few chances for small placements. In play, a green player will spend a long time learning finesse. It follows logically that the most time-consuming job should be started as soon as possible. If it is not, the learning process is stretched out over a very extended period indeed.

As soon as a player has an adequate serve and return and a rough but far from refined ability to play forehands and backhands—in sum, as soon as he can play at all—he should be introduced to slicing across the ball, spinning it a lot, and making small, restricted swing shots: the front wall shots. He should be encouraged to go into the court and fiddle with them by himself, stressing one certain shot at any given time.

This will have many beneficial effects. First, he will like it. Green players are always delighted to feel they are learning one of those "tricky shots" they have seen advanced players make. It increases their enjoyment a lot, even if they do it badly, which is almost always true. Second, most players learning squash have played tennis and have a hopelessly wild swing. Practicing finesse shots forces them to correct this in the most drastic manner, since they must take almost no backswing at all. The practice on finesse has a strong carry-over value. It improves the neatness and exactness of their big swing drives, thus increasing their skill on every shot. Third, when a ball sets up out front, they develop the good tactical habit of attempting a placement instead of just whacking it again with a basic drive. It is very important to think "shot" when the ball comes out. If a player doesn't think it he won't do it. Fourth, it has been said that a poor finesse shot is the worst mistake outside of an error in the tin. It sets up for the other fellow. But nobody can acquire finesse shots without playing a lot of bad ones in the learning process. Isn't it better to start at once getting through this crude stage, at a time when a player's opponent isn't good enough to take full advantage of miscues? If you wait, and have him make these mistakes against more advanced players, the shots will be pretty much killed every time. Many good players try to add a drop shot to their arsenal after they have reached tournament or team caliber. They give up rather quickly. "I get killed every time I try it." This is true, at that level, until they make it really well, which of course they cannot do for quite a while. Most can't stand the punishment that is unavoidable in the learning process if they take it up late. It is hard to blame them. Their best hope is to drill a lot by themselves in the court, so each failure isn't rammed down their throat by an aggressive rival. Even so, they will have trouble integrating it effectively into their tactical scheme—they'll get hurt.

That this approach actually succeeds is not theory. It is tried and true. One year in the early sixties Harvard graduated its first five players. The Freshmen had good potential, but they were all tennis players who had never seen a squash court before coming to Harvard. One of our rivals had a powerful team with two champions at the top (Intercollegiate and Junior) and seven others with good prep school backgrounds in squash. What could Harvard do with nothing but green beginners? A team meeting was held in which the sophomores were in effect told, "We have two choices. We can call this "a building year"—i.e., admit we don't have a chance until next year—or you fellows can make up your minds to learn the game faster than it ever has been learned so we'll have a shot at winning. Which way do you want it?" Of course there was only one answer for them. The method used was as described above: they were all drilled heavily on finesse and only in the middle of the year was extra stress put on exactness in the rally. For the coach it was an experiment. He had never done it before but what could he lose in this situation? Much to his surprise it worked like a charm. Only the two champions won against us. We caught and passed the others and won 7–2. From that year on it became the "Harvard system," and the team has been Intercollegiate Team Champion for twelve of the last fourteen years. So the theory that finesse should be taught early—as early as possible—has been proved to be at least equal to any other sequential system, and it is probably the best.

Cross the Ball

The basis of finesse is slicing. This means do *not* take the racquet back: take it out and cut in, or lift it and cut down. A player should be told to make almost every string in the racquet rake the ball. He should be made to try to snap the racquet fast but make the ball go slowly. If the racquet truly crosses the ball it will not go fast—it will spin fast and go slowly. These are exaggerations of what is eventually desirable, but teaching by exaggeration is one of the best methods. If a player can put twice as much spin on the ball as is really necessary, putting the correct amount on it becomes a cinch. A player should not have to strain to get enough spin. It should be easy for him.

Progression

Any teacher worth his salt has a sequence in his mind of what he wishes to teach. This is necessary so that the game can be absorbed bite by bite, and no one helping should be so large as to be "more than he can chew." A pupil cannot leap from the ground to the roof in one jump. It is the teacher's task to provide a ladder up which he can climb, with no rung so far above another that he cannot reach it. One good progression is to have the player learn:

1. Forehand grip and basic stroke

2. Backhand grip and basic stroke (Let him rally only—no points.)

3. Service and return of service—volley

4. How to play a point and keep out of the way—basic tactics and position

5. Off the back wall drives.

6. Slicing—crossing the ball (Let him just slice at the front wall without attempting any particular shot.)

7. Specific finesse shots—one only for the forehand, one only for the backhand

8. Et seq. (Use judgment as to where the stress is needed to even out his game and foster his talents. Add additional finesse shots, from out front only.)

9. Backcourt finesse—when he is quite good—the three-wall nick, reverse corner played from off the back wall, the sidewall drop

10. Tactics—as advanced as his competence warrants, adapted to his natural abilities

Avoid Narrow Systems

The greatest limitation found in teachers is a tendency for them to teach the game the way they play it. This should be avoided. A new player may be quite differently gifted, and the teacher's personal game may be in many ways inappropriate to the pupil's talents. A good teacher assesses the mental and physical gifts of his pupil and tries to adapt to them. There is no one best way to play the game. There is only a best way to develop the conglomeration of abilities found in each individual. A player without power but with natural touch should be taught to use a lot of shots. A natural hitter should be shown how to make the best use of his power. A very quick person should be urged to stress the volley.

Fundamentals Are Rigid—Style Varies

The fundamentals of racquet work are based on physical laws. They are not subject to personal preference. What the racquet must do to the ball to achieve a certain result is a rigid matter of physics no matter who does it. After these fundamentals are learned, the manner in which a player uses them can vary a great deal, and here is where a teacher should be imaginative and able to adjust to the pupil, bringing his strengths to the fore and covering up his weaknesses.

The Game's Greatest Teacher

The greatest teacher the game has known was Harry Lee Cowles. He was coach at Harvard from 1923 to 1936. During that period Harvard men won eleven national championships plus a host of other titles. The Harvard team never lost a formal intercollegiate match. The most striking thing about Cowles' pupils was the sharp differences in style that distinguished them from each other. Palmer Dixon was a position player. He held the center immovably and retrieved everything. Herbert Rawlins was a deceptive stylist who was one of the "prettiest" amateurs ever to play. Larry and Beekman Pool must be rated (along with Diehl Mateer) as the greatest power players the amateur game has known. Germain Glidden set up the highest tempo ever seen. In each case Cowles was never fettered by any set ideas about how the game should be played. In each case he saw what this particular fellow could do, and taught him to do his own thing better than anybody else did the same or anything else at the time. Such perception can only be marvelled at. It will without a doubt, never be equalled and certainly never exceeded.

A personal anecdote will perhaps give a picture of how skillful Cowles was as an instructor. In my junior year I had risen to number seven (after beginning the game Freshman year). I was taken as an alternate to the National Championships. The first six went into the courts to practice. I was standing about with no partner. Neil Sullivan (seeded second nationally) asked Cowles if there was anyone he could practice with. Cowles replied that I was there as an alternate, but not bad. It was just what he wanted. He wanted to get used to the courts, but didn't want a hard match. We warmed up and began. I was of course all keyed up. I was playing the great Sullivan. I attacked him furiously, won the first game and built a small lead in the second. Sullivan became progressively irked, and finally settled down to really hard play. The second and third games were tough and close, but he of course won them. In the fourth, my inexperience told and the roof fell in—he crushed me. He thanked me for the match, then turned to Cowles, who had watched with owl-like solemnity while all this happened, and said, "Harry, if this kid is only the alternate, what the hell are the rest of them?" The 'rest of them' won the team title decisively while Larry Pool won the individual title. The effect on me was totally electric. All of a sudden I realized that Sullivan really had to work to beat me. "I'm good!" It had never entered my head before. There were so many that were as good or better at Harvard, and what number seven intercollegiate player considers himself as having class? I had earned the trip by winning two matches by one point in the fifth game: against our numbers 8, 9, and 10. They were as good as I. The point to the story is that Cowles was such a fine teacher that he nurtured not just one or two champions but a miniature horde of really competent players.

With his genius for developing everybody, Cowles always had depth on his teams. Players like myself were never revealed until they had achieved skill approaching real excellence, because they didn't make the team until they were that good. Observers often remarked, "Where does Harvard get all that outstanding material?" They did not realize that half of us had never seen a court before Harvard. In my senior year we won the national team title, and three of the five were "Harvard beginners." There was no recruiting of prep school stars. Cowles took who came and taught them how to play better than anybody else, year after year. It was teaching, not material. We were basically decent athletes, that was all. Most of us had the same experience that I had. We didn't realize how good we were until we got away from Harvard and suddenly found ourselves beating all but the best. The advantage that gave Harvard near total dominance for years was Harry Lee Cowles.

Cowles was a very original thinker. With Beekman Pool he resorted to a trick never used before or since (to my knowledge). Pool hit so hard that his ball would come off the back wall no matter how low he aimed. Cowles took his racquet, cut out the expensive gut, strung it with cheap silk, handed it back and told Pool to hit as hard as he wanted. Thus equipped, Pool won every major tournament in North America that year.

Germain Glidden presented another problem to Cowles. He played the ball well but was not a dream shot maker. But he was quicker than anyone else and had a phenomenal ability to anticipate. Cowles had always taught that the three-wall nick was an unsound shot that backfired too often and should be used only as an occasional surprise. Soon he had Glidden doing it all the time. Why? Because his quickness and anticipation meant he could reach almost any return and pass his opponent, running him mercilessly up and back in a wild melee of continual crisis. Nobody had ever played the game that way before. Coupled with constant volleying and iron condition it added up to an irresistible force. Glidden won the Nationals three times in a row and retired undefeated. Later he did the same in the Veterans.

Here again Cowles had departed from orthodox thinking (including his own) to exploit unusual gifts and carry them to great heights. Certainly Beekman Pool was a case in point, and not only in the matter of stringing. Cowles made him hit harder, and harder, and harder, until at his peak Pool hit the hardest ball ever known in the amateur game. And Glidden was an impatient player. At times he would hit the tin, trying for a winner when the real virtue of his game lay in its cumulative pressure. Before the National finals, Cowles took him into the court, gave him the ball, and said "Hit the tin." It made that horrible 'bong' that signals failure. "Hit it again." "I don't want to," wailed Glidden, "I hate that noise. It's awful!" "All right," Harry said, "Now go in and play your match." Glidden did not hit the tin that day! He defeated a fine opponent 3-1.

In 1936 Glidden was peaking. He played superbly one day and gave me a good licking. Cowles came to me afterwards and told me that Glidden was so fast and strong he was going to keep on beating me, and I might as well get used to it. Such was my respect that I merely said, "OK, if you say so, Harry." But of course a slow burn developed and ate into me. I soon started thinking, "*Is that so!*" The next time we played I slaughtered him. The following time Glidden played like a tornado and we had a great match. Looking back, I am quite certain Cowles planned all along to jack us up, one against the other. After I won in my turn Cowles probably told Glidden, "You might as well get used to losing to Barnaby—he's the best." By playing us off this way, needling each in turn to greater efforts, he got Glidden to such a peak that he topped the field decisively in the Nationals. Glidden and I have often talked about how time and experience have enabled us to look back and see the genius of Harry Cowles at work, doing things to us we weren't even aware of at the time. He was absolutely sound, and he was also very deep and subtle. Few people ever got one thought ahead of Harry Cowles.

Cowles' manners on and off the court were impeccable. He was literally never in the other fellow's way, he never hit anyone with ball or racquet, and always offered a let whenever there was the slightest question. His code was, "You don't want any point the other fellow questions. Play it over, even if you are certain he was wrong." Harvard players were always noted for their clean play, and Harry was behind it. He set the highest standards possible, and never deviated. The university owes him a special debt in this area.

As a teacher no one has come close to Cowles. As a player he was equally masterful. Perhaps one last anecdote will appropriately cap this recital of the amazingly high standards this man set for himself in his profession. On a trip once, we were discussing fight and toughness and how long a fellow can keep it up. Glidden asked Harry how long he thought a person should fight. Cowles thought it over, then said simply but with total conviction, "You should fight until you're dead."

Tips To Coaches

Teach everyone the habit of self-practice, so your lesson continues after you move to the next player. Use groups for beginners.

Encourage everybody who will try. The obvious best athlete in a new group does not always turn out to be the best player. There is often hidden talent—players with great competitive ability and determination. Remember the hare and the tortoise.

Never criticize a loser. Leave him alone. Criticize a winner. He is happy and receptive. You can say, "You are very good. You would be even better if. . . . ." Let the loser recover.

Analyze every squad member. Do it on paper if it helps. Show each his next immediate objective and what he must do to reach it. Show him what you wrote.

Spend a lot of time drilling in the court on individual shots. Spend a lot of time watching, to detect recurring tactical errors. Then have a conference.

Provide opportunity and justice for all. Rank should always be by merit, never by coach's preference.

Always go out to win. The phrase "building year" should be abhorred. Youth lives in the present. They want to win now, today, this year. They are quick to sense that a "building year" means "You are losers." A coach must believe in his players.

One great teacher said, "Never think of a pupil in terms of what he is, but in terms of what he can and will be."

Always be enthusiastic. Enthusiasm is the life blood of youth. They must feel you have it too. Morale dies without it.

Think long. The Freshmen and Sophomores are the Varsity of two or three years later. Work on them, encourage them, make them feel valuable. They will be all you have in a couple of years. A coach who moans about graduations deserves little sympathy. He knew years ago they would graduate exactly when they did. Has he made no provision for the gap?

A coach who thinks long can measure up to a high standard—he always has a good team. If he is lucky with his material he has a great team. It can be done, and it's much more fun to be good than to be mediocre, for coaches and players alike.

The Function of the Coach

Athletics are part of the educational process. Education means the development of the whole person. If athletics don't contribute constructively to this process then how can one justify all the money put into facilities and personnel? The coach is involved in helping young men and women develop their personalities, their ethical standards, and their performance standards. Through his activity they test themselves and prove themselves. They develop habits—habits of temperament (how to take pressure); habits of work (the persistence to reach an objective); and habits of fortitude (how to be strong when things are tough). All these add up to that very big word "maturity."

The coach is an educator whose function goes far beyond showing people how to hold and wield a racquet in a court. Every young person wants to prove himself. He has selected your activity as a means to this end. If he is a candidate for a team he means business. He wants to be good, as contrasted with fooling around to get some pleasant exercise. It is often one of the most important things in his life at that particular time. Therefore the coach is to him a very important person.

It is of very small import whether one team beats another in a given contest. It doesn't matter at all to speak of. Then why do athletes, teams, and spectators get so excited about it? It is because the *effort* is important. The match is a challenge, a test. It puts one to the proof. Therefore to give it all you've got is the only way to react. President Lowell of Harvard said many years ago that it is not important that Harvard should win any particular contest; but if Harvard players ever take the field without expecting to win and being determined to win, that would be a disaster for Harvard.

The function of the coach is to help people so they expect to win and are determined to succeed at whatever they do. The carry-over factor is the real significance of coaching.

A Coaching Anecdote

Sometimes one wonders if this business of coaching and all that goes with it is really worthwhile? The author had an experience that pretty well answered the question.

During World War II all formal athletics ceased at Harvard for four or five years. The University plunged 100% into the war effort. All the coaches of course disappeared. But the college still continued to function, the students wanted teams, and informal teams were encouraged. Whenever possible, a grad student who knew a little was provided as a coach. A very nice fellow handled squash. He was an expert in his field of study but knew only a little about squash and had never coached. He organized well but could not teach what he didn't know. The year before I returned, the team lost every match it played even though the opposition was very much weakened by the war. When I returned there were only two or three players who even knew enough to try to hold the center. Some were already adopting a rationalized, casual view that they just played for fun, they didn't really care about winning. It was quite a situation at a university whose team had always been the best or nearly the best.

A meeting was called and in speaking I hoped to develop a little morale—just to get started. I went on about how grateful I was that the team still existed and that their coach had kept things organized. It gave us a basis from which to start. Perhaps they thought they were poor material because they had lost. Not so. There is no such thing as poor material. They were green material, but without knowing them at all I would guarantee there was in this group the potential for a good team. All they needed was guidance. That was my business. We had every excuse for a losing season, but winning is much more fun than losing, and Harvard had a great squash tradition. I asked the team how they liked the proposition that we forget all about losing and aim, right now, this very year, for the top where Harvard belonged?

The reaction was astonishing. There was an explosion of clapping and yelling and whistling. It was clear that underneath their defensive, debonair attitude of not really caring, they were in reality yearning for leadership. They wanted to go at it hard. They just couldn't wait. They became beavers, morale was terrific and the team moved from the bottom of the league to second place in one season, winning several cliff hangers along the way. Never was a year more rewarding to me as a coach. Never was it more clearly shown that coaching is important, that it is very significant in the lives of those students who elect athletics as their personal proving ground. The question is not if a coach is needed, but whether he can live up to the need—the tremendous demands of youth.

Summary

1. There must be rapport, based on understanding, between teacher and pupil.

2. Lessons are for missing and success only comes after many failures.

3. The natural functioning of the mind and the need for muscle knowledge urge that coaches teach one thing at a time in a sequential way.

4. Rhythm and power will come by themselves as excellence is achieved.

5. Finesse should be taught early, not left until later. This speeds the learning process in many ways.

6. Crossing the ball is fundamental to finesse.

7. Every teacher should have a progression in his mind, a ladder pupils can climb.

8. Narrow systems should be avoided. Fundamentals are quite rigid but styles can vary widely.

9. Harry Lee Cowles of Harvard was the game's greatest teacher.

10. A coach should provide justice, opportunity, inspiration, guidance, and encouragement to all. He is primarily an educator, secondly a technician. His importance is unquestionable.

14

Successful Learning

This chapter is aimed directly at anyone, from beginner to advanced player, who wishes to improve his game, whether working by himself or with a teacher. The discussions which follow, covering false impressions and misunderstandings that inhibit and undermine the learning process, are based on forty-four years of experience in teaching men and women at all levels of excellence. Each category represents hundreds of individuals each of whom suffered from the same difficulty or lack of understanding. Each reason for failure is not exceptional. Rather, it is commonplace. The greatest problem any teacher has is the pupil's ignorance of what is involved in learning.

"Ignorance" is a strong word. Many resent it. They should not resent it; there is nothing disgraceful or offensive about not knowing something. You either know a fact or you don't know a fact. Facts are not to be feared—they are merely something that is true. It is a fact that most people must learn how to learn before much progress is possible. This may seem like a play on words. What does it all mean?

The Process of Learning—The Concept

There are three steps in learning. The first is to know with real clarity what you wish to do. This is a mental process, and it is by far the easiest and quickest to master. However, it requires sharp attention and exact visualisation. If it is the technical execution of a shot, the picture must include the preparation, the execution, and the finish. A tremendous amount of time is wasted by futilely practicing a shot in a manner that will never make the shot well. This is another fact that people do not like to admit. They are in a great hurry to practice the shot before they even know how to do it.

The Drilling

A player learning a shot should realize that the mental grasp of the needed technique is only the beginning. He then must do it, slowly and methodically, a large number of times, in order to create muscle habits. Players tend to be impatient. "Now let's play and see if I can do that when the occasion arises." It is much better to set the ball up and play another hundred (yes, a hundred) before they think of playing. Why is this? It's because everybody's muscles work through habit. Hitting a few does not create a habit. Only hitting hundreds will do it. It is exactly like learning the piano. Constant repetition of scales, arpeggios, and other exercises is the only way to develop clever fingers. In passing I might mention that musicians usually learn a racquet game more quickly than others, because most of them have, through music, learned how to learn. They understand that mental knowledge is useless, that it must be drilled into the muscles.

Misunderstanding

Those who do not understand the muscle problem tend to get very angry and impatient (at themselves). They understand mentally and think therefore it is inexcusable that they cannot at once do something in the context of actual play. They see a finished player execute it neatly, and do not realize the work that lies behind his easy excellence. Sometimes they leap to the conclusion that the superior player is more gifted while they lack talent. This may or may not be true, but it is a non sequitur in any event. They must realize that the mental picture they have of how to make the shot well is the final objective that is at the top of a rather long ramp labelled "work" or "drill." There is no other way. Perhaps in the unforseeable future someone may devise an instant muscle learning process through hypnotism or some other presently unknown method. Up to today, the only way to get muscle knowledge is by many careful correct repetitions. Every player should realize that this is the *only* way, not just the best way. The impatient approach demands from the body what it cannot fulfill. Frustration is the only result, and frustration is one of the strongest forms of discouragement. It causes many players to give up trying to improve their technique.

Tactical Use

The third step in the learning process is to integrate a shot into your tactical scheme. This is a mental process and is much easier to learn than a physical skill. But it requires some practice. After you have learned to execute a corner shot, you must learn to think of it when a chance occurs in the course of play. Try not to have to say, "There was my chance to use that corner! He never would have got it!" "I didn't think of it." Thought habits can be called *tactical technique*.

Drill Again

In practicing the shot a player should imagine that his opponent is the farthest distance from where his shot will go. For example, in practicing a forehand straight nick he should always play the ball to himself with a backhand shot that comes to him via the front wall, right sidewall, and out into the middle, as though his opponent had just played the ball badly from the backhand corner. This means he is not only practicing the technical execution but also the proper tactical use of the shot. This perfects the competitive thinking as well as the skillful racquet work.

Think Preparation

It is well to repeat here what was said in the section on technique: the preparation controls what can and cannot happen. Incorrect preparation guarantees a poor shot. But most players visualize themselves making the shot and pay little attention to how they get ready to play the shot. To refer to the drop shot again, the further a player takes his racquet well back in getting ready to play, the more certain he will be to make a big, crude, horrible drop shot. Only after he has learned to prepare by putting his racquet *close* to the planned point of contact has he any chance of making a neat little effective drop. Getting one's mind on the preparation as contrasted with the actual playing of the ball is a new concept to many players.

They do not understand that improvement is *impossible* unless they control and alter their faulty preparation.

This seems like a strong statement, but the facts clearly bear it out. Do we not all know many players who have a strong side and a weak side? They have played for years. They have hit the ball hundreds of thousands of times. Yet the weak side is still weak. Practice seems to have no effect whatever, even over a period of years. In almost every such case the preparation is faulty. The grip is poor, or the backswing is incorrect. So they are faced forever with the gloomy option: hit it badly or don't hit it at all. It is an iron curtain.

A teaching anecdote may be pertinent. A middle-aged man came for a lesson. Asked what he wished to work on, he replied he wanted to learn finesse shots. As we warmed up it was obvious he had a weak floaty backhand. I asked him if he wouldn't like to improve, but he replied that it was no use. He said he just couldn't hit a backhand. He'd played for twenty years and lots of people had told him that he sliced under it too much so it would float high. He knew he ought to hit it more solidly, but he couldn't do it. He said not to bother about his backhand, he was stuck with it. But I persisted. I asked him if anyone had ever told him that his grip was wrong, and that by changing it he would inevitably hit flatter and more solidly. No, he hadn't tried that. Would he try it? Sure, he'd try it but it probably wouldn't do any good—his backhand was hopeless. Of course, it did make the difference, and in the course of an hour he scored a substantial gain. Only one thing had been done: his preparation had been corrected, so that with the same swing he had used for twenty years he achieved a far more solid shot. This is a true story. The point is that twenty years of practice with bad preparation was fruitless. One hour of practice with his mind concentrated on how he got ready (not on how he hit) started him well on the road to a major improvement.

The moral is reasonably obvious. If you fail to progress with practice, you should investigate your preparation with a very suspicious eye, and consult a good pro if you can. If you don't you may practice fruitlessly for a long time.

Power

The cult of Power is a major learning deterrent with many young players. Every year the Harvard Freshman squad is filled with eager, spirited boys who identify excellence and "fight" with power. They make an incredible racket. The ball bangs madly about the court. They are trying very hard, but it is all "full of sound and fury, signifying nothing." A player can easily beat them by merely tapping the ball, if he is accurate. It is usually necessary to be cruel and to do this until they realize they are worshipping a false god. Once one can pry their minds loose from this preoccupation with force, the door to progress is open.

It is quite easy to add severity to a good stroke. It is very difficult to improve anyone's stroke unless he will slow down and play thoughtfully, experimentally, and with no intention at all of making a great shot. When a player hits very forcefully everything happens quickly. If he hits a good shot he will probably think, "That was good. How did I do it? I don't know." He has made one good shot. He has learned nothing. If he plays slowly he can become conscious of what his arm, hand, and racquet are doing. He can improve in understanding and muscle control. He can recognize what is going on and alter it as needed. He makes mediocre shots because they lack pace, but he is learning. Isn't that his objective?

As I said in the chapter on "Successful Teaching," power will come by itself as excellence is achieved, or it can be easily added. Once a player has established control, all he has to do to get power is to do exactly the same thing, but do it faster just as he plays the ball. This adds crispness, sharpness, kick, and speed to the shot. This should always be left to the last, because if sought after first it interferes with the learning process. The shortest route to excellence is to develop a good slow technique, then sharpen it up. To start with speed and try to improve it is very difficult. Speed "fogs up" learning. There is an old cliché: "Practice makes perfect." We should amend it to read: "Slow, thoughtful practice is best."

It's Up to You

No one can "make" a player. Even the best teacher in the world can only *show* the player how he can make himself better. Teaching is only five percent of the process. It is the steering wheel, and it is therefore important, but the work, desire, determination, persistence, and character must come from the player.

Everyone hears talk of successful coaches who "mold champions." This is a nice concept for the vanity of coaches, but it is a repulsive thought. Is Niederhoffer a piece of soft clay that I, that great sculptor-coach, shaped into a winner? Somehow I feel that Mr. Niederhoffer might react unfavorably to such an analysis. And if any player wins any match, does he wish to think, "I didn't win that. The coach won it"? The only true compliment any teacher can hope for is when a player says, "The coach showed me the way."

This works in reverse. Some players seem to feel a teacher will make them into a player. Of course the teacher can't do it. Each player must resolve that he is going to improve himself. Then, yes, the teacher can guide him, show him the quickest route to success, provide constructive criticism along the way, and draw attention to neglected areas. But the real job is the player's task. It's up to you.

Summary

1. Most players must learn how to learn.

2. The process of learning demands a clear concept of the objective, long drills to perfect muscle knowledge, and tactical integration of the shot into the context of play.

3. Tactical use can be drilled simultaneously with muscle knowledge.

4. Correct preparation (getting ready to play) controls what can and cannot be done. Concentration on preparation is often neglected with fatal results. It is indispensable.

5. Preoccupation with power diverts many players from addressing their minds to other more constructive methods of progressing. Slow, thoughtful practice will bring results more quickly than practice devoted to hitting hard.

6. Control is the objective. Pace can be added after control is established.

7. In achieving excellence the teacher can function only as a guide. He cannot "make" anybody into a player.

8. Each individual must make himself the player he wants to be.

15

Drills

The objective of drilling is the achievement of skillful racquet work. During each drill the player should pay attention to the preparation, the stroke, and the follow-through. A good many drills should include practicing proper moves to avoid being in the way after the shot leaves the racquet. Often this move is simultaneous with the execution of the shot, so that an opponent is blocked until the ball is played but not even for an instant after it is played. This moving is of extreme importance in offensive play because, without it, a player may find himself merely causing "lets" on his best chances instead of punishing his opponent and winning points. A player who moves properly will almost never be in the way. If his opponent runs into him he is running the wrong way, away from the ball, not towards it. Thus a "clean" player (one who seldom blocks after playing the ball) is not only a better sport and more fun to play against, he is also a more effective player who makes the most of his openings. Crowding loses friends and potential points as well.

Beginner Drills—Use Groups

1. *Basic Forehand.* Get the grip correct for forehand, cock the racquet back, crouch, arrange the feet correctly, and make the swing in the air near the floor without a ball. It is important to do this without the ball so your mind can be on how you use the racquet without worrying about lin-

ing up the ball or timing it. You don't have to watch the ball. You can watch and think only of what the racquet is doing. Emphasis should be placed on a slightly open-faced racquet, there should be minimal use of the arm on the backswing, and a low open-faced follow-through. Maintain a crouched position throughout.

2. *Forehand with tossed ball.* Prepare the racquet and feet to play *before* tossing the ball. Toss the ball almost head high straight up above contact point. Play once and catch the rebound; but do not play it again.

This drill adds timing to the basic swing. The player must *wait*, after he is ready to play, until the ball has bounced up and started down. This teaches him to prepare early and select the best instant to release his stroke. This is timing. The toss should be pretty high just so that the player will learn to wait. The player must not drop the ball: he should toss it up quite high (five or six feet to get a good bounce).

3. *Forehand on the rebound.* Prepare for a forehand, toss the ball, play it quite high (four feet above the tin) so it returns nicely to the forehand. Practice lining it up and timing it on the rebound.

Players should be told *not* to hit hard and low. The action should be slow, the rebound easy and convenient so that they are not pressed and can think and try to get it right. This is the beginning of the rally.

4. *Basic Backhand.* Use the same three progressive drills as for the forehand.

5. *Changing Grips.* Prepare the racquet for a forehand. Snap the racquet to the backhand prepared position, then back to the forehand, etc. Emphasize loosening the third, fourth, and fifth fingers just a little to allow the butt of the racquet handle to move a little more under the hand for a backhand, and back to the forehand position. This should be practiced without a ball so the mind can concentrate on what the hand is doing. It should be done as slowly at first as is necessary to get it right, then should gradually be sped up until it becomes a quick snap into whichever prepared position is desired. Enough of this should be done to assure that when the ball comes, you will fall quickly into the proper preparation.

6. *The Easy "V" Rally.* Play gently and high, forehand to backhand to forehand to backhand, etc. This adds aiming, changing grips, changing feet. Emphasize *not* doing it hard and low. Do it at half speed and try to

keep it going slightly crosscourt, paying attention to the details of execution and avoiding the speed that doesn't give time enough for thought.

This, for beginners, is a very advanced drill. Beginners should vary it by starting sometimes with the forehand, sometimes with the backhand. Teachers should stress that they are not trying for excellence but merely to develop good habits in reacting to balls coming to either side. The objective is to keep the ball going so they get a lot of practice.

7. *Rallying with a Partner.* Players should play quite high and at half speed so each gives the other a good chance at the ball. They should keep the ball going—not try for winners. This adds two important elements: not knowing where the other fellow will hit his shot, and the need to get out of the way after playing.

Teachers should talk to a group before starting this practice. Great stress should be put on never swinging if an accident threatens due to proximity. Always call "let." Reemphasize taking the ball low and keeping the racquet low for safety. Mention to them that they should get as near the T as is consistent with keeping out of the way.

8. *The Volley.* Play the ball into the front wall high enough (above the service line) and hard enough so it will rebound in a manner that invites a volley. Volley it straight down the wall.

Teachers should emphasize the differences between basic strokes and the volley: high, closed, forward preparation compared to low, open, back preparation. Do it on one side at a time, keeping the ball well in the open. Have separate drills for forehand and backhand. Encourage volleying in the rally.

9. *Service and Return.* The lob service and how to volley it should come first. Emphasize smooth lifting in the service execution. The return of service requires the most drilling, particularly on the backhand. The lob serve must be volleyed well before or well after it touches the wall. This drill adds the need to play a ball after it strikes the wall.

Beginners must be trained to let it come out rather than to rush in and try to scrape it off the wall. If a succession of serves is made, all of which touch the wall too high to be volleyed, this will teach them to wait. A succession of serves can be made that are not quite on the wall, training a player to move up and intercept them well in the open. Only when a player has established a clear understanding of the two different situations should the teacher "mix them up," forcing the retriever to make a quick judgment and choice. Separate drills for forehand and backhand are advisable. Putting the racquet close to the ball and pressing it must constantly be stressed since beginners always tend to take a swipe at it and miss it entirely or play it off the wood.

10. *Taking the Ball off the Sidewalls.* As on service, a beginner tends to rush to the wall instead of letting the ball come out. A very effective drill is for the teacher to make a series of bad corner shots that come well off the third wall and have the player play them. Teachers should stress waiting for the ball to get low. Point out how the spin makes it jump up some off the sidewall so it takes longer to get low and will come out farther than one would at first expect. Point out how letting the ball come out increases one's time, one's options, improves position, and sometimes boxes an opponent. The drill should stress "Get ready, *wait*, play" and "Stay back—let it come out."

11. *Off the Back Wall.* This and drill number 12 are the best for learning to take the ball off the walls. They are the most difficult wall drills because the presence of the backwall inhibits any large swing and forces a player to develop a compact controlled technique. It also forces a player to *wait* for the ball to come out, because there otherwise isn't room in which to play. The ball should be fed so it hits the floor first and comes well off the wall, and stress should be laid on getting back behind the ball so as to follow it out as contrasted with letting the ball come out to the player. Facing diagonally into the backwall (about 45 degrees) is important to allow a backswing that doesn't hit the wall, and to permit taking the racquet out of the way to let the ball go in and out. The player's reply should be high enough to reach the floor service line for its first bounce. Practicing the crosscourt shot emphasizes the pivot and return to ready position. Teachers should end a long drill on these skills by telling the player to play every ball that comes off any wall in this way, so the skills apply all over the court.

12. *Around the Corner.*   This is the same as number 11 except that the ball strikes the sidewall, then the floor, then comes off the back wall. The spin makes it jump towards a player much more than he would expect, so this drill teaches him to stress getting far back away from the ball to avoid being cramped. This shot should be played straight into the open side of the court with good depth.

13. *Directly off the Back Wall.* The ball is fed so it strikes the back wall before striking the floor. It will tend to race out fast, and an around-the-corner shot will not jump way over as it does when it strikes the floor first. This drill uses the same techniques as 11 and 12, but should never precede them since the action is much faster and it is hard to learn under the time pressure.

Intermediate Drills

14. *Slicing.*   Teachers, have the player make a slicing motion with his racquet without the ball. Stress should be placed on getting him to visualize the fact that his racquet goes primarily out and in, not back and forth. Then have him make a series of slices directly into the middle of the front wall with no attempt to make any particular shot. Tell him to make five or six strings cut across the ball, so the motion of the racquet spins the ball rather than hits it. Point out that as the racquet cuts across, the weight moves forward, almost at a right angle to the motion of the racquet, and that this, not the racquet swing, is the "hit" or what makes the ball go forward. Encourage him to fiddle a lot with this trick, making it with quite a bit of wrist with his forehand and less wrist and more of an arm pull on his backhand. He should place himself four to six feet in front of the red line to do this and should feel that the shot is tricky, not powerful. Tell him to slice it just as much as he can without actually missing it. This is a situation where exaggeration speeds learning.

15. *The Slice (or Roll) Corner.*   Study Figure 15.1 carefully. Note that the player feeding the ball places himself so that the shot goes as far as possible from him. This means the striker learns when to play it as well as how to play it.

Teachers, stress letting the ball drop low and slicing it *up* into the sidewall. Make the player play it a full foot over the tin and still slice it enough so it will not come off the third wall. This cultivates the habit of aiming away from the tin and relying on spin rather than low aim to get a dead ball. He should of course cut it finer as he gets good. Use separate drills for forehand and backhand. Vary the feed: play a bad short shot directly to him in the open and then play a bad reverse corner that comes out off the third wall. Both these situations often occur in actual play, so this is realistic teaching. The player should be told to experiment with the amount of sidewall he takes until he gets a sense of good width.

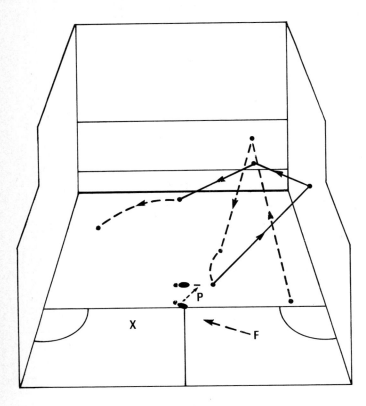

Figure 15.1 Slice Corner Drill. This is often called "Roll Corner." Feeder F plays a soft setup, boxing himself. Player P slices around corner. (Coaches should teach players to "clear" as *part of the shot*.) By taking his right foot forward as he plays (dotted arrow), the player opens the path for F to run and avoids a let. If P is positioned farther back (towards X) then he should take his left foot back, again as part of the shot. After the shot is too late—F will be into him and call "Let!" Block your man until you play, but remember: the instant you play, *he* has the right of way.

16. *The Reverse Corner.* The most common opportunity for this shot in actual play occurs when an opponent has hit a crosscourt drive too wide so it breaks out and he can be backed a little into the side from which he played. Therefore, the ball should be fed exactly this way, and the player should back the feeder off and play the opening thus created. Again the ball should be allowed to drop fairly low and should be played up into the corner—away from the tin. This shot does not need heavy side slice like the slice corner. It can be played sharply with a more direct stroke that starts on the back of the ball and goes a little under to get backspin to pull it down. It should be aimed as close as possible to the corner so it seems to squirt out across the court after striking sidewall and front wall almost simultaneously. Stress should be put on a "checked" follow-through, making it a light shot which, even though it is quick, does not have the weight in it to give it the length that will make it come off extra walls (Fig. 15.2).

Figure 15.2 Reverse Corner Drill. Note that Player P plays the ball so that it goes the farthest possible distance from Opponent F. Do not play this shot when opponent is at X—it goes towards him. (Coaches, feed slow return setups to perfect technique, make them lower and faster later.) P must also learn to move with his shot (dotted arrow) to unblock F and avoid lets.

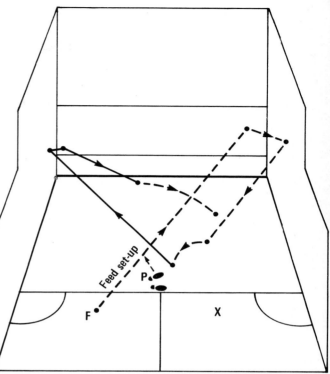

17. *The Straight Feathery Drop.* This shot is best used at first from fairly near the front wall. It is then a rather quick shot even though very gentle, because it hasn't far to go. Played from far back it must be very expertly done or it is a setup. Also, learning the easier one from up close lays the ground work for expanding it to more of an all court weapon.

The feathered drop is excellent training because it exaggerates the need for a very small swing, a very restrained stroke, and the tiniest amount of weight push. The racquet should be prepared *at* the point of contact. The ball should literally be allowed to land on the racquet, and just as it lands a little cross-tweak under it plays it up at quite a sharp angle but so softly it arcs and is going down when it reaches the front wall. The most difficult part of learning this shot is to eliminate *all* the tendency to hit the ball. It is only "feathered" by the racquet, and leg push gets it up there. Again the motion of the racquet is at right angles to the movement of the weight. The ball should be aimed to touch the front wall very close to the sidewall to help kill the rebound and perhaps get a nick.

This drill should be coordinated with number 14—Slicing. Once a player learns to slice, point out that all a good drop consists of is a tiny soft slice aimed very near the wall.

18. *Nicks.*   These are often called 'hard drop shots.' Actually they are not drop shots at all: they go straight to the front wall with no drop. They consist of a sharp chop played low near the sidewall in an attempt to hit the nick for a winner. They are among the best shots in the game. The ball is taken higher and cut sharply so it has a heavy spin. This makes it go down as quickly as possible after it hits the front wall. If it catches the sidewall just before the floor it is called a nick. The nick shots are most appropriate for setups that must be taken higher in order not to lose position. Again, the feeder should position himself the farthest possible (the diagonal) away from the destination of the shot so as to teach tactics as well as technique. The stress should be on using a closed racquet face, a higher preparation than for other finesse shots and a vertical chop swing that gives a heavy backspin. Again the racquet does not go back and forth —it goes up, then down, and the weight pushes the ball. The drill is: ready, *up,* wait, *down.* The shot is more of a "strike" with the forehand, more of a heavy, quick pull with the backhand. Basically this is slicing: the racquet crosses the ball from above to below instead of from outside to inside.

Advanced Drills

19. *Gaining the Center.*   One player feeds the ball to a corner so it comes off the back wall. The player's job is to play crosscourt hard enough and wide enough to get it around the feeder so he cannot hold his position and play the ball. This should be done repeatedly to both sides until width, depth, and pace are good. This is a bread and butter play in any match.

20. *Holding the Center.*   Teachers, play rather bad crosscourts and straight shots from behind the player. His job is to cut them off, stay in front, and run the feeder from side to side. Stress stepping out from the center always with the foot nearest the ball. Move as little as possible.

21. *Advanced Volley Drill.*   Teachers, play high crosscourt from behind the player, not too wide. His job is to step diagonally forward, in-

Drills   199

tercept the ball, and "bury" it along the wall. This involves closing the face by changing the grip to an eastern as the racquet is lifted forward to play. Any player, in learning this, will overdo it some and hit the tin at times. Tell him this is all right: he must experiment to find out how far he can safely carry this business of hitting down on higher shots. A second drill is to play a floater straight and have him cut it down crosscourt. In this drill, getting well onto the outside of the ball and taking it early must be stressed: both these skills ensure that it will really go crosscourt and not just down the middle.

22. *Retrieving Drill.* The feeder should stand at the T, with the player behind. Crack the ball hard, low, and short. The player should stand crouched, with the head of his racquet almost on the floor. He should reach forward and across to the ball with no backswing, picking the ball up with the head of his racquet as though with a long handled basket and flipping or tossing it high down the wall with a wristy follow-through. It is "lunge and flip." There is no stroke because there is no time. Drill both sides.

23. *Counterattack Drills.* This exercise also teaches the most effective tactical answers to finesse shots.

Place the receiver slightly out of position to the left. Play a forehand reverse corner from slightly behind him on the right. His task is to run up and make a straight feathery drop, then recover back and to the left to be in position to volley (Fig. 5.3).

This is one of the most difficult, exacting, and valuable drills. It demands a very fast start which includes shoving the racquet out *in front.* This shoving serves two purposes: it tends to pull the player up there, and it gets the racquet head close to the ball as it must be for a drop. It also involves bracing the wrist far back so that one can play straight even though reaching far forward. (The natural tendency is to hit crosscourt.) It involves "flattening out" so the ball is reached with a minimum loss of position. Under the pressure of all this skillful and quick physical action the player must nevertheless make a tiny, tweaky drop shot that barely drips off the front wall. After all that he must instantly recover poise and position to be ready to volley the next shot.

This sounds like too much. At first it definitely is. Therefore the corner shot should purposely be made high (two feet?) and soft so the player can have time to think and get the routine going in all its sequential particulars: racquet out front, wrist braced, hand palm up so the racquet is open (he must play up), low crouch, small quick steps to avoid galumphing awkwardly, flattening out so the armpit touches the forward knee, a tiny

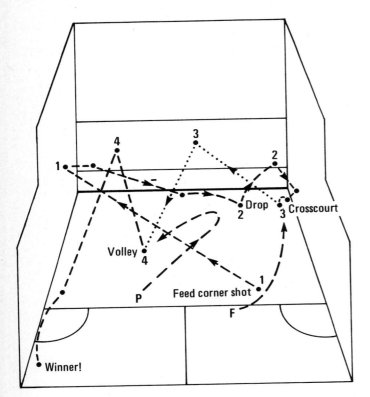

Figure 15.3 Advanced Retrieve, Drop, and Volley Drill. Player F plays a good corner shot (1). Player P runs up, and makes feathery drop (2). After P has learned this, F should follow his corner up the wall (2) and play into the open off the drop (3). P must have recovered poise, balance, and position in time to make the volley (4). (Coaches, as skill is attained, make the feed shots [1 and 3] tougher and tougher.) As the action gets very fast, it forces P to "flatten out" to make his drop and spring back instantly (never turn around) to be ready to volley.

cross slice and push, and a backward shove with the forward leg to recover position.

The Harvard boys call this drill "the gut tearer." It is just that. As proficiency improves the corner shot is played lower and lower, more and more zippy, until the action is at top speed.

And that isn't all. Once the player is getting the hang of playing skillfully at high speed, the feeder should run up the wall and whack the drop shot crosscourt. It is up to the player to have recovered position enough to volley or stroke it down the backhand wall (Fig. 5.4).

Any player who masters these maneuvers and racquet skills at high speed has acquired one of the attributes of real class: he does not merely retrieve an opponent's best shots: he makes winners off them or at least effects a turnover that gets the other fellow in trouble.

This drill develops speed markedly. Many players have no idea how potentially quick they are. They will say, "I can't even get that shot, never mind do something with it." This is true at first: they run without reaching forward, so although they move forward they fail to get the head of the rac-

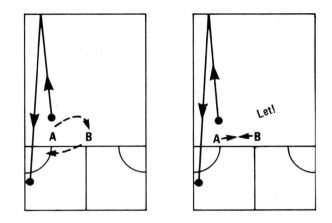

Figure 15.4a Correct—Player A hits down the wall, moves forward out of the way, so that Player B can go straight for the ball. (*Left*)

Figure 15.4b Incorrect—Player A tried to force Player B to "go around." (*Right*)

quet to the ball. When they learn to shove the racquet ahead of them plus flattening out their reach, their ability to play the shot increases by four to six feet. They get shots they never got before. It is often a revelation to them that method can markedly improve speed, since speed is usually considered to be a God-given attribute that one has or one hasn't. Speed like that of many of the champions (Glidden, Ben Hechscher, Ralph Howe, Salaun, Nayar) is indeed a gift. But reasonable speed, so that it can be said, "He's pretty fast in the court," is open to *anyone* willing to develop it.

Adding to the speed the ability to make a dangerously skillful counter shot can often move a player up from being "a good fighter" to a player who is worthy of being called "really good."

I clearly recall my own experience. I looked upon the corner shots as winners. Occasionally I would manage to dig one up but would then be so out of position that I would be slaughtered by the subsequent hard, deep shot. I looked upon the game as dependent on who got the first good chance. That was pretty much the end if the opponent played the ball at all well. Then I learned the techniques described above. I began to realize I *could* get those corners and not merely get them—I could destroy them. When I made a poor shot I would think, "I hope he plays a corner—I'll put it away." The change in confidence and morale was phenomenal. And an additional boost to anyone's ego is the very fat feeling, "He made his best shot and I took it apart." The reader must appreciate one other point: I was an ordinary average athlete, far from a "superathlete" with unusual physical gifts.

This drill, while hard to master and frustrating at first, is what can separate the men from the boys. It is strongly recommended for all players who have achieved an advanced game that has mastered the basics of general play, but who need the added ability to counterattack under almost any pressure, and the enhanced speed in getting to short low balls.

24. *Dropping the Three-Wall Nick.* This is the same as drill number 23, except that the feeder makes a three-wall nick from the back corner. It is merely another application.

25. *Run Up and Hit Straight.* Frequently an opponent will play a short ball when he is well in front of the red line—four feet or more. A player can still run up and drop the ball, hoping to catch the opponent moving back. But he is really more open to being passed by a hard deep shot. This can be done by hitting straight. It is very important not to hit crosscourt into an easy deadly volley. This drill is rather easy on the backhand, because the hitting arm is in front of the player. It is much more difficult on the forehand because the hitting arm is the back arm. The player must reach far forward and lay the wrist so far back that the ball still goes straight. Putting the arm forward and simultaneously laying the wrist way back and opening the racquet must be learned. It is not a natural thing to do. It should be practiced separately, without a ball. Then the arm and wrist should be prepared *before* the feeder plays the corner shot, and should be held motionless that way as the player runs for the shot. The point is that it does little good to hustle and get there if the racquet is not ready when the player arrives.

26. *Combining Counter-Attack Drills.* If a player masters drills 23 and 25 he can run up to a short ball ready *both* to hit it or drop it. If he gets to the ball he now has a contrasting combination, a double threat that offers an opportunity to fool his opponent. He should be in command. He should practice varying his shot.

27. *The Twister Drill.* The player is fed a setup well in front of the red line. He should put his racquet close to the ball exactly as though he planned a drop shot. At the last moment he should snap the ball crosscourt. The idea is to pull an opponent forward then make him twist back. The secret of success is identical preparation: if the racquet is close to the ball and the wrist is cocked back, one can play either a perfect drop or a sudden sharp snapped drive. If the preparation is exactly the same, how can an opponent "read" the planned attack? A detective needs a clue, and there is none. It takes a lot of practice to achieve total sameness in preparing for two different shots. Drill both sides, stress quick setting up so there can be

a deceptive hesitation before the ball is played. The reverse corner and the crosscourt drive can be combined in the same way.

28. *Finesse off the Back Wall.* Play balls that strike the floor first then loop off the back wall. Using the same technique as in drill 11, the player should make reverse corners, sidewall drops, straight feathered drops, and three-wall nicks. A very important aspect of these drills is that the preparation should be identical with the preparation for a drive, so it is never obvious what is intended. Drill only one particular shot at a time. There is no need for a feeder on this drill: the player can feed it himself.

29. *Moving Drills.* These are very important in achieving clean play and avoiding lets. In each drill feed the ball to the spot shown in the diagrams, have the player block the feeder until he plays, then move out of the way *simultaneously* with playing the ball, so that his opponent cannot run into him if he goes to the ball. The principle of simultaneity is most basic. A player cannot play the ball and then move out of the way. He must *be out of the way* when the ball leaves his racquet, because the opponent, by the rules, has the right of way not later but the very instant the ball leaves the racquet. Thus "clearing," as it is called, is actually part of the stroke. It is not a separate and subsequent action (Figs. 15.5–15.7).

Figure 15.5a Correct—Player A hits down the wall, allowing Player B to go in front of him directly to the ball. (*Left*)

Figure 15.5b Incorrect—Player A tries to force in front of Player B thus getting in the way. (*Right*)

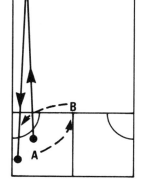 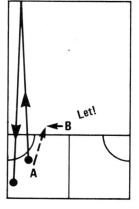

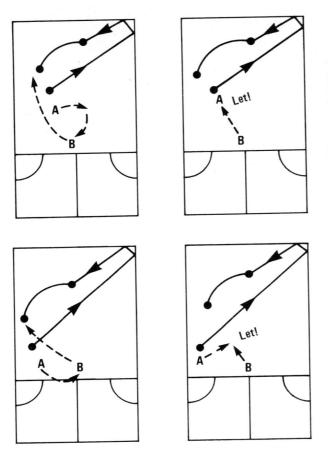

Figure 15.6a From the Center. Correct—Player A blocks Player B until he hits the ball, then moves out of the way. (*Left*)

Figure 15.6b From the Center. Incorrect—Player A continues to block Player B after striking the ball. (*Right*)

Figure 15.7a From the Side. Correct—Player A moves to the center in such a way as not to block Player B. (*Left*)

Figure 15.7b From the side. Incorrect—Player A, in moving back into position, collides with Player B. Holding your position does not justify hindering your opponent. (*Right*)

Learning to slide with the shot has a dual value. It means a player is a good sport, fun to play with, seldom irritatingly in the way. It also means that the other fellow has no alibi if the shot is good. He can never escape from a predicament by asserting, "You were in my way. I want a let. Let's start the point over." A let is very much to the striker's disadvantage: there he was, on top of the point, running his opponent with a good prospect of finishing him off—now he must start over, and perhaps it is the other fellow's serve. Who has lost out when there is a let? Blocking after the shot does not pay except against green players who don't know enough to stick up for their rights by demanding the freedom to run for the ball. If they know their rights, all the striker gets on his fine shot is a bump and the cry, "Let, please!"

It is quite important to drill this skill in moving. Green players tend to run all over the place in their anxiety to clear. Actually in most cases all one needs do is move one foot. By taking the back foot forward, the back leg is pulled out of the way if that is what blocks the opponent. Or the front foot can be drawn back if that is the leg that is doing the holding. A player is only as wide as his shoulders. That's all the room he needs to get by. If this one-foot move is made smoothly as part of the shot—a play-and-step stroke—the striker keeps his poise and his position without ever getting tangled up with his opponent. A player can be very aggressive and box his opponent thoroughly, and still seldom, if ever, be in the way.

Discussing this with the players helps. Some are so worried about being good sports they start leaning or falling out of the way before they play the ball. They spoil their shot, and they are not asserting their rights. They should block the opponent mercilessly until they play. The moment the ball leaves their racquet the traffic signal turns from green to red: there is no yellow light in squash. The other fellow *at once* has the right of way. The knack of boxing an opponent without blocking him illegitimately (after the ball is struck) is the basis of both sportsmanship and successful offensive play.

30. *Playing Drills.* These combine the preceding drills. Have an agreement: "We'll play. I'll intermittently set the ball up. You block me, play, and clear. I'll be nasty and make a let out of it if you give me half a chance." This type of playing drill can be applied to any particular shot. It teaches good tactical thinking and clarifies the player's understanding both of his rights and his obligations to his opponent, so he learns to be both a tough competitor and a clean player. Many intermediate to advanced players need help of this sort to clean up their conduct in the court by clearly learning when, how, where, and how much they should move— whether behind, even with, or in front of their opponents.

16

Sportsmanship

Two Players in the Same Space

Squash racquets is one of the most difficult games to play hard and, at the same time, play cleanly. In tennis the opponent is far away on the other side of the net. A player runs no risk of impeding him or hitting him with a big swing. In squash both players occupy the same area and must be considerate even while they are straining to defeat one another. One must learn to take the court the instant the ball leaves an opponent's racquet, and to give the court up the instant one has played. Particular attention has been given to this in the moving drills in chapter 15 (Drills 29 and 30). These are expressly calculated to show how a player can move without blocking.

Clearing Takes Precedence over Position

Many players block frequently because they have been taught to play and move to the center. The real rule is to play and move to position in such a way that you do not hinder your opponent. If the most direct move to position hinders him, you do not have the right to make it. The direct route to the ball is his, and if that interferes with your move you are obligated to give way. Players, when told they are in the way, often say, "I was only holding my position." This is an invalid excuse.

Hitting and Standing

The most common cause of lets is the tendency of many players to hit and then not move. Often they are blocking the route to the ball. They would not think of cheating by a positive move, after they play, into the path of their opponent. But they do not understand that just staying there in many cases has the same effect. A player must plan so that his shot and his subsequent move (or standing) clears the path to the ball. Otherwise he is at fault.

Players often say, "Every time I play that shot he calls a let. Don't I have a right to play it?" Of course they have a right to play it. They do not have a right to play and block, which causes the many lets. This kind of trouble occurs most frequently on the red line. A player will be on the line, near the wall, playing a straight shot. He plays, and moves back along the line to the T. The other fellow, who was at the T, moves along the line to go for the straight shot. It is a solid collision every time. The striker should move forward a couple of feet with his follow-through, keeping his opponent behind him but leaving open the direct path to the ball. He returns to position in a slight curve instead of a straight line. There is then no more trouble and play is uninterrupted. Misunderstanding of one's rights and obligations on the red line can turn a match into a real mess that can even involve personal animosity. Both players think they are within their rights. The striker is almost always at fault.

Your Job Is to Call It

It is not good manners to try for a ball and then say, "I'm not sure if I got it. Shall we play a let?" It is your job to call it, to know if you reached it in time or not. Even with a referee, a player should call a ball "not up" on himself if he knows he didn't get it on the first bounce. Frequently a player's body cuts off the view of the referee at the crucial instant, and he needs this help.

Arguing Lets

Arguing about lets is also bad manners. If an opponent asks for a let, a player should grant it even if in his private opinion there was no just cause for a let. To do otherwise means he is setting himself up as judge and jury over both himself and his opponent—a very arrogant procedure indeed.

The "Gentlemen's Game"

The phrase "Gentlemen's Game" is always taken to have a snobbish meaning, either that only the rich play or that only those in the social register are admitted to the inner sanctum and ordinary, honest people are invited out. This is totally a misinterpretation. Squash racquets is played without a referee in almost all cases. Even in intercollegiate team matches, there is no referee. And yet there are all these fine points about calling the ball down, getting out of the way, restraining one's swing, and in general having quite scrupulous consideration for an opponent at all times, no matter how close they play. There is every opportunity for an infinite variety of cheating, from blatant to subtle, and there is no referee to do anything about it except in big tournaments. This means the obligation to be ethical is entirely the responsibility of each individual player. He must be a gentleman in his attitude and actions toward his opponents, or in a short time he will find it extremely difficult to persuade anyone to play with him. A match filled with physical contact and numerous lets is no fun at all. Squash raquets is a poor game played that way, and would attract no following at all without the code of gentlemanly behavior that governs play in general. A player must be a "gentleman" in the court or he is frozen out. This applies equally in social clubs, in many local YMCAs, and in all colleges and schools where the game is played. In squash, the word "gentleman" is used in its most democratic and universal sense.

On Your Honor

On several occasions directors of athletics, seeing for the first time the numerous matches taking place without referees, have expressed their astonishment that this could happen with a minimum of altercations and incidents. Most games have umpires who quickly penalize any behavior that is out of line. The sight of scores of young men (and lately young women) striving their utmost to win, and still playing it straight with rare exceptions, impressed them more than anything else about the event. Without exception, they felt such an honor system was one of the strong points of the game as an intercollegiate or interscholastic sport. The much touted and often questioned assertion that sports build character is, in this case at least, a demonstrable fact.

Ethics

Young people will often react to a talk on sportsmanship with the question, "That's all fine, but what do you do when the other fellow cheats?" It must be explained that a player's conduct derives from his code of ethics, from his basic concepts of right and wrong, from his religion. His behavior is not elastic, subject to modification according to any opponent of the moment. Each player must decide how he will act, and stick to it against *all* opponents. No matter what his opponent's conduct, a player should remember that he represents himself and often a school, college, or club, and that to do this creditably is his primary obligation. It is easy to be a good sport when the other fellow is equally scrupulous. Playing a cheater is the real test of sportsmanship: if a player still adheres to his code, he is then a real sportsman.

Retaliation

This normal human reaction, defended by the furious assertion, "He started it!" is no solution at all. Now the pot calls the kettle black, everyone is down in the mud together, and the game is hopelessly spoiled. The proper procedure varies with the circumstances. If it is merely a social game, play "hard to get" the next time that person asks for a game. If it is a tournament or team match, ask for a referee, but only if it becomes absolutely necessary.

Firmness

Being a sportsman doesn't mean being weak. Sometimes a player will block, then when a let is requested assert, "I don't think you would have got it." In this argument he doesn't have a leg to stand on. He cannot contest the reply, "If you will clear so I can try for it, and I fail to reach it, I'll not argue the point—it's yours. But until I get a chance to try for it, I'm going to call 'Let'." The best sportsmen will not hesitate to insist on their rights as repeatedly as necessary against a blocker. With a referee, the blocker runs the additional risk of having a "Let Point" awarded to the other fellow as a penalty for his blocking. Now it is a fact that on some of these "blocks" the retriever would not have reached the ball. Therefore, the blocker has lost out, not his opponent. Thus, it is quite possible to play very strictly by the rules and still counter bad behavior effectively. It is notable that most champions are clean players.

Playing Too Close

Some players overanticipate. In their eagerness to start for the ball, they do not quite wait for the striker to play it. They start early. If a straight shot is played they are on your back, going through you for it almost before the ball is struck. It is impossible to clear the ball before you strike the ball, so frequent lets occur. A player's natural reaction is that he has a right to play straight if he wishes and he is determined to do it. This only results in a lot more lets. It is far more effective to keep cool and play crosscourt. If an opponent is insisting on attempting to occupy the same space you are occupying, then the farthest distance from him is the farthest distance from yourself. He cannot move ahead of time to cover the straight shot without opening up the other side of the court. The more he "plays close," the bigger the opening must be. Figure 16.1 is slightly exaggerated to stress the argument. The wide crosscourt is the sure answer to the crowder. He is forced to stay far enough away to cover the crosscourt, whereupon the straight shot is again a possibility.

Think—Don't Emote

This is yet another instance of the efficacy of cool thinking as opposed to raging about an apparent injustice. It is quite true an opponent may be robbing you of your straight shot. But he cannot do this without laying himself wide open to the contrasting shot, in this case, the crosscourt. Similarly if he follows you up to cover a drop shot, the long ball will defeat him. If he crowds you into the deep backhand corner, the three-wall nick or the sidewall drop will catch him leaning the wrong way. In every instance the more he moves towards the striker, the more confounded he is by the proper reply. Also, he is made to look foolish by the fact that he is constantly moving away from the ball, not towards it. The best way to deal with a player who "plays the man" instead of the ball is to make him suffer for it. He is not only defeated, but perhaps after awhile he knows better, and learns to curb his impulse to commit himself too soon.

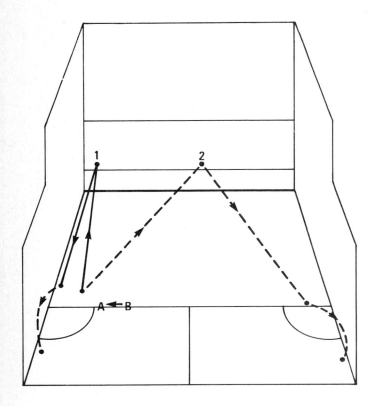

Figure 16.1a The answer to crowding: play crosscourt. If Player B stations himself so close to Player A that A finds it impossible to clear quickly enough to avoid constant lets, then B is wide open for a devastating crosscourt (2). The natural reaction to such crowding is for A to become angry and insist on his right to play straight. He is looking to the left, does not see the opening to the right. It is much more effective to keep cool and say, "You insist on having this side of the court. OK—I'll use the other side." Many players cover up the backhand—and are vulnerable on the forehand as a result.

Gamesmanship

No game offers so many opportunities to indulge in that practice which has been so aptly described as "how to win without actually cheating." The various ploys begin as psychological attacks in the locker room while dressing for the match. There are two main avenues: to establish superiority or to establish inferiority.

Superiority

The superior approach suggests sympathetic remarks about the opponent's defective strokes, hoping past problems have been ameliorated; allusions to one's proposed tactics against opponents in later rounds, implying clearly that the outcome of this match involves no doubt at all; and a general breezy manner with a touch of quiet arrogance. This hopefully in-

Figure 16.1b The answer to crowding on finesse shots: play *wide* crosscourt. If Player B, sensing a drop (1) crowds close, he is wide open for a dog-leg crosscourt that twists him unmercifully (2). A crowder is, roughly speaking, trying to occupy the same space you are. Therefore, the answer is to play the ball the farthest distance from yourself. Above all, don't loose your cool and fight for your rights. The crowder is used to that, and is probably better at it. Fool him instead. It's more fun and *very* effective. It also avoids "wrestling matches."

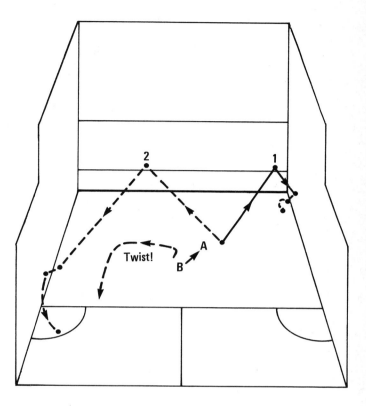

duces such rage and determination in the opponent that he loses his cool and plays like a mad bull, or it may actually intimidate him.

Inferiority

The inferior ploy is more subtle. Usually it involves various pseudomedical equipment, such as a long ace bandage wound with time-consuming concentration about a supposedly doubtful knee. This should be accompanied by several testings and flexings implying that if it isn't right one can scarcely move at all. A casual remark to a third person about the late party the previous night, complaints about one's latest racquet not having a good "feel," careful attention to an apparently painful blister on the racquet hand, plus any other little pebbles one can cast into the scale—all these serve to induce overconfidence in the intended victim. He becomes relaxed and unprepared for a furious attack in the first game.

The Warm-Up

The Warm-Up of course offers many opportunities for suggestive maneuvers. The superior ploy often calls for frequent put-away shots—low corners, three-wall nicks, and a general exhibitionistic display of seemingly inexhaustible technical resources. If some of these are casually made on the volley or half volley, the impression of maestro-like dexterity is augmented. A faint air of boredom also helps. The watchful opponent is convinced that a barrage of finesse shots is sure to occur, and is easily confounded by simply playing down the wall and crosscourt.

The inferiority persuader, after the careful locker room activity, continues his campaign systematically during the warm-up. He plays each drive at half-speed but emits a slight grunt suggesting it was a major effort. If he attempts a corner shot, he is careful to play it very high or into the tin. He tries a little experimental retrieving, exhibiting a very slight limp and just failing to reach the ball. When his opponent makes a fine shot he says, "Wow!" in a low tone, as though to suggest, "What can a fellow do about that?" He takes pains to cough a few times, as though his cigarette-clogged lungs were already feeling the pressure. His practice serves are all a bit on the mediocre side. When play starts, he attacks at once, hopefully getting a big jump to rattle his opponent into a state of nerves.

The Ace Bandage

This can be used judiciously throughout a match. It must not be over-done, but should be reserved for major crises. It is good to carry a lesser tool, such as a small bandage on one playing finger. The objective is to disturb an opponent's momentum without apparently being guilty of stalling. If the other fellow wins a couple of points and seems eager to serve, a ten-second rewinding of the bandage injects just that little delay that disturbs and flow and lessens the probability that he will "get rolling." It forces the match to stutter just a little, gives time for thought, and slightly interrupts concentration. If the opponent thinks about the bandage instead of his next service, much has been gained. The ace bandage should be used only when all other ploys have failed, an opponent is in the groove, and nothing will avail short of a major interruption of play. At this point one should smile apologetically while unrolling the bandage, and remark, "Gee, I'm sorry. This thing loosens up now and then." An ace bandage is quite long. One can apparently be unwinding and rewinding with commendable speed and industry and still take up a significant period of time. The match has stopped. The opponent has been forced to stand there, cool off, and think about all sorts of things (such as ace bandages, your personality, probable ancestry, etc.) not connected with the context of the match. Often, enough of an inner burn develops so that subsequent play is seriously impaired by irresistible emotion. Many a match has been turned around by the proper insertion of this key maneuver when all seemed lost.

The Burp Serve

This is a vulgar ploy that is eschewed by the fastidious, but is amazingly effective if one has no compunction about appearances. I witnessed a match that was clearly won through the constant and virtuosic use of this method. The player used the lob serve, bent very low, and as he lifted the ball high on the front wall released a somewhat protracted burp that suggested he was on the verge of being overcome by a digestive disorder. His innocent opponent was a Harvard sophomore who was a terrific player but totally unseasoned in the more subtle aspects of gamesmanship. He was instantly concerned for his adversary, and was torn between playing the ball and going to his aid. He missed the serve entirely. This continued for quite a stretch of points, the young man still being less worried about points than about his opponent's obvious suffering. Of course, the gamesman maintained a facial expression indicating an internal agony repressed only by a major effort of the will. Now and again the Harvard player would awaken to his own peril and run off a string of points, evening the match. So it went until it was about 11–all in the fifth game. At this point the middle-aged gamesman pulled out all the stops. He bent almost to the floor to prolong the action, and made a beautiful lob serve accompanied by a prolonged emission that rose and fell and finally dwindled for all the world like a Himalayan skyline. "He really is sick!" the polite Harvard boy must have thought for he missed the serve—and lost the match. Only in the locker room did he awaken to the realization that he had been had, but the subsequent gnashing of teeth was indeed too little and too late.

The Rude Warm-Up

This is another ploy which I have frequently witnessed. The technique is to play the ball to yourself five or six times, then whale it crosscourt very wide so it is unplayable on the wall. The ball comes around the court back to you. This continues until you are ready, and your opponent has scarcely played a ball. At this point you say with finality, "All set! Let's go!" If this can be bulldozed through it almost guarantees winning the first game. On at least one occasion it backfired. In the finals of the National Team Championships with the matches 2–all, and the games 2–all in the fifth and deciding match, a Harvard boy was playing a more seasoned opponent who was sadly not above using almost any means to gain his end. He had already struck his opponent in the mouth with a high follow-through. He had been hit so hard that the coach insisted a doctor be called to verify the boy could continue safely. After this interlude they began to warm up. The gamesman used the system outlined above. But the Harvard boy rose heroically to the occasion. After the crosscourt slam had gone around him five times he turned to the referee and said politely that he seemed unable to warm up in this court. He requested permission to go into the next court and warm up by himself. "Permission granted," stated the referee, with a certain warmth that was not lost on anybody. The boy took plenty of time, during which the gamesman was left to wander about the exhibition court under the malevolent stares of a completely antagonistic gallery. The Harvard boy returned to the court, sweetly thanked the referee, and won the match handily. The Moral: nice guys often win, particularly if they keep their cool and reason out the best answer.

There Are Many Others

The foregoing are merely a few of the endless subterfuges dreamed up by the fertile imaginations of that constitutionally devious type called the "gamesman." There is pretended fatigue; the feigned injury; the break while the referee is asked to examine the ball; walking in a circle instead of straight to pick up the ball; the super-slow serve that isn't quite officially stalling; the insinuating remark such as "Isn't it time you come down out of the clouds?"; the pretended "This isn't my day. I give up!" attitude that precedes the attempt at a comeback; towelling off (if the referee let's you—it's illegal); wiping the glasses; and the prematch heating or cooling of the ball. This little passage cannot begin to catalogue the total resources of misguided human ingenuity.

The Weakness

There is one huge and basic fallacy in all types of gamesmanship. The gamesman, like everyone else, secretly values his reputation and the esteem of his fellow man. There are few exceptions to this statement.

Therefore he resorts to his tricks only when things are not going well. No matter what form his machinations may take, they are always an admission that he is in trouble, that he is beginning to sense that playing it straight isn't going to win for him. This should be a signal to the intended victim that he is winning and will win if he avoids the traps set with a view to breaking and diverting his momentum and concentration. Nothing so discourages a gamesman as a delay followed by superlative, aggressive play by his opponent on the very next point. If he feels his opponent is too good and also impervious to his most subtle blandishments, he is left without a hope. Often he will resign himself to "losing gracefully" and abandon whatever campaign he had in mind, stolidly submitting to the subsequent execution. Any player should look upon displays of gamesmanship as a reason for feeling encouraged as well as a warning to be alert for incidents. "He is scraping the bottom of the barrel. If I keep after him I'll win." The gamesman is admitting he is the weaker player.

Reverse Gamesmanship

It is sometimes possible (and a great pleasure) to hoist a gamesman by his own petard. The author once witnessed a classic example. One player had a slight lead. The other began to take longer between points, delaying a bit here and there, darting furious glances at his opponent, calling lets whenever possible, and generally attempting to draw attention to himself by being disagreeable, thereby diverting attention from the game. Each time the winning player waited it out, then just before serving gave his opponent a delighted smile, seeming to say, "That was really well done! I loved it! You should be on Broadway!" Then he played the point with excellent concentration. The gamesman's attitude became blacker and blacker as he redoubled his efforts to dent this genial, comradely attitude, the winner's reaction ever more pleased and beatific. In the end the loser fell apart completely, enraged less at losing than at the total futility of his effort to psych his opponent. It pays to laugh at them much more than to cry, and a frustrated gamesman is one of the funniest sights in the court. And—he knows it.

Gamesmanship Literature

The wiles of gamesmanship have long been a fertile field for conversation amongst devotees of the game. On one occasion a keen and articulate observer (one hesitates to risk libel by saying "practitioner") was moved to formalize his experiences into a short essay. The following quote from Neil Powell's monograph is included here with his blessing, and without comment beyond the remark that Neil seems to get into the spirit of the thing with more than a mere observer's enthusiasm. He not only writes well and with delightful whimsy, one also feels *he knows*!

Neil Powell on Gamesmanship in Squash

The world of sports is eternally indebted to many people for their concepts of Gamesmanship as they relate to normal, civilized athletic contests, the practice of which removes some of the element of chance from victory, and which has been defined as "how to win without actually cheating." In underworld circles it is known as the "equalizer." Very little attempt has been made, to date, to formally describe the variations of this technique as it applies to the game of squash racquets, although it has been used with devastating effect by all the better players since the inception of the game. Squash racquets is to Gamesmanship what a culture of agar is to a colony of bacilli. There seems to be a direct relationship between the degree of civilization inherent in any given game and the incidence of Gamesmanship. It is significant that a leading anthropologist remarked, on seeing his first squash match, that this game was further conclusive proof that we're not long out of the trees. One thing is certain: the player who attempts serious competitive squash without employing Gamesmanship is as underequipped as a modern rifleman armed with only a crossbow.

What then is this open sesame to victory? Many otherwise finished squash players are content to perfect their strokes, footwork, basic tactics, and physical condition only to find themselves unranked at the end of the year. This limited concept of the game can only result in a discouraging proportion of defeats. Indeed, the only time victory may be tasted without Gamesmanship occurs when the opponent is a class or two inferior, or, in that isolated instance when a player may be vulgarly described as "being in a trance"—that is, when, through no special effort on his part, the majority of his shots in a given match terminate in a "nick."

Let us proceed now to an orderly consideration of the various classic gambits, or ploys, as one might term them.

I Prematch Gamesmanship

1. This takes place in the locker room and is probably the most difficult for the novice to detect, but when used by an expert

it is unquestionably the most effective form. It is hard for the average, decent, clean-cut athlete to believe, the first time he experiences it, that his affable, smiling host-opponent would take ten minutes to apply an Ace bandage laboriously to a knee which is completely uninjured. (This use of the bandage can be overplayed, however, as evidenced by the following incident witnessed during the past season. As the player applied the bandage, a teammate on cue, asked him how his knee felt. He replied carelessly, "Oh, pretty well, now that the cast is off.") One final word of caution in this particular bandage gambit: if you're going to attempt this, find out in practice on which knee it feels most comfortable, and *stick to that leg*. Your opponent may be building up a dossier on you for future matches.

2. A Bandaid applied to the racquet hand in the presence of the opponent is usually worth a couple of points in a game, as well as use of the racking cough, the blinding hangover, and the three-hundred-mile drive.

3. Regulation of court temperature is a must for any club with team championship aspirations, and contrary to popular belief, this does not require a degree in thermodynamics—although it helps. It consists simply of keeping a chart of the mean average court temperatures of opposing clubs and making very sure that the guest team gets the opposite of its normal conditions. One local club has a court which is known as the "Meat Locker," used as a battleground only for hot court guests. Another club has gone to considerable trouble to install ducts by which the steam room and swimming pool air can be exhausted into the exhibition court in a matter of minutes by simply throwing a switch.

II   The Warm-Up

1. Never tip your hand in warming up. If you're a hitter, show your opponent a lot of soft finesse, the sloppier the better. It's good practice to allow your opponent practically no opportunity to hit the ball. Pound three down the wall to yourself, then break a roll corner across to him, playing for the nick, of course. (Just a word here. You'd better have your own ball along in case your opponent is a sorehead. You may find yourself warming yourself up alone with your own ball if you let the situation get out of hand.)

2. If the opportunity presents itself, turn on a ball that breaks wide behind the red line, without warning, and bury it between your foe's shoulder blades. You'll find that when play gets underway, he will be alternately flattened against the back wall or mentally digging a fox hole in the floor every time you start your backswing.

3. If you are a member of the host team, you will improve your position immeasurably by a verbose explanation of the local regulations regarding the ball striking the lights during play; that is, a let will be played if the ball strikes either one of the front lights on a rebound from the front wall; but not on a ball going straight to, or bounding off the sidewall toward the front wall. Improvise anything you like about the rear lights. Just make it fast and complicated. You are now ready for the payoff.

III   The Match Proper

1. If you have carried out the above hints, the match is already in the bag. If, however, you do not establish a commanding lead fairly easily, run into the back wall on a ball that's hit past you, being careful to extend your racquet so that its entire length will strike the wall simultaneously with a resounding clatter. Slump to the floor. Close your eyes and check your fundamentals.

2. It is barely possible that your opponent is working on you, too. In this event, the best actor usually wins. Following is a list of suggestions that have pulled out many a close match:

a. The Hurt Look. This is used when your opponent has legitimately backed you off and has made his best put-away. The effectiveness of the hurt look lies in the chance that your opponent may glance at you after the put-away. Seeing your expression, his better nature may trap him into offering you a let on the chance that he may have blocked you. If he does, quickly accept it. If you hesitate an instant, saying, "Well, maybe you couldn't have gotten to the ball," the truth may dawn on him that you're not entitled to the let, and he'll agree with you and take the point which he'd earned in the first place. Use the hurt look automatically on every point you lose, and you'll develop a nice spontaneity, in time. The best counter to the hurt look is, of course, to avoid looking directly into your opponent's eyes during the match.

b. The Back-Step Pinion.   As you finish your shot, step back quickly coming down heavily on your opponent's toes. Maintain a firm, even pressure for a second or two, allowing him to struggle a bit. The stylists in this particular technique usually work in an apology as the victim roars by, insuring maximum distraction.

c. The Inadvertant Groan.   If you have hit a setup, you can turn adversity into success by uttering a carefully timed groan just as your foe is measuring the ball for the kill. The Groan may be alternated with the Barely Audible Curse.

d. Crowding, or the Move-In.   This is not for the timid. It is calculated to separate the men from the boys. This method consists of standing so close to your opponent that he cannot complete his follow-through without striking you with his racquet. It is a well established fact that the striker is usually more upset than the strikee (especially if there is a gallery) and as many as five quick points can be picked up before your adversary can get his mind back on the game. Under no circumstances attempt this daring maneuver without the proper research on the length, severity, and particularly the terminal height of the racquet on completion of the follow-through of the several opponents you will meet during the season. A catcher's mask may be worn in practice, if desired.

e. Lensmanship.   This ploy will round out your bag of tricks by giving you a legal excuse for stalling by cleaning your lenses. All you need is a pair of eye glasses and a hand towel. The player who is handicapped by perfect vision need have no hesitation about going out and buying a pair of shatterproof spectacles with automative safety glass for lenses. A study of the local players ranked for the last ten years reveals that 80 percent never wore glasses until they became A players. In fact, one of this group admitted that he played for ten years with no lenses at all, while another revealed a set of cross hairs on the glasses which he used to line up his corner shots.

So, now you're ready for the tournament circuit. If you don't improve by 10 points a game in a season, this game is not for you.

Summary

1. Because both players occupy the same space, squash is a difficult game to play cleanly yet competitively.

2. Clearing takes precedence over position. Hitting and standing is poor conduct if it impedes an opponent.

3. All players should practice the moving drills (29 and 30, in chapter 15), and should study illustrations 15.5–16.1.

4. You should make calls, not avoid them.

5. It is bad manners to argue a let.

6. Squash is called "the gentleman's game" because you are on your honor, with no referee, to play straight and call them straight.

7. Retaliation against cheating is the poorest answer.

8. Firmness without retaliation *is* the answer.

9. Gamesmanship is not recommended but is a fun subject.

17

Women's Squash

Women are opposing the male prerogative in sports, and it is just as apparent in the small world of squash racquets as in the more publicized areas such as tennis. Wherever the game is played, the expansion of women's teams and women's leagues is obvious. The general participation by women is growing. The original patronizing tolerance of the men, usually taking the form of faint amusement, is beginning to be replaced by interest and even respect. The astonished exclamation, "Hey! She can really play the ball!" is becoming more common (and less astonished) as women move from rank beginners towards competence. It is clear that while a lot has happened, the most is yet to come. The statistical line on the graph has only moved a little way, but it is pointed almost vertically upwards.

The Difference

This chapter is very short, not because women's squash is considered of small significance but because everything in the book applies equally to both sexes, so the only justification for a separate chapter is the need to point out one area in which women's play varies sharply from men's play. Since the drive towards excellence in squash has only recently begun amongst the women, it is natural for them to seek to imitate the men. In general, this is the best course for them to pursue until they have established themselves, but following blindly without any discrimination is not advisable.

Power

Most men are much stronger than women. A great many of their tactical maneuvers are based on being able to play the ball very sharply, so the ball, though aimed fairly low, will go far back into a corner. Most women cannot do this. They simply cannot hit the ball hard enough to get the desired depth without aiming much higher. By aiming where they see the men aim they merely make a continuous series of medium short balls that are the easiest possible shots for an opponent to play. This is the kind of imitation that is profitless because it misses the point.

Depth and Height

The man's objective is not to achieve a certain optimum miles-per-hour in the speed of the ball. His objective is to force his opponent back into a corner. If the court is very "dead" (i.e., a slow front wall), he will aim higher. A very hard hitter will aim lower than a player of average strength in any court. The tactical objective is to get the ball deep. Since women (with some but not many exceptions) cannot get much speed on the ball, they should use height on their drives far more than men. The ball will then go deep unless it is very feeble indeed. They should imitate the men's tactical objective, not their means of doing it, since that requires a degree of power that most women just don't have.

A good player has an effective "long game"—wide depth—and a "short game"—little front wall shots. The primary consideration is where the ball goes, not how fast it gets there. Women should think in these terms, and aim their long shots high enough so they actually are long rather than ineffective half-length shots.

The Old Pro's Game

Elderly professionals often play surprisingly well. They no longer have the energy of youth to streak the ball along the walls. How is it, then, that they can enter the court and totally confound most of the young fire-eaters who take them on? They do it with a judicious use of height, so that without blasting the ball they nevertheless can put it far back into the corner, and can also drop it very short. They use no more power than most women possess, yet they can defeat everyone up to class A tournament players. Women should give this much thought. It is what they *can* do that's important, not what they might wish to do but can't.

Brains

The old pro plays a "brainy game." In this department women need make no concessions to the men. Women should, from the outset, stress intelligent play and forget about the noisy power that characterizes the average man's game. The brainy game requires skill, "touch," and a clear understanding of how to use the long ball, the walls, and the short shots. It does not require much power.

The Exception

Now and then a woman appears in the game of squash who, like a few in tennis, can hit very hard. Such a woman should not be inhibited by anything said in this chapter, which is directed at women of average strength rather than those women who, indeed, can successfully play a powerful game.

The Half-Lob

The technical skill needed to implement the brainy game involves learning to play what might be called a half-lob. It is a ball that is played from four to eight feet above the telltale (roughly from two feet below to two feet above the service line) just hard enough so it will carry back somewhat behind the floor service line before bouncing, so it goes all the way back but doesn't come out much if at all off the back wall. A player must learn to use the sidewalls, so the ball is on or near the wall as it approaches the floor service line. This makes it difficult to volley, and an opponent is forced back deep.

The height on the front wall should vary with each individual. The stronger the player, the lower the shot may be and still have good depth. This is the skill the old pro always has: the ability to hit what, in terms of men's squash, might be termed a half-speed shot and yet inhibit a cut-off volley and get good depth. He continually plays these harmless looking shots and yet the opponent has great difficulty in doing much with them. Even if the opponent vollies it is hard to put away, and if he doesn't volley, the ball goes way back and often cramps him into making a poor shot from the back corner. At once the pro tweaks a drop or a corner and has his opponent running all over the court.

Men Do It Too

Many men who lack power adopt this game and enjoy surprising success. A true coaching story will illustrate. A young man came out for the Harvard team. He was short, somewhat rolly-polly in build, could not "break a paper bag" as they say, was only moderately fast, seemed to have little talent beyond a good natural touch and quick hands. He loved the game and was very competitive. He was also astute, and totally determined to make the team if there was any way he could do it. For a long time he was frustrated as he tried to out-muscle stronger opponents. The coach at first wrote him off in his mind as just not having enough natural ability to make a good team. But the coach also hated to see so dedicated a person fail in his objective. What could he do for this boy? Finally the light dawned, and the coach taught him the old pro's game: forget power, just think of where you want the ball to end up, use the walls, and get it there. The boy made the team, and in one match came up against a first string tackle who was a foot bigger and blasted every ball like a cannon. It was Mutt (a very husky Mutt) against a Jeff that looked hopelessly outranked. The contrast was almost ludicrous, as his opponent's shot made a loud wham followed by a faint tap as he played his creepy wall floater in reply. Finally one of the big fellow's furious shots would be wild and come out into the open. Again there was the tiny tap—even fainter—as the ball was dropped deftly up front. The little fellow won the match decisively without losing a game, a clear case of mind over matter, and the realization of the goal he had set for himself—to prove he could be a good player. Power is loud, obvious, impressive, very athletic, and seemingly irresistible to a green player. Brainy play is subtle, often not obvious except to experienced observers. It is there for clever women if they will make it their target. It is "their thing" if they will see it and pursue it. And just think how much smoother it is to use a slim rapier rather than a great bludgeon!

Summary

1. Women's squash is booming.
2. The game is the same as for men with one great exception: most women have less power.
3. They should play a brainy game, use height to get depth, and not try to play a power game, if they don't have the strength for it.

18

Spectating

Squash racquets is an exciting game to watch even if the observer is unschooled in the more sophisticated tactics of advanced play. There is so much running, turning, twisting, so many shots barely reached, and such fast exchanges that even if one understands only the rudiments it can be quite fascinating. However, the enjoyment increases in direct proportion to the increase in the viewer's depth of understanding.

The Ball Isn't Everything

The ball tends to be hypnotic, and to hold one's eye to the exclusion of all else. One of the first steps in improving your powers of observation is to learn not to watch the ball all the time, and to think in terms greater than the point being played. Some people may be interested in the technical skills. If so, they should watch the striker's racquet to the exclusion of the ball: how he prepares, conceals his intent, snaps his shot at the last moment, and spins the ball. Most spectators are not personally involved in technique, but in the drama of the match. They are interested in what a player does and why he does it—how he does it is of no concern to them. There are quite a few things for those people to watch besides the ball.

Watch the Flow

Quite often there will be an opposition of styles. One player will wish to make shots, but the other, aware of his opponent's skill, will seek to bottle him up in a back corner. If one doesn't understand what is occurring it can appear dull: all this fellow does is pound the ball into one corner. Doesn't he have any imagination at all? But a real battle is often raging. The shot maker is constantly trying to get out front where he can use his varied weapons to greater effect. The hitter is equally determined to inhibit and suppress him by the use of hard, low power, making a shot only on those rare occasions when he has a sure thing. The shot maker will try various schemes to break this bulldog grip. His opponent will be ever on the alert to counter them. If the touch player is really skillful, he will insert finesse shots now and then from behind his opponent, often precipitating a mad scramble and a crisis. The hitter will strive to cover them and maintain his position out in front, hoping to frustrate any attempt at a breakout. There is a lot of thinking and counter-thinking going on and such a match can be wholly absorbing if the spectator is truly aware.

Watch for Combinations

Almost all top players have their pet combinations. A general favorite is the hard straight drive combined with the three-wall nick. A series of drives deep to a corner can set up the nick shot by coaxing an opponent to linger a little back and over to the side where the deep ball is constantly going. The nick shot goes to the other side and as far up front as possible. If the drives persuade an opponent to hang just a half step over and a half step back, the nick will be a winner if well executed. Here again an apparently dull exchange of five or six drives down one side can actually be the essential ingredient in a scheme to create an opening. When observing such a colorless series you should always ask yourself, "What is at the back of their minds?" If they are class players each knows the other will rarely just plain miss. Each knows the other is quick and can cover almost anything. The court is small. Somehow a little extra space must be created or a winner is impossible barring outright luck such as a rare flat nick that doesn't bounce at all. The use of contrasting shots—one played constantly to create space for the other—is a policy they often adopt.

Watch for Sudden Shifts in Style

This is another ploy often used, particularly towards the end of a game, in an endeavor to gain an element of surprise for a short time. A player may be using the lob serve and be playing very conservatively in the rally, employing hard drives, volleys, and few finesse shots. All of a sudden, at about 11–all in points, he will shift to a very hard service and will make a short shot off of almost every open ball. His hope is that he will win the game before his startled opponent can adjust to this complete switch in tactics. A great many fine players do this, fighting hard and staying with their opponents, yet holding back for a final burst when the chips are down.

The opposite shift can be equally effective. A player who builds a lead by the use of finesse shots may find, after awhile, that his shots are being covered every time no matter how finely he cuts them. If he is astute he will shift to using depth. He will set up quickly, threaten the shot, but hit deep. He can often catch his opponent anticipating the short ball and pass him. As in the use of combinations it is the use of the front and back of the court in contrast to each other that is the secret of match play between two fine players. If a spectator can keep track of the flow of the play so that the reasons for the shifts are perceived, a match is far more interesting to follow. You can see not only the physical scrambling and shot making but also the changes in style that cause the initiative and control to swing from one player to the other. Being aware of the thinking that is occurring is the test of sophisticated spectating. What happens on this particular point is tied up closely with the context of preceding points, even games.

Top Play Is Mental

All the best players are conditioned, fast, strong, and, for the most part, have the ability to play short or long. The decisive factor is thinking: how do they put it together, how do they vary the emphasis on this or that, and how alert are they to counter similar planning by their opponents. Once a spectator reaches a level of sophistication that permits him to comprehend the thinking as well as the actual play, he will fully appreciate what a subtle and fascinating sport squash racquets can be. Of course many matches are routine, but a really good one between two tough athletes who are also thinkers, is a spectacle that is unexcelled in the world of sport.

19

Some Great Players

A hundred times I have been asked, "Is this champion as good as so-and-so used to be?" This is an unfair question. The champion has beaten everybody. How can anyone do better than that? When a player becomes champion he has reached the top of the mountain. There is no way he can go higher. If these other supposedly greater players were here today, and pushed him to climb even higher, who can say he wouldn't do it? Any player who achieves the number one status in the game deserves to be applauded without any cheapening reservations such as, "This was a weak year."

There is one test, however, which sets some champions apart even from their fellow winners. That is that they win more than once. There is no way one can impeach the record of a repeat winner. Surely there are flukey tournaments in which a great player suffers injury and a dark horse wins, or two great players so weaken each other in the semifinals that the winner is only half there in the final match and is upset by an underdog. But a champion who repeats has driven the nail all the way home and silenced his critics. Typical of these was Ben Heckscher. He won the championship in a final match over Henri Salaun in which people felt Salaun had been disturbed by some altercations with the referee. After listening for a couple of years to gossip about "a fluke," Ben apparently became irked. He mounted a campaign of training, peaked for the Nationals, and won it again. Since that time the doubters have been notably silent. Ben was very strong, about as fast in the court as anyone the game has known, had a very good

233

touch and was a fierce competitor under any pressure. Getting a point from him was like pulling a crooked wisdom tooth—it wouldn't come.

This chapter is personal, subjective, and limited. My reminiscences are confined to what I know; therefore I necessarily omit, neglect, and fail to do justice to many fine players. For instance, I was never a spectator at matches played by Myles Baker, Stanley W. Pearson (six times champion) and those who preceded Pearson as amateur champions; nor did I ever watch Tully, Ramsay, Warzycki, Chassard, Kerim, or Widelski amongst the pros (between them they won thirteen pro titles). Therefore I wish to emphasize at the outset that the chapter is not offered as a history of all the best players. The objective is to give enough of a picture to illustrate the fascinating diversity of styles which can carry a player to great heights of excellence. It is hoped that the reader's concept of the richness of the inherent possibilities of the game will be broadened and that perhaps the enjoyment of squash as a spectator sport will be enhanced. To treat all great players with equal justice would require a separate book (and a great deal of research). It would be a fine thing if someone would write such a book, comparable to *Kings of the Court* in the field of tennis literature. Therefore I repeat: the omission of any player here is merely an admission of ignorance, not to be taken as an unfavorable judgment.

Going Back—Palmer Dixon

My experience does not go back beyond Palmer Dixon, the first champion coached by Harry Cowles. He was a master at taking command of the court, making no errors, and keeping his opponent out of position until the point came his way. He was one of the most difficult players to get out of the center, and he was so quick that a winner was scarcely to be thought of unless one did get him out. Of all sound percentage players who without an instant's hesitation made the right shot on every occasion, Palmer Dixon was probably the most solid. He won the title twice in succession.

Herby Rawlins

This man, the next "Cowles Champion" was totally different. He was one of those very rare players—a "pretty" player who was also tough. He is often referred to as the game's greatest stylist. He used his quickness to set up instantly for every shot, so that he seemed always to wait quite a while before he played the ball. Having a magic touch that made every possible finesse shot from anywhere in the court, as well as a flair for deception that rivalled that of Harry Cowles, his coach, Rawlins played with a maddening smoothness that made any opponent appear clumsy and inept by comparison. He was a total delight to watch in the court, never hurrying, waiting on every shot, controlling the ball with impeccable accuracy, out-thinking his opponent continually with double threats and last instant turns of the racquet. He did it all with such relaxed physical ease one scarcely realized he was actually trying. Of course he was concentrating intensely, sensing with never-ending astuteness just what his opponent most feared, threatening to do it, then doing the exact opposite. No one ever "twisted" people more inexorably than Rawlins, unless it was his mentor, Cowles. He continually persuaded even the best to take a wrong step only to have to reverse themselves violently to go the other way. There is no punishment in the game more severe than this, an isometric wrench as a player fights his own momentum. Rawlins won the title twice and is remembered with admiration by those privileged to watch his truly artistic exhibitions of skill.

Larry Pool

The following "Cowles champion" was the elder of the two Pool brothers, J. Lawrence Pool. He was often referred to as a slugger, but the term does him only limited justice. He hit very hard down the walls, and retrieved indefatigably, but he was also quite capable of executing a neat little corner shot on those occasions when his opponent chose to linger too far back. Above all his strokes were so sound and grooved that one felt he could play five games, hit every ball hard if he wished, and never make an error. Larry was one of the toughest players who ever competed. In the finals of his second championship he was up against the brilliant Philadelphia player, Don Strachan. Strachan led 14–10 in the fifth game, but Pool only played harder. Then a famous "let" occurred, which has long been a subject of controversy. Pool made a poor shot that came around off the back wall and Strachan backed off, boxing Pool dead against the forehand sidewall. Strachan blasted it down the backhand side, hoping for the clincher. But after playing the ball he continued to hold his follow-through fully extended, so Pool was hindered in starting across the court. Pool bumped into his arm, then ducked down under it (it was still there), and dashed for the ball. Strachan's shot came off the back wall and could have been retrieved, but Pool had been delayed too long, and held up his finger as he tried, too late, to play it. The referee hesitated, then decided that since the ball came off it could have been retrieved, and awarded the let. In my opinion, it was a tough but correct decision, because the ball did come well off the wall (I saw it clearly) and any fast man, unimpeded, could have dug it up. If the ball had laid down, a let would have been a great injustice to Strachan, but it didn't. Pool went on to win—by only one point. It is nice to report that Strachan won the title twice in later years. It is a tribute to both that they played possibly the most exciting final on record—they were both great champions.

Beekman Pool

Many thought Larry Pool was the hardest hitter the game would see. His accurate streaking drives appeared to have reached the ultimate in a style of play that suppresses all opposition with infallible and unremittent depth. But Beekman Pool hit harder—much harder. He continually broke the ball, so that when I was privileged to score a match for him I always made sure I had at least six in reserve (this was in the days when the ball did not break easily). He hit so hard it became a problem. Even a ball a couple of inches above the tin would come off the backwall and be easy to retrieve. That coaching genius Cowles substituted cheap dead silk for gut in his racquet, and he became invincible. The ball went like a streak of light—and was dead. His service was so fast it frequently hit the quickest players on the fly for a point. At other times it rebounded so fast they couldn't catch up to it. It was very hard to volley it because it was so fast, and he had a good eye for the nick if one did not volley. And Pool was not without other resources. Every now and then he would leave his opponent far back, worrying about another streaker, by flicking a little reverse corner or drop shot. Beek was far from being a mere slugger.

Beeky hit so hard that it led to some amusing incidents. On one occasion he was playing his hardest and the ball hit a drop of sweat and the instant skid caused him to miss it completely. There was no sound of impact, but his racquet made a distinct *voove* noise as it whistled through the air, much like a violent wind in telephone wires. The gallery broke up and Beek joined in the laugh. It resembled a Disney cartoon sound effect. On another occasion he streaked a straight backhand that his opponent barely retrieved. It set up again on Pool's backhand. The first backhand had seemed to be about as fast as humanly possible, but Beek apparently thought, "I'm not hitting it hard enough." The next one went much faster, so fast to the same place that his opponent, although he was still standing there and the ball went dead right at his feet, couldn't flick his racquet fast enough to get under it. He threw up his hands and remarked, "You can't hit what you can't see."

Along with this awesome power Pool trained until he was in iron condition, retrieved endlessly when in trouble, and could keep increasing the pressure up, up, up, until he topped the opposition's best attempts to stay with it. In 1932, he won every major tournament in North America. He won the national title twice, but did not wish to continue the rigorous practice and training without which he would tire himself out, from heavy hitting, in a couple of games. At his peak he most certainly represented the "irresistible force."

Don Strachan

The Philadelphians were great challengers to Cowles pupils during this era. Don Strachan was one of their greatest. His backhand, a powerful flawless stroke, was a byword in the squash world, and his deadly eye made him one of the game's all-time best shot makers. He was a total pressure player, perhaps the most aggressive the game has known in going for the throat with every stroke. He played as though he had never heard that conservative phrase "keep the ball in play." Every shot seemed labelled "death—right now!" If he made a fine shot and the ball came back, the next one was an even better shot. He did not hesitate to take the risk of striking out for a winner on the dead run. Glidden defeated him in 1936 by rushing him so fast that Strachan could not get set to aim his death-ray shots, but Glidden told me afterwards that he won three straight and was ahead all the time, but every instant he could feel this awful *thing,* right there, ready to be unleashed if he gave it the slightest chance. Glidden wasn't kidding. When Don Strachan rolled it was like a scythe. He was always a leading threat, won the Nationals in 1934 and 1939 and a host of other titles. A truly great player, when really "on" he was awesomely impressive to watch.

Neil Sullivan

If few could compete with Strachan's backhand the same could be said for Sullivan's forehand. Sharp and deadly accurate, he could place this stroke anywhere in the court, short or long. A fine tactician and a great competitor, Sullivan was a leading contender for many years in all major events. He won the Nationals once, came close other times, and won many other titles. The Harvard players greatly feared Strachan and Sullivan. Much time was spent analyzing and planning how to cope with their deadly attacks. If the Cowles pupils came out on top a little more than half the time, it was only by a hair and after the most homeric struggles. The Strachan-Sullivan era is a proud chapter in Philadelphia squash, and it is to be hoped someone will do them fuller justice than I could hope to accomplish since I only saw them intermittently in a few tournaments. This was enough to show me their outstanding class.

Germain G. Glidden

"G3," as he is affectionately known, was perhaps the most extraordinary player in the history of the amateur game. He brought to it a combination of mental and physical talents that has not been seen before or since. He was quick almost beyond belief, but almost all champions have the attribute of excellent mobility. Germain's mind and hand were as quick as his legs. He carried the knack of aggressive anticipation to a height not seen before or since. He often seemed to play as much as four feet in front of the red line—and yet he was seldom passed. Stewart Brauns made a great crack when he remarked that Glidden was the first man he had ever seen volley with one foot on the telltale. In addition to this speed of foot, mind, and hand, Germain had a beautiful touch. His corners, drops, and three-wall knicks were deadly. His strokes were sound.

Aided by the great insight of Harry Cowles, Glidden combined these talents into a tactical style that was an innovation in itself. It was based on tempo. His anticipation enabled him to be on the other fellow's shot and play it almost before he had completed his follow-through. A person could listen, without watching, and hear a peculiar sequence of hits: the opponent's ball would strike the front wall and almost at once Glidden's reply would be heard. A slight interval would occur, then the two hits again. It was hit, hit, pause—hit, hit, pause. This would often end with a scramble involving a mad series of rapid hits, usually ending in a groan from a frustrated opponent.

Volleying everything wasn't enough. At every opportunity Glidden would use the front wall, running his man up, then anticipating to run him instantly back, then up again. His anticipation was so keen that even if he made a poor front wall shot, he would often convert an opponent's "kill" into a deep forcing shot of his own. He used the three-wall nick more than any player before or since, as a means to force this up-and-back play even on those who tried to suppress him with steady depth. With most players this would have been unsound tactics, giving an opponent too many chances out front. With Glidden, who could cover his mistakes with incredible retrieving and anticipation, it became a major weapon. Particularly near the end of a match, if an opponent became even a little slowed up, Glidden would precipitate crisis after crisis that made it impossible for the victim to slow the pace. Up, up, up went the tempo until no one could stay with it.

Many observers did not understand Glidden's excellence. "He doesn't seem to hit the ball unusually well." "I think so and so has more deadly drives." This was true. The virtue of his play was in the cumulative effect of time pressure. Every opponent gradually became hurried and harassed, unable to set up to make his best shots, and unable to win a majority of the crisis situations brought about by Glidden's use of the front wall from all over the court. Every tough match developed, not into a grim exchange of basic drives leading to a weak return and a crisis, but rather, into a mad whirling dervish up-and-back scramble—a mess of quick volleys, shots, and nicks that seemed all wrong but was somehow unbeatable. People used to ask, "How does he win with that crazy game?" Crazy—yes—like a fox.

"G3" won the national championship three times in a row, then announced that three times is enough and retired undefeated. When he reached the age of forty he won the Veteran's title three times in a row, and again retired undefeated. In between he won the National Doubles title with Dick Remsen, a former Dartmouth number one player.

Many have opined that Glidden's success was based on sheer talent. Certainly he was a superathlete in terms of iron condition, mobility, and intuitive competitive ability. But he also had what all champions have: desire, determination, persistence, and the guts to overcome major obstacles. When he reached Harvard he had a totally unsound backhand. He couldn't win a game from any A player who had sense enough to press this glaring weakness. He worked daily, for three entire seasons, on changing his whole stroke radically until he emerged, late in his junior year, with a really sound stroke. It was only after this was accomplished that he scored his first big tournament win, the Boston Open.

It is very difficult for a prep school star to accept that he must start all over again, like a beginner, and learn how to play the ball in an entirely new way. Germain, being human, didn't like the idea. I finally told him, "Look—I'll play you and agree to hit every ball to your backhand no matter what other chances I have, and you won't win a game." "You can't do it!" he blazed. But I did—rather easily, too. That's how bad his technical deficiency really was. When he recovered from this humiliation he gritted his teeth and admitted defeat. But then he asked me what he had to do. We started, right then, on the long grim road of total change. Improvement was very gradual—everything was strange and against all his well entrenched muscle habits. But, inspite of an occasional emotional cry that he couldn't do it, he tried and he did. His senior year his backhand could stay with anybody's, the yawning gulf in his technique had been bridged, and there was no stopping him. His teacher was one of his early victims as he beat me 3-2 in the finals of the Boston Open.

The road to the top is always rocky. People watching a great champion never see what is underneath—the obstacles overcome, the determination, and the hard labor that eventually produces a finished product that looks smooth and invincible in the court. Every champion is a human being who began by being far from perfect, but who had the inner drive to overcome all obstacles, even if, as with Glidden's backhand, it was like chewing granite. Like all great champions, "G3" had real character, and would not have otherwise got to the top.

The impression that Glidden's game was "all talent" is extremely superficial. Underneath the dazzling physical display was great imagination, unusual intensity, a touch of wild, but disciplined, Irish daring, a blazing will to win, and that indefinable but indispensable quality we call "character."

Arthur Willing Patterson

In 1940, when Glidden had retired and Strachan was getting on in years, a new generation of Philadelphians was emerging. Stanley Pearson and Charlie Brinton were the new duo, but before they reached maturity the old guard had one more word to say. Willing Patterson had played number two behind Beekman Pool at Harvard in 1932. In that year Pool was at his greatest and won almost all the tournaments he entered—except one. Patterson beat him in the final of the Harvard University Championship in a tremendous battle of power against persistence. It was a surprise to all, except those who knew him well, when he won the title in 1940 over a tough field. Patterson combined excellent conditioning with total soundness and great cool—he never rattled. If he had not been a little overshadowed by Pool he would have enjoyed much greater fame. There was nothing extraordinary about his game. He just had an all-round toughness that would give way to nothing less than great brilliance. He always seemed to be fighting "up" to flashier players, but he also always seemed to win eleven out of twenty-one points. As a boxing critic once said about Rocky Marciano that he wasn't a great boxer, didn't have an impressive style, couldn't hit as hard as some others, and wasn't really fast on his feet—he beat hell out of everybody who went with him into the ring. Patterson was that kind of player, and no one knows it better than the group of us who attended Harvard with him.

Charles M. Brinton, Jr.

Charlie was the ideal champion. Not very large, neat, wiry, quick, and sharp, he was exactly what one would expect a champion to be. A gentleman on and off the court, his fluid strokes and classy style of play were a joy to behold. Many of his drives were masterpieces, played with pistol shot crispness and so accurate they would glue to the wall after bouncing. His reverse corner was made with so decisive a last instant flick that often his opponents were caught flat. Like Rawlins, he was a master at positioning himself so quickly that he always seemed able to wait before striking the ball. People still argue, "Who had the best backhand—Strachan or Brinton?" Certainly Charlie must rank with the top stylists of all time.

The quick positioning that makes possible a long deceptive wait before playing is a very difficult art. It is a simple concept, but requires twinkle toes footwork and an absolutely dead-eye judgment of an opponent's shot the instant it leaves his racquet. Any player will jump into position quickly, but nine out of ten won't get it just right—they get it roughly right but must then make further adjustments. Not Brinton. With one hop and a flick of his feet he would come down in perfect position, racquet cocked, crouched, waiting for the ball, with plenty of time to make his play with deadly, fastidious perfection and with a preparation that never gave a clue as to what that play would be. Charlie had heavy black eyebrows, and when they drew together in intense concentration it was time to take to the hills. Like Strachan, he was truly lethal.

Many observers opined that Brinton won just through technical excellence. Nothing could be more superficial. He was an absolute master at combining long and short shots, setting up a fear of his depth in an opponent's mind by cracking his setups, then at the perfect moment flicking the short one. He seemed to have antennae in the back of his head that could read his opponent's thought—and he played the opposite way. It made the game look easy, as his hard drives forced weak returns which were put away, after that wait, with such smooth deception.

To this I must add that Brinton was a great match player. He was capable of a prolonged intensity of concentration, and he never until near the end of a game put all his chips on the table. Many a game was decided in his favor by the fact that he switched to the hard serve and put it right in the crack or rushed his man into sloppy play just when the crisis was at hand in the last few points. He was very keen to vary the emphasis from long to short or vice versa if he sensed his opponent was ripe for a change. Few players, if any, outthought him in the court. Competitors don't come any tougher than Charlie Brinton.

His record justifies these superlatives. He won the title in 1941 and 1942, then after three years at war won it twice more in 1946 and 1947. Four in succession, like Glidden's three in a row, qualifies for the very top.

Stanley W. Pearson, Jr.

Like Willing Patterson, Pearson was a truly fine player who had been held down by a teammate at Princeton, namely Brinton. With another of those inimitable Philadelphia backhands, great strength, speed, and endurance (he was a star halfback in school), Pearson played a hard game that swept the field in 1948. He also had a great rivalry with his friend Brinton and ran him close on almost every occasion. Again, like Patterson, Pearson was not truly appreciated (who esteems number two?) until he won the title and put his name on the list of the best.

H. Hunter Lott, Jr.

Another in this string of Philadelphians, Lott had been a prominent player for years without quite winning the big one. His forehand was so good everybody stayed away from it as though it were poison, which it was. Unfortunately Lott's backhand was not quite top class, and this had tripped him up repeatedly in the biggest matches. It was by no means bad, but it was also not really forcing, not good enough to sustain the top pressure he could apply with his forehand. But, in 1949, he perfected a rarely used shot, the true boast which hits both sidewalls before dripping off the front wall. Suddenly there was a lethal double threat where before there had merely been steadiness. There was no longer a weaker side to which a harassed player might resort for some relief. He swept the tournament and for that particular year was a great player, reminiscent of Strachan and Brinton in the deadly aggression of his play.

Edward J. Hahn

Detroit had never been heard from in terms of top squash. All of a sudden here was this fellow Ed Hahn, with neither the Philadelphia style nor the Harvard coaching system, winning the Nationals in 1950. It must be a fluke! But it was totally convincing in 1951 when he beat none other than Salaun in the final to repeat. What did this fellow have? Ed had a straight wide mouth that turned up a bit at the corners. His eyes always twinkled as though he were ready to smile and enjoy a joke. He was totally calm, infinitely patient, steady as a rock, and a master tactician. Ten, fifteen times he would force his man back deep, preferably on the backhand side, anticipating all returns and putting them back there again. Finally, just as one was thinking, "Doesn't he *ever* do anything else?" he would slip a neat, beautifully unexpected shot around the corner for a winner. He never hauled off and hit a backhand to end all backhands like Strachan or Brinton. He never rushed his man ferociously, like Glidden, or powdered the ball, like Pool. In fact, he didn't seem to do much of anything, except—the ball always went out of the center, it always had just enough pace to prevent a volley, it always had good depth. And there was Ed, absolutely always in the dead center of the court, invulnerable in his perfect control of position. People used to say, "I don't see what's so good about *him*"—that is, until they played him. And, of course, there was always that Irish twinkle and slight imperturbable smile on his jolly face as he inexorably ground down the shot makers, the hitters, and the retrievers alike. Ed Hahn was like a glacier. He didn't seem to be going anywhere very fast but he always got there; and he made you love him, too.

Harry Conlon

This boy was the son of a Buffalo professional. He was skinny to the point of emaciation, but what there was of him was all wire. He had a spidery quickness that made him a tremendous retriever, and big strokes that whistled the ball with great speed. He had a famous trick, when up front, of turning his back to the ball just as he played a corner shot, staring at his opponent with his mouth slightly open and his eyes large and wide. It was hypnotic—nobody ever ran for his corner shot! It also entranced the gallery. Harry won the Nationals in 1952 when very young, but Air Force commitments prevented him from maintaining his game at peak level; so one will never know what else he might have done if the opportunity was offered. Certainly his speed, strokes, and concentration were first class. The year he won the Nationals the field was very strong and his opponent in the finals was Diehl Mateer.

Earnest Howard

If Ernie let more than one ball a game go past him, he was angry. He volleyed everything—slow, fast, high, low. It was a rapid-fire game that kept him always on top of his opponent, never giving him a moment's rest. He just kept pouring it on from the first point to the last. Like Glidden, he played a tempo game, relying on the cumulative effect of his shots rather than the individual excellence of any single stroke. He accumulated our championship and took it to Canada for the first time in 1953.

G. Diehl Mateer, Jr.

Mateer had everything: strength, stamina, power, touch, size, mobility, and toughness. Above all, he was a power player, and reminded many oldsters of the great days of the Pools. No one ever looked more impressive in the court or applied more continuous pressure throughout a match. Forehand and backhand and volley—all were very severe and well executed. He also had early training. He won the Intercollegiates in his sophomore year, figuratively, without taking off his sweater. He was obviously a coming champion, and it was freely predicted that he would win it as soon as he got out of college. But it was not that easy. Only after he experienced the pressure of top play, stopped being in love with power to the exclusion of everything else, and added that double threat—the frontwall shots—did he overcome the field. From then on the squash world was treated to a long series of terrific battles between Mateer and that great touch player Henri Salaun. The opposition of two contrasting styles made for an ideal rivalry, each playing his own game with masterful skill. Mateer always attempted to crush Salaun with overpowering force, Salaun always retrieved indefatigably, so that the next one couldn't be quite a winner, inserting deft placements of his own whenever he had half a chance. Almost always these contests were long and bitter with the issue in doubt to the end. Mateer won three Nationals, Salaun won four; Mateer won two Open titles, Salaun won one. The rivalry must be called a draw, and both must be numbered among the greatest champions, each representing the epitomy of his own style of play.

Henri R. Salaun

This man was one of the smoothest and most astute players the game has known. Henri never hit a ball harder than necessary. Every ball had just enough pace so that it could not be cut off, and his accuracy in keeping it out of the center was as near one hundred percent as a human being can achieve. His touch was fabulous—he could take a "hot" ball in the middle of a furious rally and drip it off the front wall so gently it made an opponent run the very last inch to reach it. His retrieving, patience, willingness (like Ed Hahn) to play long points, and his deft use of front wall shots put him above all other amateurs of his time except Mateer.

Salaun was small but extremely and smoothly mobile. It was always a pleasure to watch him slide back and forth at the red line, intercepting and holding position until a mistake by his opponent presented an opportunity for the use of his deft touch and astute deception. Henri's game was so effortless and inevitable that he usually won with a smooth ease that baffled almost all comers except when he was subjected to the terrific pressure of Mateer's power game at its peak. It then became a classic case of the irresistible force against the immovable object. Sometimes the object cracked a little, then broke under the sustained strain. Sometimes it gave, bent, and was reduced to a thread, but the thread held and Salaun emerged triumphant. The two had many dramatic encounters, and each was so good at his own game that predictions were useless. When two great players with sharply contrasting styles meet, the gallery is usually in for a rare treat. There were many in the Mateer-Salaun era.

Benjamin H. Heckscher

A third player muscled in to interrupt the dominance of Salaun and Mateer. Ben Heckscher was very fast—faster than either Salaun or Mateer, was very strong, had a fine touch at the front wall, and used rifle-like drives off both wings. Twice he intervened to win the championship, once over Salaun himself in the final, when he ended the match with a beautiful sidewall drop shot that fooled even the little maestro himself. Ben must be recorded as one of the toughest competitors the game has seen. In 1963, he repeated as champion in very convincing fashion, subduing the field with a pistol-shot offense sustained by an impenetrable defense. Ben at his best was about as good as they come.

Samuel P. Howe III

A new generation was now rising to challenge the long supremacy of Mateer and Salaun. The Howe brothers were the most impressive in this group of stars. Sam was a stylist and a shot maker in the finest Philadelphia tradition, bringing to the game another of those superb backhands for which the Friendly City is so famous. Like Strachan and Brinton he attacked with every shot, preferring always the calculated risk to the waiting game. Sam was not as fast in the court as someone like Heckscher, but he attacked with such consistent accuracy that few could wrest the initiative from him often enough to capitalize on this shortcoming. Sam, like the old general, "aimed to git thar fustest with the mostest" on every occasion. His attack was totally versatile from anywhere in the court, his stroking and style were impeccable, and his daring and refusal to compromise made him one of the most exciting players to watch. Sam was one of the real masters of the racquet and of the art of using every inch of the court.

Ralph E. Howe

Ralph was quite different from Sam. A superathlete in his lightning mobility, deadly with his quick volley and flickering corner shots, his style was less fluid with his use of the shorter, quicker strokes reminiscent of Glidden's. Like the latter, he seized every chance to use his quickness offensively, following one shot instantly with the next to create a tempo that rushed his opponents mercilessly at all times. Ralph won the Nationals once and also the Open. Sam won the Nationals twice. Sam won six doubles titles; Ralph five. They were both high or top seeds in all tournaments for years. Each in his way was an exciting player to watch, Sam for his beautiful execution of placements from everywhere, Ralph for his lethal quickness with foot and racquet.

Stephen Vehslage

Meanwhile a young fellow called Vehslage was winning the Intercollegiates three times in succession (the first player to accomplish this feat). Steve was quick and had very severe sliced drives off both wings. Primarily a pressure player, he literally crushed his opponents, his low powerful drives totally inhibiting their hopes for shot making until he was able himself to make a winner. Winning in this manner requires iron conditioning, and after copping the title once, Steve did not wish to make the effort to reach the peak again. Like other hard hitters before him, he knew that the only way is to initiate a long conditioning program that finally enables the player to sustain high-level pressure for ten games (two matches a day). Many hard hitters find too many other things in life that they do not wish to put aside, year after year. Steve had the distinction of defeating Niederhoffer in the final, so who can blame him for resting on his laurels?

Colin Adair

Colin was a strong man. In Montreal they called him "the bull." Big, solidly built, hardened by systematic conditioning, he pounded the ball to the back corners, stuck to his position like a barnacle to a rock, and capped it off with an unexpected, cute little corner shot here and there. He was tireless, relentless, powerful, and he never stopped coming at his man. He was the Rocky Marciano of squash—not stylish, seldom brilliant, fast but not easily swift like a Ralph Howe or a Heckscher, he was simply unvarnished fight all the way. Many have downgraded his play because he wasn't as fast as Glidden, as smooth as Sam Howe, or as deadly accurate as Brinton. But in his own way, he was a tremendous force in the court, never too tired in the fifth, always ready for the next round, afraid of no one. He was the type of champion who is always rated below his worth because he didn't have a "pretty" style. He went home to Canada twice with our title, leaving all the stylists licking their wounds.

Anil Nayar

Meanwhile a phenomenon had appeared at Harvard. A very polite young man from Bombay, India, stood in line and humbly requested permission to try out for the Freshman team. Only persistent questioning forced him to reveal that he had already twice won the Men's Championship of India, where the tough English game is played very well.

One look at the man in the court convinced any spectator that here was a future champion. Moving with the litheness of a Bengal tiger, perfectly poised at all times, flattening out like a snake to reach unreachable front wall shots, possessing already a bullet-like English forehand and a deft feathery drop shot, all he needed was an improved backhand and a little knowledge of American tactics.

Great praise is due his Indian coach, Yusuf Khan, who taught him perfect conditioning habits, impeccable court manners, and match toughness. All Harvard had to do was adapt his strokes and tactics to the American game. In his sophomore year he was Intercollegiate Champion, in his senior year National Champion. He repeated the following year, then returned to India.

As usual, inspite of mind-boggling physical talent, Nayar did not find the road to the top easy. He began to play our tournaments, and quickly reached the semis by sheer unbeatable retrieving. But these were the days of Sam Howe at his peak. Three times Nayar met him. Three times he lost 3–0. Analysis showed his thinking was impatient, nonpercentage, and gave a great shot artist too many good chances. Even with quicksilver in his feet, this was fatal against a master at exploiting opportunity such as Howe. The matches were marvellous, with the unsophisticated but mercurial Nayar retrieving impossible balls all over the court while Howe gave the gallery exhibitions of racquet artistry and tactical variations that were a separate show all by themselves. But Sam won all the games.

This was exactly what Nayar needed: to learn the percentages, how to use his service and return of service, how to press his opponent so severely that his offense would be dampened and less effective, how to use his speed aggressively rather than merely defensively, how to develop a total match plan as contrasted with merely trying hard on each individual point. As sophistication came his way, Nayar's victories became more and more inevitable. No one could make many winners against him, no one could tire him. It was merely a matter of how long it would be before one of his shots was a winner.

It is a great regret to American squash that Nayar was lost to our game. A Niederhoffer-Nayar rivalry would have been as fabulous as the great Mateer-Salaun series, as each pushed the other to ever greater heights. It is certain that even though he still was improving Nayar was one of our very great champions.

Victor Niederhoffer

Victor Neiderhoffer has been champion five times. People always want to watch him play. Anyone seeing him for the first time is frequently astonished. Having heard of his prowess they have a mental image of a terrifically fleet superathlete. Often one hears a newcomer say, "Is *that*

Niederhoffer?'' They can't believe it. Vic is not a superathlete. He is not the fastest player, or the hardest hitter, nor does he have a dashing presence in the court. He looks like just another ordinary squash player with none of the aura of a five-time champion. What has he got, and how does he do it?

Niederhoffer's assets are numerous and very real, but they are for the most part, invisible. He is a terrific competitor, asking and giving no quarter in a tournament match. Once a player got in front of him when he was leading 12–3, so he couldn't make the shot he wished to make. He played that shot, hit him with the ball, and took the penalty point. The other player asked, "At 12–3?'' "At 14–0,'' replied Niederhoffer. To many this seemed to lack sporting generosity. Vic doesn't believe in fake graciousness. Both players are in there to win, the rules are the rules and the score doesn't matter. He plays hard, *all* the time, and expects the same from his opponent.

Another great asset is long range determination. As a Freshman at Harvard he announced that he was going to be a champion at this game. Since he was a beginner who had never seen the court before Harvard, this seemed to savour of premature arrogance. To Niederhoffer it was simply a statement of fact, comparable to what any of us might say, such as, "I'm now going to the Post Office.'' He was National Junior Champion fourteen months later.

When Vic made this apparently pretentious statement he did not make it from a shallow base. He knew he would have to acquire, by long hard work, a complex and difficult technique. He knew he would have to take his lumps on the way up, since there is no substitute for experience. He also knew he was willing to make the effort. One of his mottoes is "No pain, no gain.'' He is an unbelievable worker at anything he seriously undertakes. He was just stating, "I'm going to do it,'' with a pretty deep realization of what the statement included. He has character quite similar to that of Hashim Khan in the pursuit of his objectives. He does not make casual statements.

A third great asset is comprehension. Niederhoffer realized early that anyone can talk a great game but that a tactical concept is worthless in the court unless it can be executed and executed well. He set himself to learn every shot in the game, spending a considerable time *every day* in the court by himself, perfecting what is recognized as the most versatile technique in the game today. Every thought he has in the court is also at the tip of his racquet. He is a virtuoso with his instrument. Therefore, his tactical and strategic assets know no limits beyond the game itself and his own astuteness. If there is any way to win a match and he can perceive it, he can also do it. How many players can merit the same statement? That he perceived clearly the basic need for total technical excellence when he was a seventeen-year-old Freshman is a tribute to his understanding of the broad picture in his attack on the game.

Another invisible asset is Niederhoffer's anticipation. Although, as has been said, he is by no means the fastest player, he is a great getter. No one seems able to fool him, make him run the wrong way, or outclass him. Quite a few players look more athletically impressive in the court and often put him under great pressure, but his anticipation is so keen he always stays with them until in his turn he can attack. Not since Germain Glidden has there been anyone who can intuit so infallibly what is coming next from an opponent's racquet. Vic is much faster than he looks in the court.

Undoubtedly his greatest asset is the ability to analyze and think under pressure. Most of us are great staircase wits. "I was thinking about that match. If I had used more shots I could have won." With Vic, it is usually a statement like "I realized I wasn't using enough shots, so I changed and was able to win," or "At the start I could see he was watching for my shots, so I played patiently using depth. In the third game he was hanging back more, so I pulled out the shots." The combination of being able to see the picture as clearly as if he were an unoccupied spectator plus the ability to put into effect any plan that gives promise of success makes him the most consistently formidable competitor in the amateur game today.

But Vic was not content with four national titles. "The best" qualified by the word "amateur" was not his goal. The best of all, with no qualifications, was what he wanted. The Open title had been won six times in a row by that great professional, Sharif Khan, who combined relentless power, swift retrieving, and great touch to turn back all challengers. Sharif was the established king of professional squash, and had little fear of being dethroned until age caught up with him.

Niederhoffer announced that his goal was to beat Sharif. Few thought it possible. After all, squash was Sharif's life. Niederhoffer worked over ten hours a day at his business and had to confine squash to the periphery of his preoccupations. He was strictly an amateur in the time he could allot to the game. What chance did he have against this superathlete with his iron condition and relentless polished game? But Vic did it. He ran through the streets of New York to and from work, carrying a racquet at night against the threat of the streets, and worked out daily at the Harvard Club. And in 1975 he defeated Sharif to win the Open in a great match. At one point in the match Sharif lost a contact lens, and the question of default arose. Vic immediately insisted Sharif be given whatever time was needed, since he did not wish to have it said he had defeated a handicapped opponent.

Niederhoffer won the Juniors after playing for one and one quarter seasons. He won the Intercollegiates his fourth year. He graduated magna cum laude, with a summa on his thesis. He earned a Ph.D at Chicago, incidentally winning the Nationals. He became a member of the faculty at Berkeley, giving courses on the stock market and infant behavior (are these subjects closely related?). Simultaneously (flying back and forth to New York) he founded and still presides over a vastly successful firm, Niederhoffer, Cross and Zeckhauser, that executes complicated mergers on Wall Street. Incidentally, he is a good piano player and excellent on the clarinet—two extremely demanding techniques. And, by the by, he has won our Nationals for four years and also the Open in 1975, by giving squash possibly fifteen percent of his attention.

The Professionals

There have been many great professional players. Their prowess goes far back to the days of Tom Pettitt, who dazzled the world of court tennis and found squash racquets so easy he sometimes used the leg of a chair instead of a racquet so his hapless opponent could make a game of it against him. Then there was Harry Cowles, who coached so many champions at Harvard and usually, just after they won the title, took them into the court and whipped them just to balance their egos properly. Then there was that terrific fighter, Jack Summers; the wizard volleyer Skillman; Lester Cummings and his brothers Al and George, all beautiful stylists; Ed Reid (now coach at Bowdoin), who won his third title without the loss of a game; Jim Tully who won in 1936, then repeated in 1951; Al Ramsay with numerous wins; John Warzycki; Al Chassard; Mahmoud Kerim; Ray Widelski—all these followed by the Khans (Hashim, Mohibullah, Azzim, Roshan and Sharif). There is no way these players can be treated justly without another whole book, and I am familiar with only a few. In my limited experience and strictly subjective view, a few stand out.

Harry Cowles

For immaculate footwork, perfect execution of every shot, total versatility in technique, and the power to deceive, this man has never been equalled. He was also as quick as the quickest. No one before or since has used the front wall from deep in the court with such devastating effects as Harry. He seemed able to find the nick with his drop shots from anywhere with both forehand and backhand. I once asked him, "How did you develop this game?" He replied that opponents tended to crowd and hog the center, and he found that this was impossible if they were forced to go to the front wall. His dew-drop tactic was derided until, in an exhibition, he defeated the national champion (a fearsome slugger) 3-0, and 15-0 in the third game.

When he became coach at Harvard he gave up all tournament play and confined himself to teaching. His fabulous row of champions, a record that will never be equalled, dims the fact that he could play at least as well as he could coach.

Hashim Khan

This man was written up in the *New Yorker* as a candidate for "athlete of the century." He was as fast as a mongoose and he could strike like a cobra. Like Harry Cowles, he would wait, then snap with the sharpness of a pistol or the delicacy of a floating feather. Like Harry Cowles, he kept in perfect condition, never tired, and set for himself nothing but the highest standards. When he came to this country he was past his prime, yet dominated the tournaments for several years as soon as he mastered the new game. It is my understanding that Hashim was never defeated at the English game, and for quite a time was seldom defeated at our game even though by regular standards he was "over the hill."

On one occasion he was practicing for a tournament at the Merion Cricket Club in Philadelphia. He defeated Mateer, then Brinton, then the Intercollegiate Champion Roger Campbell—one after the other without pause. There was no one else available. Hashim looked up, said, "That is all?" and left the court with no visible sign of fatigue. Someone said, "Hashim, how do you *do* it?" and he merely remarked that he was a professional. There was a certain emphasis on that word "professional" which somehow carried a world of meaning. To Hashim it meant being absolutely tops in every aspect of the game. That was his standard.

I once asked Hashim, "We all think you are very fast in the court, but, Hashim, when you were in your twenties you must have been even faster, not so?" Hashim, who never brags, looked at me quickly. Opening his eyes wide he said that he was *much* faster! One can only imagine the incredible frustration that must have been the lot of all players of the English game as they found their finest shots were, to Hashim, merely another means of keeping the ball in play.

I once had an Indian, Yehangir Jal Mugaseth, on the Harvard team. I told him tales of the wondrous exploits of Harry Cowles, of his quickness, masterful technique, analytical powers, and deception. Muggy told me that there was a man in Pakistan who was exactly like that. He was so quick he was there as soon as the ball left anyone's racquet. What he did was *wait*, and no one could know where he would put the ball. He beat everybody with ease. His name was Hashim Khan, and if he ever came to the United States, I would see. He came, I saw, and it is impossible to choose between the two. They are undoubtedly the two greatest players in my experience. Harry Cowles had the most finished technique at the American game, which Hashim learned late. Whether Hashim's speed could have overcome this could only be proved by the event. Certainly the two of them tower above all others that it has been my privilege to witness.

Professional Eras

The professional game has gone through several phases. In the earlier stages professionals were poorly paid. Some clubs had several simultaneously, and their games reached great heights of excellence through playing each other. In the pre-income-tax days it was common practice for members to wager on the outcome of matches between professionals. Often, of course, the gambler would spur on his champion by offering him a share of any winnings. With this pecuniary incentive most professionals trained hard and became terrific competitors. There were no open tournaments whereby they could achieve fame, but anyone who has played Jack Summers anytime before he was fifty will attest that these were great days for the playing pros, and anyone who has been volleyed right into the floor by John Skillman will say the same.

There followed a period when professionals acted more as teachers than players. Each was for the most part alone at his club or educational institution. There was as a rule no opposition available that could push a talented player to the realization of his full potential. That some of them, such as Ed Reid and Lester Cummings, managed to sharpen their games to true excellence is a great tribute to these champions. If they had had the opportunities provided by todays' open events there is no telling how far their games would have developed. What would Ed Reid have done? Certainly he had beautiful strokes for every shot, was a great "long point" tactician, and was fast in the court. He once won the professional title without the loss of a game in the whole tournament. He won the Boston Open twice. What more can a man do than beat everybody decisively? His legs went just before the open era arrived. Lester Cummings was another four-time winner, a beautiful stylist who coupled speed with an immaculate technique, but his day passed before open squash arrived. Al Chassard won four titles with his lithe swiftness and beautiful strokes.

The arrival of the Khans revived the concept of the "playing pro." They did not teach. They travelled about, playing exhibitions and tournaments, seldom bothered with lessons, thinking only of the excellence of their personal games. The great continual battles that characterized the days of Jack Summers and Johnny Skillman were again commonplace, open events proliferated, and there is today great opportunity for talented professionals and amateurs to go as far as their talent permits.

Mohibullah Khan is a lefty who holds his racquet very short—some say "halfway up the handle" though this is an overstatement. He is gifted with mercurial quickness, dramatic flair, and considerable imagination. He is one of the most entertaining players to watch, since he is a master at putting on a show. He varies his play at will from soft to bullet speed, inserting sudden changes, swinging at the ball hard and whiffing it on purpose only to take an instant, second swing that makes a soft drop, and he covers the court like an excited squirrel. These actions are all accompanied by appropriate facial expressions purposely varied from the lifted eyebrow to the heavy frown. His short grip, reducing the leverage of the racquet against his wrist, enables him to change the direction of his shot at the very last second. Mo dominated the professional field for about four years, even though the field became ever stronger, and is without doubt the game's greatest dramatist besides being one of its best players.

Sharif Khan

In this atmosphere of opportunity and challenge the recent and present exploits of Sharif Khan, son of the great Hashim, must rank him as one of the all time greats. Six consecutive times he won the U.S. Open (1969–1974) until finally defeated in 1975 by Niederhoffer. His other victories are too numerous to mention. He combines tremendous power with iron conditioning, and he is also extremely deceptive when near the front wall. His game is very straightforward: he applies heavy pressure, augmented by volleying at every opportunity, until something gives. His hard drives and volleys keep him continually in front of his opponents; his quickness (and he is very quick) covers anything they can do from behind him; and his condition enables him to sustain and even raise the pressure as the match goes on. Like all superplayers, he makes the game look easy, because he does it so well that it is only occasionally that anyone can give him real trouble. The shot makers are so suppressed they cannot make use of their wiles. The retrievers are kept retrieving until they fail to reach one. The power players are outpowered and out conditioned. He wins most matches with such ease that he is always fresh for the final in a big event, so he is never in a weakened condition when the big test comes. This is extremely important, since many events are weekend affairs that require two matches a day, and squash racquets is one of the most taxing games known when play is thus compressed. Upsets of favorites occur constantly because the higher seed does not have "enough left" after a difficult encounter in an earlier round. This makes the dominance of Sharif Khan truly impressive. Not only does he defeat everyone, but he does it with plenty to spare for the next, and the next, to the end. This is true greatness, from which nothing can detract. Today there is Sharif—and everybody else. In a period when there are more fine players than ever before, this is indeed remarkable.

The Future

The growth of the game assures an ever-increasing stream of talented players. Not only is the volume much enlarged, but the base has broadened. No longer is Philadelphia the source of almost all promising juniors, with the New England prep schools and Harvard the only intermittent threat. Toronto, Montreal, British Columbia, and Seattle are coming up with a stream of talented youth. The game has taken Mexico by storm, and already Juan DeVillafranca is a top-class player and two-time winner of the U.S. Intercollegiates. In particular, Toronto seems to be getting young players and giving them good training with fine professionals, so they become accomplished while still only in high school. The junior tournaments host ever-increasing numbers and the level of play improves. Good instruction is far more widespread as more and more schools, clubs, and colleges provide professional guidance.

Women's squash in particular seems to have entered on a period of rapid growth. There have been many superb female players, but seldom more than one at a time. Women's squash has been a small world that was often dominated by a single player of outstanding talent. With the present increase in numbers, it would seem inevitable that the future will bring more top-class players to the fore so that exciting duels such as the Mateer-Salaun series and the old Harvard-Philadelphia rivalry will lift the level of spectator interest to a par with men's squash.

Overall one can only be optimistic. Every indicator of play is showing marked increases: new construction; the number of clubs, schools, colleges, and Ys participating; entries in junior, men, womens, senior, professional, interscholastic and intercollegiate events; sales of balls and equipment; and inquiries received by the national office. The recent attempts to establish regulations for a ball that might be acceptable world-wide is a development with exciting possibilities, and players are hoping for standard courts and balls everywhere, as with tennis. It is quite possible squash is entering on a wholly new era that will make the past pale by comparison. While such a concept is without a doubt premature, since progress tends always to lag possibilities because of financial and other practical difficulties, it can be said that, at least for the near term, the future of the game is assured.

Recent Developments

Even while this book was being written, exciting events have transpired. Niederhoffer has turned professional and has challenged Sharif Khan for the top honors. Sharif still dominates the field but by a narrower margin. Peter Briggs, with Niederhoffer gone, won our amateur national title with impressive decision—he didn't lose a game. Now he, too, has turned professional and is one of a large group of fine pros who threaten Sharif and Vic at the top. A pro tournament is now very tough—from the first round all the way through. The increase in the number of class players is quite astonishing. There are more open events, more sponsors, more money prizes. Squash is really "taking off."

The Very Latest Is the Best

A new champion appeared in 1978 who looks to be one of the all-time greats. Mike DeSaulniers, from Canada, while a mere sophomore at Harvard, swept the U. S., Canadian, and Intercollegiate titles without the loss of even one game.

I originally stated that the like of the great Germain Glidden has not been seen "before or since." The "since" must now be eliminated. DeSaulniers has equal quickness, equal technique, and, most importantly, equally daring imagination. He volleys everything, uses all the shots constantly, and sets up such a high tempo that even the best opponents become baffled, confused, even totally overwhelmed. He turns an orderly match into a wild melee in which, after a bit, he is the only one who knows what is going on. If you would enjoy seeing an intelligent tornado operating in a squash court, watch Mike DeSaulniers. He is the most exciting player to appear since Neiderhoffer.

20

Conditioning

This subject is complex and is evolving rapidly. Every day we hear more about ingenious exercises that are good for warming up, for stamina, for special muscles, for quickness, for fast starts, for building strength, for agility (turning, twisting, reversing direction rapidly), and for warming down (after the match).

Playing

The simplest conditioning process is to play yourself into condition. This means, however, that you must play furiously—or you don't get the job done. Most people don't play that hard except in a match, so the system doesn't work. Also, this too simple approach neglects the fact that conditioning uses in general a type of overload system: it compresses into a short period of time stresses that could only be equalled by many hours of play, if at all.

Running

A second approach is running. Anyone in poor shape should start by jogging, then move up to a lope. Push yourself a little but don't overdo it. It takes time to develop stamina. After awhile you will be able to run for longer and longer—it builds up. After (not before) you have developed reasonably good stamina you can move into sprints. Harry Hopman has a famous exercise: run (lope) twenty steps, then sprint (just as fast as you can) twenty steps, then lope twenty, etc. This develops quickness and fast starts as well as putting a lot more pressure on your stamina. It should be said again: don't try this until you are already in fair or good shape. It's a killer: you must work up to it. But, in general, simply running is excellent conditioning. Note that jogging is only suggested as a means of working up to running.

Relating Conditioning to Play

A third approach is to relate the conditioning to the particular game you are playing. It is possible to develop exercises that combine building stamina plus agility. In squash racquets, agility is of supreme importance. Lots of players who have good stamina are very slow at turning, twisting, and above all at reversing direction. But this reversing process is just what a squash player must constantly do. He seldom takes more than four or five steps in any one direction—usually only two or three. He is constantly jumping to one place, then instantly back the other way: stopping, starting, turning, twisting, flattening out low, rebounding back to a more balanced stance, ever ready for another quick move. The same is true in good tennis.

One exercise that combines these factors of stamina and agility can be run with a group on any fairly large space such as a tennis court or a basketball court. Everybody lines up on one sideline. They sprint to the other sideline, touch it with their hand, reverse and sprint to the other sideline and touch it (with the hand, forcing a low bend) reverse again, etc. If this is done at top speed about twenty times, emphasizing the fastest possible reversal each time, it increases the speed of recovery on the court and also builds stamina. It is very taxing. The reversals are even more emphasized if this drill is run in a squash court.

Another even more specific exercise of this sort, which actually involves playing the ball, is found in drills 20 and 21 in the chapter on drills. The player must start fast, go up and play the ball, recover position and volley. As the player's racquet skill improves to make it possible to perform this drill fast, it is a fine conditioner and at the same time teaches advanced counter-attack tactics, fast take-off, special racquet skills, and good thinking under pressure.

Other well-known exercises are good: jump rope, push-ups, running up to the net and back on a tennis court on only one foot (that's a toughie), and jumping jacks (these work the arms too). Some stomach exercises should be included: lie on your back, with knees bent, and do sit-ups (with hands behind your head). But the best—for squash—are those exercises that actually relate specifically to action in the court.

The Warm-Up

Many players have a poor concept of what this means. They think it means practice your shots. It doesn't, it means loosen up your arms, legs, back, shoulders, and neck. Get the blood flowing to them so you are loose, pliant, and efficient when you start, as contrasted with being stiff and having that feeling, "I couldn't get going in that first game." Additionally, it is not without significance that an insufficiently warmed-up player is far more injury prone than one who is properly prepared. The point being made here, however, is that the word "warm-up" refers to you, physically, not to your skills with the racquet. There are other considerations, which will be mentioned, but this physical preparation is the primary concern.

Stretching exercises are important. You may need to rush to the front wall and flatten out for a get on the first exchange. Stretch one leg out as far as you can while bending the other knee. Then the other leg. Stand erect, hold your arms out horizontally, and twist each way at the waist as far as you can without discomfort. Swing your arm (playing arm particularly) in a full vertical circle. You can feel it pull a little under the arm as you loosen up. You can feel your arm and hand get warm as the centrifugal action aids circulation. Rotate your head in an exaggerated manner, slowly. Lift your legs as high as you can—if you are very supple, don't knee yourself in the face! When you enter the court take huge slow swings—to stretch and loosen rather than to practice technique. Continue lifting your legs (bending the knees) as you stand there.

All this sounds like a lot. It isn't. It only requires five to ten minutes to do all these things, and it makes a huge difference. The author was always known as a fast starter who played at peak skill and speed from the first point. Many asked, "How do you start like that? I can never get going instantly in a match." The answer was always, "I get myself ready, physically, as well as mentally." And, many a match is decided by who gets the jump, even as in a track meet. Of course some of it can be temperament—some people don't get involved until they've been trodden on for awhile—but a substantial part of it is certainly physical preparation.

The other aspects of warm-up have nothing to do with conditioning.

In a strange court, one should always try out the various walls—are they slow, fast, medium? Are they good for shots? How hard and high must one hit to get good depth? How do serves act? How is the footing—slippery? Most players are very aware of these important questions and tend to favor them to the point where they neglect proper physical warm-up.

It is crucial not to do any of these warm-up routines violently. You should treat yourself just as you'd treat a machine (which in a sense you are). You run the motor gently, rev it a little in short bursts to get it running, the oil (circulation) flowing smoothly. The motor and its moving parts are brought gradually and carefully to the point where they are prepared for high performance. No one should put himself to any test in the warm-up—you are getting *ready* to do that, you are not doing it.

Lastly, people differ not fundamentally, but in degree. Some people need a lot of warm-up. Some even need to play a practice game before they start the match. Others, like me, need much less. Therefore, as in everything, know thyself: experiment until you find what gets *you* ready to do your best from the start, and stick to it. It is perhaps also significant that, during my long playing career, I have suffered only one injury (not my fault: my foot caught under a loose tape, spraining my ankle). That is, until at about age 65, after having stopped playing hard for several years, I entered an event to fill a draw. Not being in shape, sure enough I sprained my ankle.

Diet and Prematch Food

Of all areas, this one is probably the most subject to crazy fads and a new theory every few days, including all the accompanying advertisements about instant miraculous results. So far, none of them has made good.

The fact is that medical science has, over the last four or five decades, made constant discoveries about this vitamin or that, this trace mineral or that, which was previously unknown in the body, besides increasing information about conversion into usable energy. It is also a fact that the body, being adapted to what is available, has with time developed a marvellous ability to take and hold what it needs *if* given the opportunity. Doubtless there will be further developments in medical knowledge in this area—important facts not yet discovered, specific vitamins and minerals which we need for optimum health and all round fitness. It is therefore probably very unwise to adopt a diet that says, "none of this" or "eat only a lot of that."

All this leads to a conclusion that will perhaps disappoint some, but seems the only wise course: eat a well-rounded diet that gives your body the chance to take what it needs. It will do this, including all the trace minerals that we know about and perhaps some we don't know about as yet. Anyone wishing to or having reason to depart from this broad principle should not do so without consulting a doctor—someone whose knowledge of the subject has depth. Certainly few coaches can qualify on this basis. Therefore the best advice any unqualified person can give is: consult a medical man on a medical matter, don't consult your pro.

A good example of well-meaning error committed by athletes making medical decisions is in the pre-game-meal area. For long it was thought that if you "eat the blood of a lion you will fight like a lion." The traditional meal was a steak before the game. Apparently it has now been established that other foods will digest more quickly—spaghetti, pancakes, etc.—so the steak is less in favor. It was also thought that spaghetti was an anathema, until it was found that it was the sauce, not the spaghetti, which delayed digestion and caused trouble on the field. There was also a theory that a pregame meal *must* be four hours before the game. This tradition, perhaps very good for contact sports, was handed down to noncontact sports (what's good for football had to be right for every other activity). But in tennis, for example, when matches are played over a great length of time—singles, then doubles—players would enter the doubles having had nothing to eat for six to eight hours. Some felt that empty weakness that can accompany hunger, and performed beneath their best.

Here again, it is important to know yourself. There is no hard and fast rule for all people. Temperament is very important. It is well known that nervousness interferes with digestive processes. It is also well known that some people are very nervous before a contest. For such people to eat a huge meal (steak, baked potato, etc.) before a match, then have it sit in their stomachs, heavy, undigested or only partially digested, can be devastating. It is the height of folly. For other more phlegmatic types, a good solid meal is a fine thing—it makes them feel, "I'm all set—lemme at 'em."

It has, I believe, been fairly well established that there is a considerable time lapse between ingestion and usable energy. The food must be digested and go through various processes before it becomes of use to the muscles in actual play. It has been said, "You play on Saturday with what you ate on Thursday." Whether this is the precise interval I don't know, but it seems at least to be true that doing something special just before a contest may upset your routine and hurt you, but has small chance of being of much help nutritionally.

Nonetheless, I am strongly in favor of a pregame meal, for psychological rather than physical reasons. The team gets in a group, team spirit and togetherness are augmented, everyone feels a unanimity of concentration and purpose, and each player is reinforced by this general feeling. The whole becomes greater than the sum of its parts. But what and how much each should eat is an individual matter and it is a dangerous presumption for a coach to think he knows what is best for all and to lay down a blanket rule.

A good example of the validity of individualism occurred in track. At the time when the four-minute-mile barrier was being broken, numerous articles appeared about the diet of each successive star. Most varied quite a bit. Each had learned what was best for himself, how to get himself ready for a supreme effort. No two were alike, yet all performed superbly.

Another example occurred with my own team. We were undefeated and the final match was with the only other undefeated team. This opponent was favored to beat us. Therefore there was all the emotion and tension that accompanies a climax match, which decides a national team title. We took a train. The department of athletics had generously arranged for a steak and baked potato meal at 11:00 A.M. for the team in the dining car—very expensive. I had protested, "If they don't want it, I'm not going to make them eat it." I was told that they'd better eat it—it cost plenty. I left it at that. On the train, one big aggressive fellow said that he was hungry. He needed a big meal. I told him to eat one. He ate *two* steaks and said he felt great. Another said he'd get sick if he ate that steak. Did he have to eat it? "You don't have to," I said, "How about a BLT and a cup of tea?" That's what he wanted—he was nervous and didn't want much. He got it. So it went—each boy deciding, according to how he felt, what and how much. We played very well and won (the player having had two steaks and the tea man both won decisively).

This, of course, can go too far. If someone wants to drink two big frappes a half hour before play, one must veto such insanity. But if it is made a part of coaching to teach each player to learn to know himself, so he makes intelligent decisions and develops effective habits of "getting ready," individualism has much in its favor. The blanket rule approach ignores the psychological aspects that are so different in different people. It ignores the fact that most coaches have limited knowledge in the field in question, and it ignores the fact that, basically, one is tampering with a process that nature has been perfecting, in many subtle ways, for millions of years.

How Much Conditioning?

Ever since Kennedy popularized fitness, revealing the prevalence of obesity, and, in racquet games, since the reinforcement of the significance of conditioning by Harry Hopman's great achievements, conditioning has become the in thing. Actually it is, at this moment, being given exaggerated importance. Of what avail is a lot of stamina and agility if one is mediocre at actually playing the ball? A significant conditioning program is necessary for anyone who aspires to heights in tournament play: you can't stay with the competition without it. But for the majority of players, who play for fun and exercise, moderation would seem to make sense.

Everyone should warm up before playing. This makes sense, reduces chances of ankle injuries and tennis elbows or pulling this or that muscle, and helps one to play one's best at whatever level of excellence this "best" may be. A habit of doing some running is an excellent habit just for general well being—it makes you feel good, and is beneficial whether you play squash or not. Whether or not one wishes to go beyond this is an individual decision. A daily program is excellent for teams at schools and colleges. It gets the team together and increases team spirit as well as team fitness. If you are out for a team you should be making a serious effort which contrasts sharply with casual participation. But such a daily program should be short—thirty minutes at the most. Why? I believe that most of the available time should be put on learning the game in all its facets. Any coach or teacher who thinks the road to excellence is primarily a matter of conditioning is out of focus in his thinking. Conditioning is significant, important, indispensable near the top—but it is only one of the several areas in the game of squash. Conditioning will not succeed as a substitute for skills.

Warning

Conditioning is a fine thing if used judiciously and properly. It can also be disappointing and even harmful is used unwisely. The first warning is to urge overenthusiastic people to take it easy. Improvement takes time, like walking up a ramp that is only slightly inclined. While you should push yourself a little, you should not keep pushing when your body tells you that's all it can take for now. The body's message is itself a warning not to go too far. This point will vary with each individual according to age and present fitness. If you rush out all full of determination and practically try to kill yourself—you may succeed!

Often someone will say, "I'm going into that tournament next week—I've got to get in shape." He will then punish himself severely with intensive conditioning work, and usually surprise himself by playing very badly. This is because, if you are out of shape and take to conditioning, it's first effect is to tear you down rather than build you up. You may have sore muscles, feel fatigued, and be sluggish—you are worse off than before. Over time, conditioning will unquestionably build you up and bring about a vast improvement, but it is no more good as a quick remedy than rapid dehydration is for reducing weight.

A *Little Knowledge Is a Dangerous Thing*

It is appropriate to establish boundaries to any area of expertise. A squash racquets teaching professional is a "squash doctor." He is not a medical doctor. He must know what he doesn't know and say so without hesitation. People constantly go to professionals and say, "I have a tennis elbow" (or a pulled this or that). "What should I do?" For me, there is only *one* proper answer: "Go to a doctor." For an "elbow" (there are several variations) the pro can advise a springy racquet strung not too tight with gut (more resilient) rather than nylon (stiff) to reduce impact shock. But as to whether the patient should play, rest it without play, use cortisone, acupuncture, or whatever—this is not his area of knowledge. He probably knows less about it than a medical doctor would know about how to fix up a faulty backhand.

Coaches who handle teams should carry this even farther. Young players often tend to bring all their problems to the coach—trouble with the girl friend, what decision to make about a future career, studies, and of course any injury. Some coaches are fine teachers. Few are also marriage counselors, tutors, and career choice experts. In the case of a vague or doubtful injury, the coach should not merely advise going to a doctor, he should *order* going to a doctor, and refuse permission to participate further until this has been done.

One little example: the day before a long trip a player jammed his foot against a wall. Afterwards he said that his toe hurt but he would be all right. I told him to see the doctor right away. He continued to deny the injury, but I was adamant. "See the doctor right now or you don't make the trip," I told him. The chances of anything serious were very slim, but it turned out that he had a hairline fracture, was not allowed to play, had to have a special shoe, and would have suffered permanent damage without prompt and expert diagnosis and treatment. It is foolish, even reprehensible, for a coach to take chances and make judgments in areas where his knowledge is clearly inadequate, unless he is forced to because a more expert opinion is unavailable.

Summary

1. Conditioning in moderation is strongly recommended for everybody. It markedly reduces the probability of injury, and it also contributes to daily well being and efficiency.

2. It does not need to be tremendously time consuming. Simply running is excellent.

3. Those who go in for serious conditioning should work up to the more demanding routines rather than plunge into them at once if they are in poor shape when they start.

4. Group conditioning is fine for teams but should not be overdone or substituted for skill.

5. Special diets are suspect and should never be adopted without prior medical consultation.

6. All coaches and teachers (and players) should know their limitations and avoid intruding on the area of medicine.

Note: Those who wish to learn more about this subject should go to doctors and trainers who know anatomy, know what exercise affects what specific muscle, what is beneficial and what is dangerous, and what will build this particular strength or that, what diet stresses protein, carbohydrate, vitamins, trace minerals, fat, etc. Any such treatment in depth is far outside the scope of this book and therefore has not been attempted. In can be pointed out, however, that conditioning may be approached from two points of view. You may wish only to achieve reasonable fitness and stamina so as to use your present assets to good advantage. Or, you may wish actually to increase your assets, build new strengths, and develop new physical skills. This is a personal choice.

21

An Appreciation of Squash Doubles

by Victor Niederhoffer*

The first squash racquets doubles court was built in 1907 at the Philadelphia Racquet Club by Frederich Tomkins, the great racquets and tennis professor, who formerly served as private coach to the Duke of Wellington. The space on which it was built was too small for a racquets court, it wasn't even big enough for a locker room. In addition to the doubles court, the facility had five squash racquets courts, two racquets courts, and one court-tennis court.

Philadelphia has almost totally dominated doubles since that first court was built. Of forty national championships since the event was begun in 1933, Philadelphia players have won thirty-three. It is my pleasure to have won the championship on each of the three occasions since 1958 when Philadelphia failed to receive the laurels. Some of these were memorable, as when in 1968, at age 24, I teamed with Victor Elmaleh, age 49, to win the title at the prestigious Racquet Club of St. Louis. A doubles championship entails much more than merely squash. It is a social affair also, with well-planned and well-attended festivities surrounding the matches. Considering that an average five-game match in doubles lasts two hours, and that rallies frequently remain in play for more than 100 hits, it is fortunate that the two Victors were teetotalers. We won every match in five games

* Illustrations have been omitted from this section on doubles because all the shots have been shown for singles. We would like to thank all of the doubles players who responded to our research inquiries about the game, particularly Larry Terrell from whose careful analysis Vic quoted extensively.

throughout the tournament, prevailing in the finals over the great Philadelphia team of Ralph Howe and Diehl Mateer 15–13, 15–12, 5–15, 9–15, 15–10.

Doubles suffers from essentially the same handicaps that have practically wiped out the great game of court tennis. In the seventeenth century in the era of the "Roi Soleil," Louis XIV, there were upwards of 1200 court tennis courts in Paris alone. But the fall of the aristocracy was a deadly blow to such status symbols. By the end of the revolution only one court remained. Doubles is a great game. But it is a game which unfortunately seems destined to share the same fate as court tennis. And for many of the same reasons.

A grasp of these difficulties must begin with an understanding of the dimensions of the court. The court is a rectangle twenty-five-feet wide by forty-five-feet long. The front wall is twenty-feet high with the red line fifteen-feet from the back wall. Note that the volume of the court is 22,500 cubic feet compared to 9,216 cubic feet for the singles court. This means that a doubles court will have to generate about two-and-one-half times as much revenue to warrant its construction versus a singles court.

Even if revenue is no obstacle, there is frequently an insoluble problem of available space. A great many city clubs have used all their available space, so that to add a doubles court necessitates the sacrifice of useful facilities already in place, such as singles courts. A third deterrent is the very high cost of alterations. It is not just a matter of substituting one thing for another. A doubles court is high as well as long. Main bearing beams may be in the way, and to cut these and install new bridges can add horrendously to the cost of building the court. With all these obstacles it is no wonder that while there is frequent favorable discussion about more doubles courts not many more actually get built. The game exists, players love it, but the growth is understandably slow.

This is all the more reason for readers to go out and play, watch and enjoy this game immediately. There are all too few remnants of the good old days left. So let us turn together to the appreciating and possible playing of doubles with a spirit of optimism and benevolence.

Fundamental Differences From Singles

The red line in doubles is fifteen feet from the back wall. The average hard hit drive off the back wall in doubles that hits the front wall first followed by a bounce on the floor, then hitting the back wall will land about three feet behind the red line. This places it twelve feet from the back wall.

A player must defend against the deep shot by stationing himself close enough to the back wall to retrieve this shot. Position play in an average point tends to be near the red line itself which is thirty feet from the front wall. This compares to twenty-two feet from the front wall to red line in singles.

This opens up the possibility of much more effective use of shots in doubles than singles. The average retriever has about as great a distance to travel lengthwise for a short shot as he would face if he were standing flush against the back wall in a singles court. Larry Terrell, who was schooled in Philadelphia and Harvard, has expressed this point by saying that winning shots in doubles, unlike singles, are often ordinary affairs, like a deep rail or a mediocre straight or cross court drop shot. In singles, a fast man caught in a bad position can retrieve anything if hit poorly. But in doubles, the same man can be so far out of position that even a humdrum winner will suffice.

The striker has a much greater advantage in going for shots in doubles. And in fact, almost all of the greatest doubles champions have been shot makers rather than retrievers. Diehl Mateer, who won the doubles title on 11 occasions, is probably the greatest left court player. He goes for winners at least once in four hits. Jim Zug is probably the greatest right court player. Again, his ratio of attempts for winners to drives is phenomenally high. The major adjustment a singles player must make in doubles is a realization that the reward risk ratio is different. A good shot should win the point in doubles. In singles, almost all shots can be retrieved. A good singles player must expect to be accurate on at least six attempts at winners for each error on shots made. A good doubles player, on the other hand, might be content with a ratio of five in seven winners to losers.

One of the most striking examples of how implementation of this can make a decisive difference came in the semifinals of the Nationals in 1975 at the Buffalo Tennis and Squash Club. I teamed with Colin Adair, the frequent Canadian Amateur Singles and twice U.S. Amateur Singles Champion. Our opponents were Diehl Mateer Jr., age 50, and his 19 year old son Gil. Both Adair and myself hardly ever commit an error. In singles this is an extremely effective strategy. Ultimately, the opponent will make an error or will give an opening for an attempt at a shot that will have a winner to error ratio of over ten to one. In the meantime, any shot by the opponent can be returned. It is interesting that neither Diehl, at 50, nor his talented but comparatively unseasoned son Gil, at 19, could probably have won more than five points a game from Colin or myself in singles. Yet they were clearly superior in doubles as they beat us 15-10, 15-11, 12-15, 15-8, because they played more aggressively while we played more defensively. In doubles a totally defensive attitude seldom succeeds. The shots by a skilled opponent such as Diehl Mateer too often will go for winners. A good team cannot afford just to play steady. They must go for the point.

I first gleaned this fundamental difference by competing in the game of racquetball. In that game, the good players consistently make errors on a scale unprecedented in squash. A top squash player like Adair, myself, or Henri Salaun frequently will hold down the errors to an average of one a game. In racquetball, a winning player might make as many as six or seven in a game. In top squash doubles, three or four errors a player a game is common. The singles player can adopt this manner of thinking to improve his doubles game. What is the ideal proportion of opportunities for shots that should be seized? This would depend on the probability of winning the point with a shot compared to a drive, on the speed of the ball, fleetness of the opposing player, time of the shot in the game, and the ability of opposing players to affect these probabilities. The pathetic memory of Colin and myself waiting it out in doubles while our more brash opponents won point after point with shots that wouldn't have made sense in singles still hurts. All we could do was shake our heads in disbelief at their seemingly nonpercentage shots. But a good five out of seven times they did win the point.

On the other hand, when I first teamed up with Jim Zug, who also won the National Doubles Championship in 1972, the shoe was on the other foot. Our history in the National Doubles '73 was one of the most lopsided tours to victory ever. We lost one game on the route to the finals. And this was our first time playing together. The reason is simple in retrospect. Our opponents invariably tried to play Jim. Jim would move up in front of the red line and hit shot after shot from his side. A good seventy-five percent of the eight or nine he tried each game were accurate. And this was enough to determine our usual margin of victory. Again this also explains the reason that the fifty-year-old Vic Elmaleh and myself were able to win the doubles titles in 1966. Vic is a great shot maker. And my opponents would constantly hit it more and more to him as the match wore on. As the game progressed, our opponents grew more tired. The percentage of Vic's winning shots increased. We won all our matches in five games. All of them were on shots by Vic. Finally, this also explains why an older player has a chance in doubles. The point can be ended by a shot. In singles, this shot would just be the beginning of a long point which inevitably would end with an error by the older opponent as he tries for the point or game. In doubles, whenever a well-placed shot is taken, the point is in imminent danger of ending.

Winning Shots

The Forehand Reverse Corner.   Probably this is the most effective shot in doubles. It must be hit so that it eludes the left court player, the right court player, and the right side wall. Hitting the ball so that the point of contact is closer to the front wall brings the ball off the front wall so that it will end nearer the middle. Hitting the sidewall farther back will bring the ball farther towards the right. Hitting too far back on the left side will cause the ball to strike the right wall, and be easy to retrieve: in fact, it is a setup as in singles. The ideal point to hit the sidewall will vary depending on the position of the striker. The height of the point of contact with the initial sidewall should be slightly higher than in singles. The speed of the shot should be faster for those aimed to take their second bounce in the middle horizontally and slower for the sharply angled shots. The further forward in the court the reverse corner is struck from, the greater the opportunities open. A good striker will always move up to hit this shot from as far forward as possible. In fact, the closer you are to the front wall, the more effective this shot and any shot will be. A top spin imparted to the reverse corner will lift the ball up off the side wall thereby increasing the chances of it clearing the front wall. However, it is harder to control the top spin. Only one player uses this effectively—Ken Binns from Toronto.

The Forehand-Volley Drop Shot.   This is a shot that is only effective in doubles. It is very rarely used in singles. The idea is to hit the front wall first and then to nick it on the sidewall. The most frequently used shot is the forehand volley from the right side of court hit directly on the right front wall angling off to the nick on the right sidewall. The sharper the downward angle the ball is hit at, the faster it will descend to the nick which is the goal. Usually this means the volley should be taken as high in the air as possible. If you hit it from too low it will strike the sidewall too high. Underspin on the ball will both help keep the ball above the tin on the front wall and force the ball to drop faster onto and off the sidewall. The softer the ball is hit, the closer up to the front wall it will descend. The other side of playing it soft is that the softer it is hit, the more time an opponent will have to retrieve the shot. Moreover, on soft shots, there is always the danger of not hitting it with enough depth so that it clears the tin before dropping. All things considered, a crisp volley is probably the most effective and most easily acquired.

A particularly effective variation of the hard volley drop shot is a side corner drop shot. This is a shot that hits the sidewall up close enough to the front wall so that it looks like it's going to be a straight volley drop. But instead of nicking the sidewall, it goes around the corner and takes its second bounce near the middle. The deception is extremely effective. Again, the farther up this shot is hit from, the closer to the front we can expect its bounce.

Finally, a most effective volley drop shot is a cross-court drop shot. The idea here is to catch the ball as high as possible and sharply angle the ball so that it first hits the front wall and then catches the left sidewall for a nick or near nick. Spin imparted on the side of the ball by carving around it will increase the chance of this ball catching the nick close to the front wall. On a lower chance one can slice (cut) from the outside in thereby imparting a sidespin that "throws" the ball at the sidewall when it leaves the front wall. More nicks result. The cross court volley drop shot can be varied with the reverse corner to confound your opponents and prevent them from anticipating with any certainty.

Now that we've considered the shots that do work in doubles, let's consider one crucial shot in singles that doesn't work in doubles. The shot that wins the most points in singles is the three-wall nick. In a hard singles match, for example, I might win eighty percent of my points with this shot. It is particularly effective because there is so little chance of an error. Almost all of the great champions of the 1960s in fact have used this shot as the corner stone in their game. The following players, for example, probably won more than fifty percent of their winners with the three-wall nick: Sharif Khan, Victor Niederhoffer, Anil Nayar, Gordon Anderson, and Colin Adair. These players have won the last eight U.S. Singles Championships, the last seven Canadian Single Championships and the last seven Open Championships, amongst them. You can't argue with success. The three-wall nick is undoubtedly the most effective shot in the modern game at the top level of play. The three-wall nick in singles can be hit in a number of ways. But each stroke has in common that the ball is hit on the sidewall between six inches and two feet in front of the point of contact with the racquet. This does not work in doubles. The forward diagonal distance this shot must travel is too great for a winning shot from those areas of the court where the ball is most frequently in play.

The Sliced Corner Shot. The sidewall drop shot or sliced corner shot can be very effective, particularly if combined with hard, deep cross-court drives. This shot has the effect of a three-wall nick in singles, catching the player on the other side of the court lingering too deep. In talking about his limited doubles experience, my mentor Jack Barnaby indicated his surprise at how often his side corners were winners as long as enough hard wide cross-court shots were mixed in to keep the other court player worried about his depth. A heavy side spin on the side corner will tend to bring the trajectory of the shot closer to the sidewall it originally strikes. The spin also throws the ball around the walls faster, makes it drop faster, and permits a hard swing that deceives an opponent into suspecting a drive. The shot is equally effective off forehand or backhand provided the threat of a deep crosscourt is present: the player on the other side can't tell whether the ball will be short or long.

The Lob. No discussion of winning shots would be complete without the lob, the major antidote to the winner. Whenever a winner or a drive is not possible, a lob is appropriate. The lob should always be hit to the backhand opponent. The goal should be for it to end its trajectory as close to the back wall as possible. While the lob is being retrieved, both players should get back into advantageous positions. But remember that, at best, even if executed properly, the lob will enable your team only to get back to an even position in the point. It will never give your team the edge. Thus, a lob should never be hit when an attempt for a winner is possible.

The principles advanced in considering these shots can be applied to every stroke in the game, and of course all the winner shots discussed above for the forehand are applicable to the backhand player also. In each instance, consider the height above the telltale to which you aim the ball, the spin placed on the ball, the angle of contact with the first wall, the speed imparted, the height of the point of contact on the wall being aimed at, and deception. Practice adjusting these variables one at a time and your game will improve drastically, and, as a rule of thumb, hit all of these with a much bigger backswing than you would in singles. The ball generally has about fifty percent more distance to travel. This should be emphasized. Everything said about technique, spin, etc. in the rest of the book also applies to execution in doubles except for one thing—take a bigger swing. The ball always has much farther to travel, so more swing is needed on practically every shot. By a bigger swing I mean a fuller backswing.

Partnership

Doubles brings out the cooperative spirit as well as the competitive. Like life, its success is greatest where you specialize in those areas where your talents are greatest. A good doubles team must start with players who complement each other. For example, one partner might specialize in shot making while the other specializes in gets. Another excellent combination is a hard hitter with a soft hitter. A player with an excellent forehand should combine with one with an excellent backhand. Finally, age combined with youth can also work.

Perhaps the most effective combination is a right-handed partner combined with a left-handed partner. The reason this is such an excellent combination is that the reach on the forehand is about two feet greater than the backhand. Since the most difficult area to retrieve from is the area close to the sidewalls, it is important to have that extra reach extending towards the sidewall. With a right-handed player playing on the right side and a left-handed player playing on the left side, the sidewalls are best defended.

There are about ten right-handed players for every left-handed squash player. Therefore, a left-handed squash player is an extremely valuable commodity for squash doubles. If you need a partner, think first of the good lefties you know.

Mohibullah Khan, the left-handed pro at the Harvard Club of Boston has perhaps the best record among pros in open doubles. For example, in five consecutive years from 1969 through 1973, Mo won the David C. Johnson Memorial, held at the Heights Casino in Brooklyn, New York, with three different partners. This has traditionally been the stiffest doubles competition of the year. During this period, Mo won only one of the ten major singles championships. We can attribute Mo's superiority in doubles during this period to two factors: his left-handedness and his proneness to go for a shot at the drop of a hat.

The worst combination in doubles is one where both players play a similar, conservative game. Colin Adair and myself were such a team. Both of us hardly ever miss during a match. Despite this, we consistently lost during 1975 to teams consisting of players who in singles were inferior to either of us.

Probably the most important factor in choosing a doubles partner is to get together with someone you like. This has the obvious advantage of making the game fun. It also adds the psychological lift at crucial stages of a match of bringing out your best so that you can honor your partner. Conversely, the worst thing a doubles player can do is to express disgust when his partner misses. This has such a demoralizing influence on your partners. You will lose the respect of everyone in the game, and you will find that no one else wishes to play with you.

There was one partner I played with frequently who is known for his manifestations of utter disgust at every mistake during the game. He made faces whenever I missed, and bitterly complained whenever I inadvertently ran into his side of the court trying to save a point. He gave the impression that he was the kind of man who, even if he were to find himself in Heaven would immediately complain, "The gold paving these streets is hard on my feet." I finally told him, "Look, stop complaining. You're ruining my enjoyment." He remarked that he just couldn't control his emotions. And that there was nothing personal involved. Our partnership ended shortly thereafter, although we buried our hatchets long enough to capture a National Championship.

The most enjoyable combination I ever played in consisted of my partnership with Dr. James Lorie, the noted conservative investment dean who served as my thesis advisor at the University of Chicago. I would say to him that his game complemented mine. Wherever I was strong, he was weak. Period. But he saw it differently. He would point out the clearly proved superiority of his game to mine, noting that since I hit at least ninety percent of the shots our side hit, this meant our opponents knew I was the weaker player because they were obviously hitting everything to me. Every year I commuted to Chicago to play in the Christmas Invitational Doubles with him at the Chicago Racquet and Tennis Club. Finally we won it. But there was no trophy. Only a bottle of champagne. I took the liberty of going to a trophy store to purchase our own mementos. I sheepishly entered, thinking that perhaps it seemed a bit vainglorious to be purchasing one's own trophies. But the proprietor quickly informed me that at least ninety percent of the trophies and prizes purchased at his store consisted of individuals purchasing these momentos for themselves after the occasion. In any case, the trophy which I designed and paid for commemorating our success at the "Illinois Open Invitational Doubles Championship" is probably the proudest trophy that we both display.

It is even more important for good partners to like each other on the court than off the court. Larry Terrell, National Doubles Champion in 1972 with Jim Zug, expressed this point elegantly in laying down the Four Cs of Partnership as follows:

COMBINATION

. . . you must not only analyze the games, the strengths, and weaknesses of the two opposing players, but you must also analyze how those two games fit together. This is especially true where the opposing team utilizes one partner's strength to compensate for the other's weakness. You must determine how to neutralize their combination so that their games do not mesh effectively. At the same time you must analyze the games of you and your partner so that your games are optimally coordinated.

COMPENSATION

One common error of singles players on a doubles court is that they often tend to let their mind wander while their partner is hitting the ball. This is stupid, for they must compensate for the position from which their partner hits. Thus if one partner goes back to retrieve a deep ball, the other should drift forward expecting a short shot—especially if the opponents are already standing in the forecourt.

CONSERVATION

A frequently neglected precept is to vary the pace. You can't always blast a cross-court past your opponent, and even if you could, you shouldn't. It is wiser to conserve your strength and the advantage of surprise. Use lobs not just a little, but a lot, in moving your opponents to the back wall.

COMMUNICATION

For some unaccountable reason, many partners hardly exchange a word during a match. How can you expect your partner to take advantage of, or guard against, habits you have noticed unless you communicate? Also a team handles its opponents' game most effectively only when it coordinates its attack and defense. It can be dangerous to adopt unilaterally certain tactics if your partner does not know what you're up to. If, for instance, he is aware of how you might take advantage of a certain situation, then he is less apt to get in the way and cause a let, thereby giving the other team a second chance when you could have had the point outright.

Perhaps the most embarrassing part of partnership in doubles comes when two partners race in tandem from front to back, or back to front to retrieve a shot. In addition to the embarrassment, there is always the danger that your partner will clobber you with his racquet. More frequently, the ball will just drop between you. A general rule to solve this problem is this: let the partner who has struck the ball most recently hit all balls that are in question. In addition to solving the problem unequivocally, this solution has the virtue of enabling the most recently grooved partner to return the ball.

No discussion of partnership would be complete without an acknowledgement that squash doubles is a game that can be played during a whole lifetime. There is half the strain and exercise in doubles as singles.

There is more emphasis on mental strategy in doubles in comparison to singles.

Position

The essence of position in doubles is to place your team in an area where it's impossible for your opponents to go for the point with a high percentage shot. Conversely, the goal is to maneuver your opponents to a point where you can hit a winner without risking an undue chance of an error.

It's beautiful to see the two partners in a well-oiled doubles machine moving back and forth to gain this positional advantage. In fact, when both teams are playing good position, a point can last interminably. Both sets of partners will be dancing around their sides like boxers involved in a tag match. Rallies involving more than 150 separate strikes of the ball as both teams maneuver around the court are not uncommon in championships. This would mean a point of almost three minutes versus a maximum of thirty seconds and thirty strikes in singles. No wonder the best doubles matches often last more than two hours versus a one hour maximum for singles.

As discussed in the section on winners, the closer you are to the front wall, the easier it is to shoot for a winner. And at least one player on the top doubles teams will constantly be moving up front to gain this positional advantage. The goal of the partner to the man moving up front must be to adjust and promote the winner for his partner by belting the ball hard so that the opponents loft up an easy shot. Alternately he can try for a short shot attempting to set up the return so that his partner can power a winner.

There are two theories of positional play in doubles. The first is to place yourself in tandem with your partner always standing exactly the same distance from the front wall as your partner. This reduces to a minimum the area you and your partner will have to cover as your opponents attempt to drive the ball through you. Unfortunately, by playing in tandem you do open up the opportunity for your opponents to win the point with a sharp cross court that catches the sidewall before it can be cut off.

The other theory of doubles position is for one partner to work his way up front for the winning opportunity, while the other partner hangs back covering against his partner's being passed. The optimum point to stand here is at the point that guards against the cross court angle your partner is exposed to while at the same time not falling back enough to fall prey to an easy winner in your own corner (front or back or both). This position is most common for doubles teams consisting of one younger player and an older player. By moving the older player closer and closer to the front wall, the shot maker can minimize the area he is forced to cover while at the same time gaining full opportunity to use his experience to go for the early winner.

Vic Elmaleh, who has won numerous top doubles championships with partners like Mo Heckshire, Ralph Howe, and myself, was a master at this strategy. He was constantly moving up front on the right side. When the ball was hit to him, there he was, deadly, with a volley reverse corner or a volley straight drop. When a short cross court was hit to him, he either powered it deep cross court to his back hand opponent or hit a soft side corner. On those rare occasions when an opponent was able to get the ball around him, he was always there to encourage his partners with a shout of "Yours, _____." During the 1968 national doubles championships which we won in St. Louis, I covered for Vic as he moved up front and wound up covering about eighty percent of the court and hitting a good eighty-five percent of all shots. But the margin of victory was always the seven or eight winners per game that Vic Elmaleh made from up front compared to the two or three errors he committed. As an aside, our victory illustrated the importance of desire in winning major championships. We won each of our matches in five games. In total, we gave up 280 points and won 282 points. Yet that little extra that we put in at the crucial point was enough to gain the championship.

The difference between success and failure in squash doubles is probably a smaller line than in any other racquet sport. Frequently, all four of the quarter final, two semi-finals, and one final round of a doubles tournament will go the full five games. With two hours a match, and two matches a day, this means at least four hours on the court, not counting warm-up time. Desire, persistence, and good health, as well as an intuitive awareness of the principles of winning shots, partnership, and position discussed above are the keys to success.

One other important aspect of position play in doubles is clearing a lane so that your opponent can hit his shot without giving him so much room that his chances of winning a point become excessive. The most common critical position in doubles is one where three players are on one side of the court while the striker is on the other side hitting his shot. The opponent from the striker's side is then between the devil and deep blue sea. If he doesn't clear enough, the striker is likely to belt him with the ball. If he clears too much, he's likely to leave the striker an easy opportunity for a winner. Unfortunately, human nature being what it is, the tendency is not to give the striker enough room. The result is that in the most competitive doubles games all four players are likely to come out black and blue from being struck with the ball.

I have always found this the most unfortunate aspect of doubles, whether on the receiving end or the striking end. Especially so, since there is such a simple solution. All that's necessary is to adopt the singles rule of English Let. Where a striker hits the ball directly to the front wall and it catches an opponent on the way to the front wall, the *striker's* side wins the point. Singles adopted this rule in 1933. Since that time, its been rare to see more than two or three occasions in a whole tournament where the ball is drilled into the opponent. In doubles, one expects at least two or three such occasions a match. These are dangerous and disturbing. To date, the solution in doubles has been to appeal to the straight receiver to clear for the strikers so that the striker has a real chance for the winner. But a crab cannot walk straight. And it is rare to see a top doubles player who in the early phase of a two-hour, five-game battle, won't crowd and limit the playing areas of strikers. The result is a horrible shot in an unpredictable, but hopefully not lethal area. Let us hope that the powers that be in the world of doubles will adopt the change to the English Let rule posthaste.

Concluding Remarks

It is feared that, like the days of grand dukes, luxury transatlantic cruises, fine claret, thirty course meals, and named newspapers at private clubs, doubles is a great but receding activity. Yet of all the court and racquet games, I find doubles the most stimulating. I encourage you to play or watch doubles before it dies out. Your life will be enriched by the experience.

Rather than mourning for the "Dusk of Doubles," I'll end with some hopeful remarks. An appreciation of squash doubles will improve a player's abilities in all other racquet games, and hopefully life itself. A major hope for the continuation of doubles is that it will adapt itself for the 20' X 40' racquetball courts now popping up all over the United States. Racquet ball is played with a softer or smaller racquet. Squash players could be the vanguard of a trend toward a new, great racquet game, if they move now to change the game. A game played with squash doubles rules and a tin, but with racquetball equipment, would be magnificent athletic experience.

Comment by Jack Barnaby

Vic Niederhoffer's most interesting treatment of doubles offers an opportunity for anyone taking up the game to change his "singles thinking" right from the start rather than only after considerable unprofitable experience. Technique is the same except for a much enlarged backswing. Shots pay off, conservatism that wins in singles merely ignores golden opportunities. Shots made on the volley, as a rule definitely nonpercentage in singles, are standard procedure in doubles.

As in tennis, when you get a player out of position, you play the winner short or long to the same side, not to the other side as in singles where there is no partner waiting. This is one of the hardest principles to learn—it is so habitual to play away from the player in trouble that the tendency of the neophyte in doubles is to play right to the troubled player's partner—a stupid play if ever there was one. The only time to do this is when you are pretty certain one partner is rushing to cover his troubled partner, so he isn't any longer where he normally would be. Here the subtleties of the twist play and the cross up can be as prominent as in singles.

As to getting hit by the ball due to not leaving a lane open to the striker, I learned the hard way. In one of my few doubles matches, my partner hit a high hard shot that broke way around off the back wall towards my side. Being green at the game, I didn't know which way to move, so I hesitated. My opponent, Ethridge, was famous for his powerful forehand. He did not see me—he was watching the ball come off the back wall. He really whaled it, and caught me smack in the fanny. After several moments of earnest rubbing and some jumping up and down, I joined in the general laughter. But I still vividly recall that mighty blow, and urge one and all not to get in front of the ball. It's a losing tactic. I am no expert on doubles, but that much I *know*. Experience is a great teacher, but in this case it is preferable to follow the other old saw, "Wise men learn from the experience of others."

Index